Capital Wars

Michael J. Howell

Capital Wars

The Rise of Global Liquidity

Michael J. Howell
CrossBorder Capital Ltd.
London, UK

ISBN 978-3-030-39287-1   ISBN 978-3-030-39288-8   (eBook)
https://doi.org/10.1007/978-3-030-39288-8

This Palgrave Macmillan imprint is published by the registered company Springer Nature Switzerland AG
The registered company address is: Gewerbestrasse 11, 6330 Cham, Switzerland

To the Salomon Brothers' Diaspora

Preface

History, particularly financial history, is not random. The key idea in this book is that economic cycles are driven by financial flows, namely quantities of savings and credits, and not by high street inflation or the level of interest rates. Their sweeping destructive powers are expressed through Global Liquidity, a US$130 trillion pool of footloose cash. Our Central Bank policy-makers should, consequently, about-turn and focus more on financial stability than on hitting phantom consumer price inflation targets. The economist John Maynard Keynes distinguished the economy's financial and industrial spheres in a similar way to how we might, today, separate the asset economy from the real economy. Trying to stimulate the real economy with liquidity always runs the risk of creating asset price bubbles instead. In the 1930s, facing a near-identical situation to the post-GFC years, policy-makers then unleashed an analogous stimulus with the same outturn: near-flat high street prices, but soaring asset prices. A fractured, uncertain World encourages investors to hold excessive amounts of 'safe' assets, like cash and government bonds and, particularly, US dollar assets, rather than putting money to work productively. When the State fails to produce sufficient safe assets, then the private sector steps in with less good substitutes, whose values unfortunately move procyclically. Governments' austerity policies and quantitative tightening programmes might not sound such good ideas in this light? Think of this mechanism as the so-called *precautionary demand for money*, hurriedly skipped over in the traditional textbooks, but which seems to better describe the growing systemic risks we face than the better-known speculative motive, which assesses the chances of rising (as opposed to falling) interest rates and can lead to a 'liquidity trap'. I argue that Global

Liquidity is never trapped: it waves no flag, knows no boundaries and shifts all too rapidly between markets and asset classes.

What appear as two puzzling features in the latest policy debates, in fact, emphasise the importance of Global Liquidity. First, the widespread consensus view, underpinned by repeated Central Bank claims, that more QE (quantitative easing) lowers, and does not raise, term premia and hence government bond yields. The academic argument, summarised by Gagnon (2016), quantifies this as 67 basis points (bp) per 10% of GDP injected via QE. Second, many believe that the slope of the yield curve is an unambiguous predictor of the business cycle. Hence, an inverted yield curve should warn us that a recession is fast approaching. In fact, neither statement is true. The former is easily refuted by the data, which show that QE periods in the US have unequivocally been associated with higher yields, with term premia rising by an average 134 bp through each past QE phase. The efficiency of the Treasury yield curve as a predictor of the business cycle is analysed elsewhere (Howell 2018). This confirms that the standard 10-2 year yield curve slope is, at best, a flaky predictor. This analysis points out that, because different maturity spreads work at different times, what also matters is the curvature of the term structure. In other works, slope and curvature must be assessed together. A key component explaining curvature is the pattern of term premia. Term premia are liquidity phenomena, largely reflecting the excess demand for 'safe' assets.

The liquidity shocks that ricocheted across the World in 1989 as the Berlin Wall fell ultimately forced interest rates down and helped to reverse the polarity of the global financial system. Capital raced Eastwards along what I call the *Financial Silk Road*, while politics and people marched West, causing too many countries, and notably China, to lean too heavily on the US dollar and the US Treasury market for safety. Linked to these changes, today's financial markets increasingly have to serve as *refinancing mechanisms* rather than as *new financing mechanisms*, making the capacity of capital, i.e. balance sheet size, more important than the cost of capital, i.e. the level of interest rates. The heightened supply of poor quality 'safe' assets, or what I more formally describe as the *shadow monetary base*, compromises the ability of private balance sheets to roll over the huge volumes of outstanding debts left over from the GFC era. Ironically, a reduced supply of liquidity and 'safe' assets, increases the demand to hoard them. Together these features amplify the swings in Global Liquidity and explain why, as the World has got bigger, it has also become more volatile. The underlying scarcity of high-quality assets leads on to *Capital Wars*. Here, the battleground embraces money, technology and geopolitics, with the struggle fought out between the two key superpowers: Chinese industry and American finance. China's presence is weighing more and more: in the year 2000, China accounted for 5.9% of Global Liquidity, or less than one-fifth of America's share; China's share reached 10.1% at the time of the 2007–2008 GFC and, today, it has swelled to a whopping 27.5%, significantly out-pacing America's slipping 22.5% slice. China matters hugely to both the World economy and World finance. I conclude that whereas America needs to reinvigorate her industry, China has the more pressing need to rapidly develop her financial sector. Like history, these are processes, not events, but we can still ask whether the final victor in the markets will be the US dollar or a digitally based Chinese Yuan?

This book is a hybrid of economic and finance theory and real-World experience. Unlike traditional finance, which focuses on the merits of individual securities, I concentrate on asset allocation and evaluate the potential for macro-valuation shifts based on the interaction of investment crowds and monetary institutions. The approach is my own, but several people deserve a hat-tip. Among those academics that have influenced me, foremost have been Ron Smith, Richard Portes, Helene Rey and Pavol Povala. In business, I had the good luck to work with innovative researchers Henry Kaufman, Marty Leibowitz and Chris Mitchinson, and thoughtful bankers, most notably Ewen Cameron-Watt and (the late) Michael Baring. The collection and implementation of liquidity and capital flow data is the specialisation of *CrossBorder Capital*, an investment advisory firm we set up in 1996. My colleagues need special praise, most particularly Angela Cozzini. I owe a debt to Tula Weis and Lucy Kidwell, the editors at Palgrave Macmillan. Above all, heartfelt thanks to my long-suffering family for putting up with so much.

London and Oxford   Michael J. Howell
November 2019

References

Gagnon, J. 2016. Quantitative Easing: An Underappreciated Success. PIIE Policy Brief No. 16-4. Washington, DC.
Howell, Michael J. 2018. What Does the Yield Curve Slope Really Tell Us? *The Journal of Fixed Income* 27 (4): 22–33.

Contents

List of Figures

List of Tables

1

Introduction: Capital Wars

The money power preys upon the nation in times of peace and conspires against it in times of adversity. It is more despotic than monarchy, more insolent than autocracy, more selfish than bureaucracy. Abraham Lincoln (Attributed, purportedly from a letter to Colonel William F. Elkins [November, 1864] following the passage of the National Bank Act [June, 1864])

Capital Wars: The New Trade Wars

Surveying the shattered certainties of the post-2008 era, what can we learn? The 2007–2008 Global Financial Crisis[1] (GFC) was a devastating global liquidity shock. But already by the early 1980s, the warnings were there. New factors had by then evolved to displace the prevailing doctrine of *earnings power* as the main driver of stock prices: foremost among these is *money power*. We focus here on a specific type of money power that we dub *Global Liquidity*: a US$130 trillion pool of footloose capital that is currently two-thirds bigger than World GDP. See Fig. 1.1.

The 2007–2008 GFC happened when a dramatic escalation in monetary tensions triggered a frantic scramble for US dollars. Europe's demands alone exceeded a whopping US$8 trillion. Yet, there was no automatic international lender of the last resort and, with the IMF's firepower then still only counted in billions, there was no pool of reserves anywhere in the World, outside of the US Federal Reserve and its system of swap lines, that was large

© The Author(s) 2020
M. J. Howell, *Capital Wars*,
https://doi.org/10.1007/978-3-030-39288-8_1

Fig. 1.1   Global Liquidity

enough to backstop the international financial system. This gap remains and US dollar swap lines have since become even more politicised. The US authorities officially target 'favoured nations', which, for now, excludes Emerging Market economies and, pointedly, China, the biggest dollar user.[2] America's decisions to deploy Fed swap lines, and whom to allocate these to, have essentially become Nero-like choices and conditional on who sits in the White House. With close to US$17 trillion of debt now owed by non-US corporations, and with over two-thirds of this debt US dollar-denominated, these decisions matter.

In facing up to these tensions, the last decade has not surprisingly seen an explosion of monetary policy accommodation to fill the gaps left by the many private sector casualties, and rightly analogous to the billion light-ening volts that Dr. Frankenstein jolted through his slumping monster. Figure 1.2 shows that Global Liquidity continues to outpace World GDP, even besting its pre-GFC peak ratio to GDP in both 2009 and 2017. The continuing crucial role played by the US Federal Reserve means that its actions now largely dictate whether global investors move risk-on or risk-off. Consequently, US Fed-watching has turned into a much-prized skill, sometimes even serving as a dark art worthy of Hogwarts and Harry Potter. The collapse of global banks in 2007–2008; the Eurozone banking crisis of 2010–2012; the subsequent injection of over US$10 trillion into financial markets through the widespread adoption of explicit quantitative easing

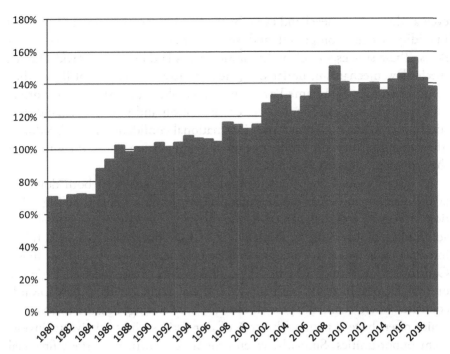

Fig. 1.2 Global Liquidity (% of World GDP), 1980–2019 (Source *CrossBorder Capital*)

(QE) policies by Central Banks, as well as their more recent dalliance with quantitative tightening (QT), all underscore the importance of monitoring and understanding liquidity conditions Worldwide. Simply put, money moves markets.

Democrat strategist James Carville shrewdly recognised how finance controls the World when he famously quipped that if there is reincarnation he wanted to "…*come back as the bond market*". These days it more obviously dominates the complex interaction between the industrial economy and the markets. But then who or what controls finance? We focus here on the drivers of Global Liquidity, namely the financial and exchange rate relationships within and between countries and the determinants of cross-border flows of money, securities, goods and services. These same factors have become the new weapons in the escalating Capital Wars between the US, Europe and China. Think of capital wars as a conflict between nations, fought out in investment markets, that parallels the more familiar concept of trade wars and which ultimately involves a battle for currency supremacy in the World economy. Global Liquidity embodies the idea that money, here meaning savings plus credit, is never entirely exogenous to the economic system, even at the national level and even for the World's largest economies. Global Liquidity shocks compound and spread internationally via cross-border flows. These shocks still obey the classical rules laid down by David Hume's specie-flow mechanism, updated to include cross-border capital flows; they continue to obey Gresham's Law,[3] where overvalued (or 'bad') money drives undervalued (or 'good') money out of circulation and into hoards, and they still respect Triffin's dilemma[4] over international confidence in the US dollar. Throughout history, the problems caused by money are always the same: it is the proposed solutions that differ.

As history's clock has swept forward, the deregulation of both domestic credit markets and cross-border capital flows, lower taxes and falling inflation rates have together helped to mobilise the swelling savings pools that accumulate in the large money-centres of London, New York and Tokyo into fast-moving and sometimes menacing cross-border capital flows. Controversy surrounds whether these flows are ultimately driven by 'push' or 'pull' factors. In truth, both apply. Financial capital tends to flow towards countries where economic growth rates are accelerating, because these economies often have a natural shortfall of domestic savings relative to investment opportunities. Similarly, when economic growth rates slow, financial capital typically quits in step with declining investment potential. However, the clustering and commonality of capital flow movements, both between countries and between asset and liability components, highlight the vital push from some Global Liquidity cycle.

For most of the period since the end of WW1, America's economic dominance meant that her external payments position could provide a convenient cushion or shock absorber for the Rest of the World against these waves of international capital. The two World Wars accelerated American economic growth and gave her a generous savings surplus, which, at first sight, resembles that of China today. But unlike our current setting, America's ability to fund post-war reconstruction in the 1920s and once again in the 1950s, coincided with huge investment and savings shortfalls elsewhere. Thus, the US could easily export her vast savings through increased foreign trade, even though this increased her vulnerability to tariff wars and a subsequent trade contraction in the 1930s.

Things changed by the late 1960s. The advanced economies, and notably Germany and Japan, had by then been rebuilt and global savings were again abundant. Instead of needing access to scarce capital, these economies now hunted out foreign export markets for their tradable goods, while at the same time protecting their home industries by limiting consumer imports. In short, they wanted to export their excess savings as capital. With their large and open financial markets and with the background already set by a progressive elimination of controls on capital flows through the 1950 and 1960s, the US and UK economies started to run ever-larger trade deficits to accommodate these Asian and Continental European surpluses, albeit at a cost to themselves of higher unemployment and more consumer debt. Ironically, these large deficits were likely a better measure of the competitiveness of British and American finance, than a signpost to their relative industrial inefficiency.

Lately, we have seemingly reached the apogee: spurred by the vast economic changes that followed the fall of the Berlin Wall, the entire World economy now enjoys excess production and abundant savings, with China alone having to deploy an annual US$6 trillion nest-egg. Not surprisingly, more and more economies are seeking to increase their trade surpluses, so becoming potentially even bigger net exporters of capital. However, this plainly requires some other economy (or economies) to run large counterpart trade deficits.[5] And, since trade deficits effectively mean deficits for domestic manufacturing industry, which is a key source of future productivity growth and remains a major urban employer, this policy creates emotive political challenges. The need to run large, persistent trade deficits may also explain why it is probably still too early for China to take America's place in the World trading system. Without the US as the facilitator, other smaller economies would be forced to run deficits to accommodate China, which could sizeably reduce their underlying rates of economic growth. Some estimates even suggest that a switch from a World trading system centred on *American deficits* to one revolving around *Chinese surpluses* could ultimately dampen World GDP growth by as much as 2% per annum.[6]

In this new World of capital abundance, we have seemingly hit an impasse. America has lost her willingness and her ability to absorb the excess savings of others. The US share of World GDP is plainly lower than it was after WW2, domestic income inequality is greater, and the geopolitical benefits of accommodating economic rivals, like China, has become far less obvious. But surely excess liquidity should drive down the price of money and help restore balance? Given that the true *price of money* is the exchange rate[7] (not the interest rate), a question related to this capital abundance is what currency arrangements now best serve the diverging interests of the US and her economic competitors? For most of the last two centuries, the US dollar and other international currencies have been pegged, initially under the gold standard (1717–1934)[8] and subsequently under the Bretton Woods (1944–1971) fixed exchange rate system. Bretton Woods was set up as a dollar-based system, although some have since argued that this outcome was not predetermined, but largely driven by British nervousness over their inability, at the time, to guarantee future sterling stability. Whether or not it came as a coincidence, the Bretton Woods era proved a comparative economic nirvana, enjoying GDP growth rates roughly twice those seen in the preceding and following decades of fluctuating currencies, modest albeit creeping inflation, the absence of major bank failures and financial crises, and more homogeneous distributions of both incomes and wealth.

Following the demise of Bretton Woods,[9] the major World currencies have now been floating for most of the last fifty years. Alongside, capital flows became progressively deregulated. Almost the first act of Britain's incoming Thatcher Government in 1979 was to abolish UK capital controls. Other countries followed. The evolution of the so-called *Washington Consensus* policies through the 1990s featured tax reform and fiscal discipline, combined with trade liberalisation and the opening-up of capital accounts to inward investment. These initiatives were led by the IMF, the World Bank and the US Treasury, all of whom encouraged their adoption by the Emerging Market economies. As we explore in a later chapter, the symbolic Fall of the Berlin Wall in 1989 and the earlier 1985 reforms in China enacted by Deng Xiaoping effectively economically enfranchised some 2–3 billion workers, across many previously State Socialist governments and formerly closed economies. China further nailed-down her rapid growth path by joining the WTO (World Trade Organisation) in 2001. The decision by several of these fast-growing countries to either officially fix their currencies to the floating US dollar, or else closely shadow it, gave the greenback a much-needed shot in the arm. It follows that the period of floating exchange rates should not be seen as part of a natural evolution into a multi-currency system, as some have suggested, but it should be viewed as three distinct eras. From 1974 until the early 1990s, the World operated on an *oil-based standard*,[10] which effectively underwrote the continuation of the US dollar system. And, from the early 1990s onwards, new demand from the Emerging Market economies has replaced currency demand from the oil producers to similarly help underwrite the US dollar. We shall argue that here-in lie the roots of our current financial instability.

The original proponents of floating exchange rates advanced several inflated claims in the 1950s and the 1960s to promote their attractions, including gradualism in terms of the scope and pace of currency movements and the greater independence for national monetary policies. Yet, even though financial crises were not unknown under the gold standard, the last 30 years have been among the most tumultuous in monetary history; the pace and scope of movements in exchange rates have been larger than ever before, with greater exchange rate 'overshooting'[11] and, yet, with a clearly failing ability to hold back the destructive waves of Global Liquidity. Whereas in the 1960s, the World economy mostly suffered labour cost shocks and, in the 1970s and 1980s, oil and commodity-price shocks, it is more often buffeted these days by Global Liquidity shocks. Financial markets spin on fragile axes and this common driver emphasises that modern financial crises tend to be neither purely national, nor simply isolated events. Moreover, the Global Liquidity shocks are typically bigger, longer-lasting and more pervasive than the calibre of shocks studied by economists and Central Banks when using their so-called DSGE[12] models of the economy. In fact, since 1980 well over sixty countries have experienced asset booms followed by banking crises, with at least six episodes of major asset price bubbles: (1) 1980s Japan; (2) early 1990s in Sweden and across much of Scandinavia; (3) Thailand and the neighbouring South-East Asian economies in the mid-1990s and (4) US in the late 1990s and, so far, twice again in the 2000s. The social and economic costs have been high, with national banking systems in many of these countries subsequently collapsing, after facing loan losses from these bubbles that on occasions exceeded a staggering one-quarter of their GDPs. As 007 agent, James Bond, keenly observed in *Goldfinger*: "*Once is happenstance. Twice is coincidence. Three times is enemy action*".

The most recent and deepest of these crises is the 2007–2008 GFC. In the event, this proved to be as much a crisis about 'bad liabilities', i.e. unreliable funding structures, as a crisis over 'bad assets', i.e. poor investments. The GFC is widely dated from the run on Bear Stearns investment bank in March 2008, with the crisis precipitated by the US Administration's September 15th decision to allow the venerable investment bank Lehman Brothers to fail. This single event caused interbank credit markets Worldwide to freeze as banks with excess reserves quickly turned more risk-averse. Indebted banks suddenly had to find alternative sources of finance to avoid shrinking their balance sheets. Yet, at the same time, there is a compelling argument that the roots of the GFC instead trail back to the 2002–2006 US real estate boom, with the trigger revealing clear Chinese fingerprints: once again underlining her growing economic and financial sway. Closer inspection of capital flow and credit data highlight the People's Bank (PBoC) tightening Chinese credit conditions in early 2008, probably to defray industrial pollution concerns and improve air quality ahead of the showcase August 2008 Beijing Olympics? Figure 1.3 tracks the rolling 12-month total of funds injected or withdrawn from Chinese money markets by the PBoC, which recorded a cumulative drawdown exceeding RMB650 billion (circa US$95 billion) or 6.3% of its balance sheet.

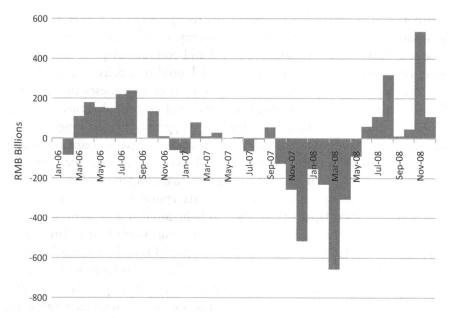

Fig. 1.3 Liquidity injections into Chinese money markets, 2007–2008 (RMB billions, rolling 12-month total) (Source *CrossBorder Capital*, People's Bank)

This forced credit-starved Chinese borrowers into the offshore Eurodollar markets in search of replacement funding. Could their demands have simultaneously clashed with the rising needs from Western borrowers, who were increasingly struggling to finance their leveraged mortgage-backed and asset-backed security portfolios, particularly following the failure of Bear Stearns?

Cross-Border Capital Flaws?

With hindsight, the pattern of all these crises looks remarkably similar. Every national crisis is preceded by an economic boom, although not every economic boom has been followed by a financial crisis. Their cause is not so much floating exchange rate regimes, per se, but the destructive effect of rapidly shifting cross-border capital flows. Those economies that suffer severe crises tend to have previously experienced above-average increases in cross-border capital inflows, which lead on to higher financial asset and real estate prices. Ahead of the 2007–2008 GFC many countries, including even the US, saw sharp jumps in their cross-border capital activity. Notwithstanding, the rising ratios between investment inflows and GDP were multiple times bigger for the smaller economies of Ireland, Greece, Spain and Iceland, with their large-scale inflows often resulting, ironically, from the whopping debts issued by their banks and corporations in the major offshore funding centres of New York, Frankfurt and London. In contrast, the parallel increase in capital inflows into America largely arrived from fast-growing Emerging Market economies, namely China and South-East Asia, and from the oil-exporting economies all eager to buy more US dollar 'safe' assets. Admittedly, these capital flows were also at times unusually large: China enjoyed a dramatic windfall increase in her exports after joining the World Trade Organization (WTO) in 2001, and the oil exporters benefitted from the tripling of crude oil prices to $90/barrel between 2001–2006.

Such risks were well-known to the architects of Bretton Woods. They deliberately restricted private capital movements, blaming the depth of the 1930s Depression and the turmoil of the interwar years on the violent swings of capital between nations. Ironically, the original case for floating exchange rates largely ignored capital movements, seeing them, at worst, as adjusting passively to current account imbalances. Not only did these experts miss the size and velocity of capital flows, but they failed to recognise that it is also likely that current accounts adjust to capital flows: a possibility that echoes an earlier debate in the 1920s about the so-called *transfer problem* over German WW1 reparation payments. There is, of course, no reason why capital flows should sum to zero. In fact, they are the necessary counterpart to current account imbalances. There is also no reason per se why large or small net capital flows tell us everything about exchange rates. What matters for the exchange rate is the net balance between overall supply and demand. A surge of capital inflows is likely to increase the exchange rate unless there is a corresponding expansion in the supply of the currency. But even when the exchange rate is bid higher, there is no guarantee that it will rebalance flows. Exchange rate movements act as a more plausible equilibrium mechanism following trade shocks than after capital flow shocks. In reality, in the wake of a capital flow shock, it is often hard to predict whether the financial system will converge or diverge from its equilibrium position, because capital flows may, at least for a period, become self-sustaining so causing currencies and asset prices to overshoot. These rapid, large-scale cross-border capital flows consequently demand equally large offsetting movements both in current accounts and potentially in exchange rates. To help ensure economic stability, many national governments have insisted on maintaining currency parities against competitor currencies, and notably by staying closely aligned with the US dollar.

It would, therefore, seem that modern financial crises have less to do with lax regulation, excessive risk-taking by imprudent bankers and policy-makers' obsession with inflation-targeting than might be presupposed. Central Banks have power, but they do not always have control. And, often they exercise unelected powers. According to an anonymous governor,[13] the ECB: "… *threaten[s] governments that misbehave with financial destruction. They cut off refinancing and threaten to kill the banking system. They create a roll-over crisis in the bond market. This is what happened to Italy in 2011*". We focus on the similar disruptive potential of Global Liquidity in aggregate; its role is raising cross-asset correlations, and its contribution towards the build-up of systemic risk. The expansion of domestic credit and heightened asset demand in each of these previous crises was largely a consequence of the inflows of cross-border capital, which substantially eased funding constraints on local banks. This extra ability to borrow allowed certain governments, businesses, households and even other banks to side-step the burdens imposed by their existing debts, often for years. Each crisis broke when the global credit providers' appetite for new debt slowed. This forced hasty liquidations of remaining assets to quickly repay debts and it often occurred alongside a sliding national currency unit when the direction of capital flows suddenly reversed. At the same time, the collapse in their capital bases forced banks to sharply shrink their loan books, which, in turn, led on to further falls in the value of bank capital and ever tighter credit conditions. Not only is this the very reverse of what had happened in the preceding boom years, it sounds remarkably like the classic 'debt-deflation' model described by American economist Irving Fisher in his *Booms and Depressions* (1932) written about America's Depression years, but now brought up-to-date with what Rey (2015) describes as a single *global factor* and we explain in terms of Global Liquidity.

The First Sightings: Salomon Brothers Inc.

Whether or not we can rightly claim responsibility for first coining the term *Global Liquidity*, we were certainly among its very earliest pioneers. These roots run back to the mid-1980s when Salomon Brothers,[14] the US investment bank, was set to make its big push into international financial markets. At the time, Salomon dominated securities' trading. Underpinned by a whopping balance sheet, its financial punch was led by an innovative research department, directed by the restless geniuses of Henry Kaufman and Marty Leibowitz. What Henry knew about credit and currencies, Marty matched him on bonds and duration. Investment policy was implemented by a pre-eminent team of researchers and economists, several plucked from the IMF and recruited from the Federal Reserve, among them Nick Sargen, John Lipsky, Dick Berner, Kim Schoenholtz, Robbie Feldman, Ron Napier, Chris Mitchinson and Laszlo Birinyi. All now form part of the far-reaching Salomon Diaspora.

Many of Salomon's traders believed that watching money and capital flows was the nearest thing to obtaining *insider information*. What's more, it was perfectly legal. In planning its mid-1980s business expansion, Salomon needed estimates of the size of cross-border investment and trading flows and this writer, brilliantly assisted by Angela Cozzini, was tasked with gathering the data. Our researches ultimately led to an annual publication (now defunct) called *International Equity Flows* that surveyed the cross-border capital markets and featured estimates of what we dubbed *Global Liquidity* and defined, in the Salomon tradition, as the total inflow of savings and credit into domestic and cross-border financial markets. Salomon Research Head, Henry Kaufman's famous dictum is of course: "*...money matters, but credit counts*". The first Salomon Brothers publication tracking *Global Liquidity* was published in 1986.

Global Liquidity can be split functionally, as well as geographically, by type of liquidity, which helps to isolate its changing quality. In other words, certain components exercise a greater influence over the future size and direction of the total pool than others. We focus on three liquidity components: (1) Central Bank provision; (2) private sector supply and (3) cross-border inflows. We think in terms of three broad liquidity transmission channels, with each one affecting or amplifying risk-taking behaviour. First, the sum of domestic Central Bank and private sector liquidity tends to affect the relative prices of 'safe' assets, through a *risk-taking channel*. By reducing the odds of systemic risk, more domestic liquidity increases the term premia on government bonds as the demand for safety falls, while simultaneously reducing the equivalent premia assigned to risk assets. When the 'safe' asset is used internationally, cross-border inflows are also likely to come into play. Second, the *exchange rate channel* reflects the changing quality-mix of liquidity between the private and public sectors. More private sector or 'good' liquidity strengthens a currency unit, whereas more Central Bank or 'bad' liquidity weakens it. Third, the spillovers of domestic liquidity from the core economies into outward cross-border capital flows are typically amplified both by offshore funding markets and by other policy-makers in the periphery economies into bigger increases in Global Liquidity and more risk-taking by investors. This latter *cross-border capital flow channel* is shaped by the current institutional make-up of the World economy and embodies many of the structural differences between America and China.

Although conventional finance theory typically ignores the impact of liquidity factors, a straightforward example can show their importance. Between the start of the Reagan Presidency in 1981 and the end of the Clinton Presidency in 2001, or some twenty years later, Wall Street jumped by almost tenfold. Yet, profits increased by a miserly 236% and so could justify less than one-quarter of this rise. The increase in investors' appetite for risk assets proved more decisive, with equities (held directly and indirectly) rising from a little over 14% of aggregate US financial wealth to more than 42% and safe asset holdings correspondingly tumbling. Similar experiences are shared Worldwide and even in Emerging Markets, such as India, near-flat earnings have not deterred waves of foreign money and domestic mutual funds, fuelled by aspiring middle-class investors, from driving-up stock prices. Now with Central Banks actively pursuing QE policies, industrial corporations flush with cash and aggressively buying-in their equity, and wealth levels rising among Emerging Market investors, the liquidity theory of investment has never been more important. Yet, the sources and uses of liquidity need to be better understood by investors and policy-makers alike. It is these macro-valuation shifts in asset markets that liquidity analysis seeks to explain.

Global Liquidity: Endless River or High-Water Mark?

Putting this into context, the US, the main supplier of the global currency to World markets, is a large, low productivity growth economy, with highly developed financial system and a capital surplus. In direct contrast to the US, China is a large, high productivity growth economy, with underdeveloped financial markets and a far greater need for 'intelligent' and risk-seeking capital. China increasingly dominates World industrial production and has become the major international user of the global currency, through her supply chains and logistic companies that span Asia, Europe and the Americas. The resulting vast capital flows into China describe what we call *The Financial Silk Road*, echoing the monetary factors that drove capital and trade flows along the dusty, historic caravan routes between the West and China during the sixteenth and eighteenth centuries. After the Fall of Constantinople to the Ottomans (1453), the old Silk Road became as much about China's lust for silver as the West's demand for paper, silk and spices. China's monetary system became tied to the silver peso, with at times, more coins circulating in China than in Mexico itself. In the late 1590s, the gold/silver ratio in China stood around 6:1, or more than twice the 13:1 ratio that then prevailed in Spain. In the more than 50 years that it took to eliminate this huge silver arbitrage, large-scale trade and capital flows reshaped the historic World economy. This was to happen again in the early 1700s, when a Chinese population boom, literally fed by the new American crops (maize, peanuts and sweet potatoes), triggered further large demands for silver coin. And, it is happening once more right now through the US dollar.

Yet, the modern international monetary system is becoming evermore ill-suited to intermediate our current vast capital and trade flows. It evolved from a pragmatic mish-mash of various agreements, whose origins primarily lie in the WW2 institutions, such as the IMF. It is not designed for a billion hard-working, high savings Chinese determined to rapidly pull their country out of poverty. Not surprisingly, China, for one, is eager to displace both the US dollar and America's financial imprint, especially in Asia:

> ...we should promote the Renminbi[15] to be the primary currency of Asia, just as the US dollar first became the currency of North America and then the currency of the World ... Every globalisation was initiated by a rising empire ... As a rising super power, the 'One Belt, One Road' strategy is the beginning of China's own globalisation ... it is a counter-measure to the US strategy of shifting focus to the East. (Excerpts from a speech by Major-General Qiao Liang, Chinese PLA, April 2015)

China needs to create an alternative international means of payment that looks more like the Swiss Franc than the Argentinean peso, but whether or not she can ever get herself off the US dollar hook, the challenge adds a geopolitical dimension to the latest monetary trends. It also highlights the great importance of *seigniorage*, namely the facility of national monies to command a greater purchasing power. Put another way, this describes the ability of, say, the US authorities to buy real resources with a US$100 bill that costs the US Treasury only a few cents to print. International financial systems, from ancient Greece and Rome, through to the nineteenth-century dominance of Britain's pound sterling are always built around a key currency that embodies *seigniorage*. China now wants its slice. We shall argue that a key risk to international financial market stability is that China is too hooked on the US unit: she effectively re-exports US dollars, when she should export Yuan. This will likely have big cross-border effects as it forces China to open up her domestic bond market to foreign capital; invoice more and lend more in Yuan; onshore or regionalise more of her supply chains and establish and promote a digital Yuan currency.

If capital is power, capital also needs power. Put another way, what exactly constitutes a 'safe' asset embodies a crucial geopolitical dimension. Thus, the British pound sterling dominated the nineteenth century in many ways because of her vast navy. Both expected to dominate the twentieth. On 26 June 1897, 165 ships of the Royal Navy lined up at Spithead to mark Queen Victoria's Diamond Jubilee. The assembled fleet stretched for miles. Their bunting gracefully receding into the sun-blazed horizon. This armada included 21 battleships and 44 cruisers, their names projecting the arrogant confidence of a global Empire: Victorious, Renown, Powerful, Terrible, Majestic and Mars. It was an emphatic message sent out to friends as well as foes, and one that projected the persistence of British imperial power alongside the continuing integrity and soundness of the pound sterling. The Prince of Wales, soon to become Edward VII, took the salute from the quarterdeck of the royal yacht on behalf of his mother. Her Majesty the Queen, then 78 years old, had perhaps wisely opted to observe the great fleet by telescope from nearby Osborne House on the Isle of Wight. For this vast, intimidating military presence took fully eight hours to sail past, and yet its assembly still did not require the recall of one single ship from the Mediterranean or from those distant squadrons guarding Britain's imperial sea lanes in India and Asia. Capital wars are not simply the battles for currency supremacy.

Sceptics who dismiss China's future threat might recall that just over a hundred years ago, around the outbreak of World War One, the US dollar was quoted and convertible in far fewer international markets than was the contemporary Austro-Hungarian krone. In 1984, Shenzhen's Special Economic Zones (SEZ) were a tiny blip that barely registered on the radar of World trade. The latest US$4½ trillion annual rate of Chinese exports dramatically emphasises the impact of three decades of breakneck growth and economic 'catch-up'. On many measures of financial might, China has already overtaken America, as Fig. 1.4 confirms. Economic adjustment is being channelled through a weaker US dollar and a loose US monetary policy/tight fiscal policy mix, into a heightened and more fragile Global Liquidity cycle. America's domestic policy imperative alongside China's productivity catch-up essentially results in an unstable financial World. The tension between the strength of the Chinese economy and the evermore inadequate supplies of US Treasuries, for 'safe' savings assets, incentivises more and more dangerously complex forms of financial engineering. The Global Liquidity cycle vents these tensions. Our mantras are—don't ignore liquidity and don't underestimate China. These subliminal messages of the past two decades have now become the explicit warnings for the future.

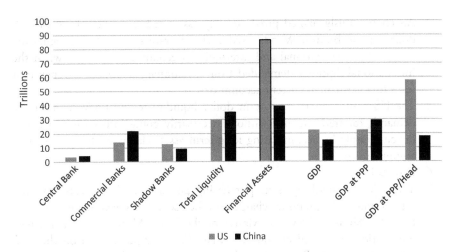

Fig. 1.4 China's relative financial power, mid-2019 (US$ in trillions, except PPP/head in US$ '000s) (Source *CrossBorder Capital*)

In the following chapters, the second tries to put Global Liquidity into context. In Chapter 3, we trace the key forces of change and summarise our argument. Chapter 4 analyses the economics of flow of funds accounting that lies at the heart of our approach. The real exchange rate adjustment mechanism is explained in Chapter 5. Chapters 6–8 consider in more detail the three main sources of Global Liquidity: private sector funding, Central Bank provision and cross-border capital flows. It specifically identifies the rise of CICPs. Chapter 9 looks more closely at the immature financial systems in China and the Emerging Market economies. How liquidity shocks are transmitted is examined in Chapter 10. Chapter 11 revisits questions over the safe asset shortage. Chapter 12 discusses globalisation, FDI and questions over the direction of Europe, and Chapter 13 explains the use of global liquidity index (GLI) data. Chapter 14 concludes.

Notes

1. The accepted appellation for the financial and economic turmoil that struck in 2007–2008 is the *Global Financial Crisis (GFC) and Great Recession.*
2. See Adam Tooze, *Crashed*, 2018.
3. Gresham's Law, namely after the Elizabethan financier, states that "*bad money drives out good*" from circulation, so that coins with a higher intrinsic than their face value are withdrawn from circulation and hoarded.

4. An eponymously named puzzle usually associated with the role of the US dollar in the Bretton Woods fixed exchange rate system. It highlights the conflict between national and international economic objectives, when the international liquidity demanded from a nationally supplied currency unit leads to a permanent current account deficit.

5. The US could export short-term dollar liquidity to the RoW to meet the demands for trade finance without necessarily going into current account deficit, simply by accumulating long-term assets claims on foreigners. This argument is different.

6. IMF estimate.

7. The 'price' of anything is its purchasing power, i.e. what it can buy. The interest rate is the premium charged on the use of borrowed money.

8. In 1717, Sir Isaac Newton, Master of the Royal Mint, established a new mint ratio between silver and gold that effectively put Britain on the gold standard. President Roosevelt took America off the gold standard by introducing the Gold Reserve Act, 30 January 1934.

9. It was over when President Nixon ended US dollar convertibility into gold on 15 August 1971.

10. In July 1974, US Treasury Secretary William Simon (another Salomon Brothers' alumnus) agreed with Saudi Arabia and subsequently OPEC that crude oil would in future be priced solely in US dollars. It still remains true that the Saudi holdings of US Treasury securities are not separately disclosed.

11. Measured, say, by the differences between market and purchasing power parity (PPP) or trend exchange rates.

12. Dynamic Stochastic General Equilibrium (DSGE) are the workhorse models used in many Central Banks to better understand how the economy responds to policy changes.

13. Quoted by Ambrose Evans-Pritchard, Telegraph, October 30, 2019.

14. Salomon Brothers Inc. was eventually acquired and absorbed into Citigroup in 1996.

15. 'RMB' or 'Renminbi' and 'Yuan' can be considered as alternative terms and used, respectively, in the same manner as 'Sterling' and 'British pound'. Chinese prices are denominated in Yuan.

Reference

Rey, Hélène. 2015. IMF Mundell Fleming Lecture.

2

Global Money

How Big Is the Pool of Global Liquidity?

The wealth of modern capitalist societies appears as an immense collection of stocks, bonds and short-term liquid instruments. Most of these financial assets have seen a huge growth over the past three decades. Global financial markets now total some US$250 trillion of listed assets (primary securities) or roughly 3½ times World GDP, even ignoring the sizeable pools of unlisted and off-market OTC[1] instruments. This is equivalent to a potential nest-egg of more than US$40,000 for every living person on the planet. Or, advertising our 'green' credentials, a hefty US$42 of paper wealth for every tree growing in every country in the World. Figure 2.1 reports the ratio between US households' net financial wealth (i.e. excluding housing) and GDP since 1950 and highlights its recent parabolic rise to test an impressive ratio of four-times income. Never has the World enjoyed such a rapid increase in its average per capita wealth.

The equivalent more than 10-fold leap in the size of World financial markets that has occurred since the early 1980s has been paced by a similar-sized explosion in Global Liquidity, with much of these flows criss-crossing international borders. This pool of liquidity alone, covering retail and wholesale liquid assets, totals close to US$130 trillion, making it some two-thirds bigger than World GDP. See Fig. 2.2. Alongside, World credit markets have become both more international and more interconnected, spanned by complex intermediation chains, involving so-called *shadow banks*, and financed by the increasing use of market-based collateral. The cross-border dimension

© The Author(s) 2020
M. J. Howell, *Capital Wars*,
https://doi.org/10.1007/978-3-030-39288-8_2

Fig. 2.1 US household wealth (net, excluding housing) as multiple of GDP, 1950–2019 (quarterly) (*Source* US Federal Reserve)

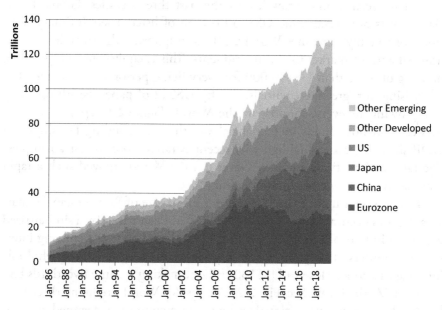

Fig. 2.2 The pool of Global Liquidity, 1986–2019 (US$ in trillions) (Source *CrossBorder Capital*)

is especially important because it links the fortunes of Emerging Markets to the gyrations of Western wholesale money markets in the core economies. Through a network of foreign currency loans made to local and regional banks, large *global banks* domiciled in the major financial centres are funded through repos and commercial paper, usually denominated in US dollars. These funds are on-lent often against local currency collateral, which means that US dollar devaluation (itself commonly associated with American monetary expansions) encourages still greater leverage. On top, local policy-makers in the Emerging Markets typically try to monetise these capital inflows, so further fuelling the Global Liquidity cycle.

Global Liquidity represents a pool of funds bigger than the annual flows of World savings, as reported by the IMF and shown as a percentage of World GDP in Fig. 2.3. Within this total, the pool of Emerging Market Liquidity is near US$50 trillion according to Table 2.1, or some 38% of the total. However, China makes up almost US$36 trillion of this figure, or some 70% of Emerging Market liquidity, and she has provided most of the recent impetus, expanding by a jaw-dropping near-15-fold in less than 20 years. Figure 2.4 reports the growth rates of Global Liquidity

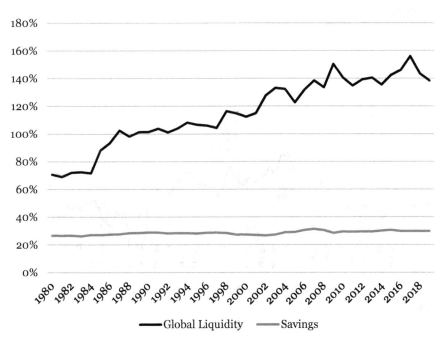

Fig. 2.3 Global Liquidity and World savings, 1980–2018 (annual, percent of GDP) (*Source* IMF, *CrossBorder Capital*)

Table 2.1 Global Liquidity—regional breakdown, 2000–2019E (US$ in trillions)

| End-year | World | Developed | Emerging | Of which | | | |
				Eurozone	China	Japan	USA
2000	37.95	32.49	5.47	12.09	2.43	5.01	12.01
2001	38.11	32.50	5.59	11.72	2.68	4.31	13.05
2002	45.03	38.68	6.32	15.42	3.03	4.72	14.26
2003	51.86	44.47	7.35	18.78	3.50	5.19	15.23
2004	57.45	48.97	8.44	21.11	3.92	5.22	16.53
2005	59.96	50.09	9.82	21.16	4.63	4.63	17.83
2006	67.73	56.15	11.51	24.43	5.39	4.34	19.51
2007	81.69	66.63	14.96	31.34	7.05	4.96	20.77
2008	82.40	66.22	16.08	29.77	8.67	6.08	22.47
2009	89.54	69.91	19.49	32.54	10.75	5.96	22.02
2010	93.69	69.43	24.10	31.97	13.71	6.54	21.26
2011	100.12	71.90	28.05	31.78	16.80	7.26	22.21
2012	104.34	72.51	31.64	32.49	19.50	6.25	22.84
2013	107.43	71.68	35.54	30.42	23.24	6.34	24.02
2014	104.77	66.71	37.85	25.17	25.91	6.23	25.25
2015	106.21	67.03	38.92	24.66	27.50	6.79	25.99
2016	112.59	70.76	41.52	25.59	29.23	8.10	26.96
2017	128.67	79.58	48.74	31.02	34.59	8.84	28.00
2018	127.65	77.99	49.26	28.94	35.18	9.20	28.56
2019E	128.90	78.51	49.99	28.61	35.58	9.41	29.24
%change 2000–19	240	142	835	137	1366	88	143

E—estimate
Source *CrossBorder Capital*

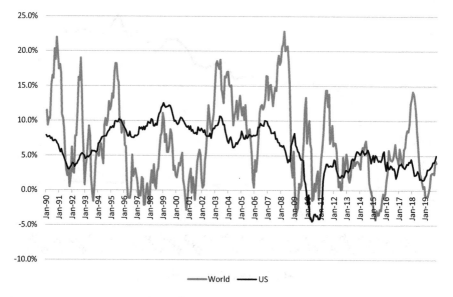

Fig. 2.4 Growth in Global Liquidity and US Liquidity, 1990–2019 (YoY% change) (Source *CrossBorder Capital*)

against benchmark US Liquidity since 1990. Global Liquidity experiences the bigger swings. Its annual growth has often been negative and generally it appears to amplify the US moves, likely operating through a mechanism linked to movements in the US dollar. While some economies, such as Japan have come and largely gone as major financial players, others continue to muscle forward, notably China, which looks ultimately set to wrestle control over global, or at least Asian, finance from the USA. As we detail later in Chapter 9, China accounted for barely 6% of Global Liquidity in 1990, but this has since leapt to a 28% share, with the other Emerging Markets adding a further 11% points. The wrinkle in this story is that China's huge financial footprint is still largely dollar-based, and her future challenge is to encourage a commensurate growth in the international use of the Yuan. The US which made up a huge 39% of Global Liquidity in 1985 is now down to under 23% or the same as the Eurozone, while Japan has skidded from her peak contribution of 21% in 1989 to just a 7% share. Over the period since the year 2000, Global Liquidity has increased by 240%, led by a huge 1366% jump in Chinese liquidity and a strong but less pacey rise in other Emerging Market liquidity of 374% (Table 2.1 and Fig. 2.4).

Figure 2.5 highlights the current distribution of the Global Liquidity pool using a block-map technique. This may better describe the concentration and hierarchy of Global Liquidity than the more conventional pie chart shown in Fig. 2.6. It is clear from these charts that China, the US, the Eurozone and Japan dominate. The UK looks comparatively small, notably when taken relative to France and Germany, although her financial influence is far greater because of the importance of the City of London as an international banking and foreign exchange trading centre, as well as through the cross-border foreign currency lending undertaken by Britain's large international banks. Switzerland also punches above her weight for similar reasons. Figure 2.7 compares the development of Chinese, US and Eurozone Liquidity, expressed in US dollar terms. Although foreign exchange movements are important in explaining some of this relative performance, the two standout facts are: (1) the surge in Eurozone Liquidity from shortly after the introduction of the Euro in 1999 until the 2007–2008 GFC and 2010–2012 Eurozone banking crisis, and (2) the exponential rise in Chinese Liquidity following her entry into the World Trade Organisation (WTO) in 2001, but particularly in the immediate post-GFC period. Eurozone banking expanded largely through rapid cross-border loan growth between banks in the core economies, such as Germany, and borrowers in the peripheral Eurozone economies, such as Spain, Ireland and Greece. Despite a renewed and sizeable policy easing from late 2008, China's liquidity expansion over

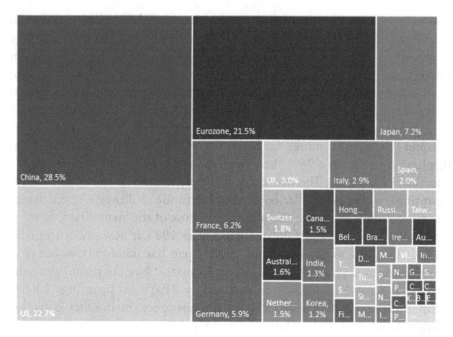

Fig. 2.5 How US$130 trillion of Global Liquidity is distributed, end-July 2019 (Source *CrossBorder Capital*)

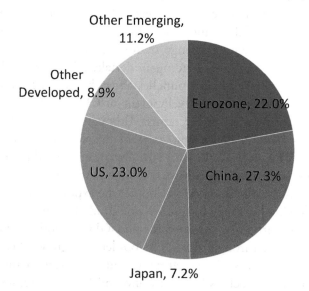

Fig. 2.6 The pool of Global Liquidity, 2019 (percent) (Source *CrossBorder Capital*)

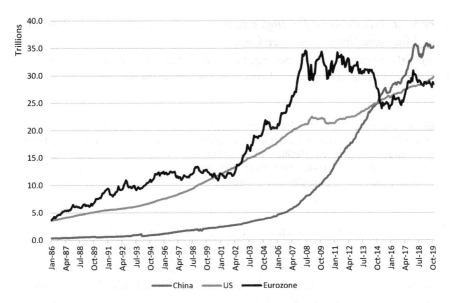

Fig. 2.7 The major players—China, US and Eurozone, 1986–2019 (US$ in trillions) (Source *CrossBorder Capital*)

the period was largely the result of the parallel rise in her foreign exchange reserves, which policy-makers monetised into major increases in domestic credit. The large jump in China's foreign exchange reserves, in turn, largely follow from her 2001 entry into the WTO; her policy of closely shadowing the US dollar, and the associated build-up of dollar-based regional supply chains. China's sophisticated and extensive industrial base sharply contrasts with her relative financial immaturity.

What Is Global Liquidity?

Although Global Liquidity itself is a much-discussed concept, it can be sometimes vaguely defined and is often hard to pin down. It does not refer to a single-minded mass of money denominated in the same currency and warehoused together in some secret offshore jurisdiction. Nor it mainly used to ease the buying and selling of goods and services. Global Liquidity is the collective term we use to describe the gross flows of credit, savings and international capital feeding through the world's banking systems and wholesale money markets and used in and between World financial markets to facilitate debt, investment and cross-border capital flows. In this study, we shall analyse three specific sources of Global Liquidity:

- *domestic private sector funding,* e.g. corporations, banks and shadow banks and financial institutions (see Chapter 6)
- *official monetary institutions,* e.g. Central Banks (see Chapter 7), and
- *foreign investors and lenders* through cross-border flows (see Chapter 8).

> **Global Liquidity** (Definition): A source of funding that measures the gross flows of credit and international capital feeding through the world's banking systems and collateral-based wholesale money markets. It is determined by the balance sheet capacity of all credit providers and represents the private sector's ability to access cash through savings and credit.

We think of liquidity in terms of the *sources of funds* available for the private sector to use, rather than the traditional way of defining money supply as bank deposits, which is technically a *use of funds.* Credit, in other words national and international IOUs, dominates Global Liquidity. Monetary savings sit more prosaically alongside. In modern economies, money is sometimes thought of as a higher form of credit that is ultimately underwritten by the State. Liquidity is a looser and more fluid concept than money, per se, because it includes what might be termed 'moneyness'. This is a qualitative attribute, much akin to the roots of the term credit from *credibility* or *belief* (origin Latin), which moves procyclically with business activity and gives liquidity more elasticity. In pure accounting terminology, liquidity measures the ability of a household, firm or investor to pay their upcoming liabilities at any point in time.[2] A useful definition comes from Lance Taylor[3]: "*Liquidity is often interpreted as a measure of the financial flexibility of an individual actor, group of actors, or the financial system as a whole. It represents the resources readily available for purposes of capital formation or financial transactions*".

A similar perspective is taken by the far-reaching *Report on the Working of the Monetary System in Great Britain* published by the Radcliffe Committee in July 1959. The essence of the Radcliffe Committee's view was that: "*... [t]hough we do not regard the supply of money as an unimportant quantity, we view it as only part of a wider structure of liquidity in the economy ... it is the whole liquidity position that is relevant to spending decisions ...*". Liquid assets are taken to refer to "*... all such assets which can be exchanged for money (or for other liquid assets, normally through the intermediation of money), at any time, at short notice, and at a relatively small transaction cost*". It concludes that: "*... decisions to spend on goods and services — the decisions that determine the level of total demand — are influenced by the liquidity of the spenders ...*

The spending is not limited by the amount of money in existence, but it is related to the amount of money people think they can get hold of whether by disposal of capital assets or by borrowing".

In practice, the term 'liquidity' is both used to describe the *ease of financing* (i.e. the availability of cash to meet expected liabilities), or so-called *funding liquidity*, and the *ease of trading* (i.e. the ability to buy and sell assets and commodities in size around current prices), or *market liquidity*. We think of *funding liquidity* as a measure of balance sheet capacity. It represents the private sector's access to finance through savings and credit, with future liquidity growth dependent both on lending by traditional banks and by the credit provided by international and collateral-based wholesale markets (often dubbed *shadow banks*). Funding liquidity and market liquidity are closely connected,[4] particularly in market-based credit systems. The fact that they can interact adversely to create dangerous downward liquidity spirals suggests that they should neither be seen in isolation, nor as independent. Although we are more interested in funding liquidity, per se, it also makes sense to cross-check our calculations with the related measures of market liquidity. From now onwards, we shall use the terms liquidity and funding liquidity interchangeably.

Market Liquidity refers to the ability to execute large transactions with limited price impact. It is also associated with low transaction costs and immediacy in execution. Liquidity in financial markets is central for effective market functioning. It facilitates the efficient allocation of economic resources through the better deployment of capital and risk, and the more effective dissemination and use of information. Low liquidity introduces frictions and costs, so potentially reducing market efficiency and disrupting economic growth. Market liquidity conditions can differ significantly across different asset classes, even in normal times. Financial assets with lower levels of liquidity tend to have higher liquidity risk premia, and investors also typically face higher transaction costs and wider bid-ask spreads when trading in these instruments. By acting as counterparties to transactions, specialised market makers, such as banks and trading firms provide a vital liquidity and risk-taking role. This often involves the buying and selling of financial securities without an immediate off-setting transaction, and therefore to carry and fund inventories.

Global Liquidity is simply another way of expressing international funding liquidity, i.e. by aggregating across economies Worldwide and including cross-border capital movements. To put our measure into context, the Bank for International Settlements (BIS) produce different Global Liquidity estimates.[5] They concentrate on the cross-border component of our definition. This they estimate[6] at US$32.5 trillion, which falls to US$16 trillion when interbank claims are excluded. It excludes domestic credit denominated in local currencies (US$68.5 trillion), but includes foreign currency lending by domestic banks (US$5 trillion). Adding these different elements together, the closest BIS data match to our Global Liquidity figure of US$128.2 trillion comes in around one-third smaller at US$85 trillion. Alternative Global Liquidity measures are also produced by other data providers, but these are far smaller. The two most popular variants are: (1) the sum of the US monetary base plus foreign official holdings of US Treasuries held at the Federal Reserve (US$7.4 trillion), and (2) an aggregate consisting of the US, Eurozone, Japanese, UK and Swiss monetary bases, plus Chinese foreign exchange reserves, plus foreign official holdings of US Treasuries held at the Federal Reserve (circa US$20 trillion).

It follows that with its strength partly dependent on the buoyancy of capital asset prices and exchange rates, Global Liquidity moves procyclically, or much like domestic funding liquidity. As well as possessing national and cross-border dimensions, Global Liquidity similarly has private and public components. Quantitatively, private sector liquidity dominates publicly created liquidity in size, but qualitatively Finance Ministries and Central Banks matter more, particularly during times of economic stress. Admittedly, traditional high street banks also hold a unique position within the financial system because their credits can create deposits. This follows because their retail deposits are guaranteed by the State, which gives the illusion that banks are always self-funding and can magically produce money out of thin air, limited only by the Central Bank's statutory reserve requirements. However, the reality is different. When these deposits are exchanged, what is really being spent is, say, a JPMorgan credit, a Citibank credit, a Barclays credit and a HSBC credit. The State's role in backstopping the balance sheets of these banks is crucial. Deposit guarantees encourage redepositing and access to emergency funding, through the official lender of the last resort facility, can provide immediate cash. These State backstops ensure that a notional Citibank dollar always exchanges at parity for a JPMorgan dollar, and a notional Barclays pound always exchanges one-to-one for a HSBC pound. Shorn of such backstops these bank credits might otherwise trade at discounts related to their perceived credit quality. Hence, funding problems can arise when the State's backstop boundaries are exceeded by, say, large-sized deposits (e.g. above America's US$250,000 limit for deposit guarantees) from corporate and institutional cash pools (CICPs), or by non-regulated banks requiring emergency funding, such as shadow banks and foreign banks operating outside their national jurisdictions. At these times credit risks can escalate, as the 2007–2008 GFC evidenced. Recent

new regulations by policy-makers aim to improve banks' capital and restrict their operations in order to mitigate these credit risks.

The dynamics behind liquidity can be understood by digging still-deeper into the evolution of money. Historically, money appears in two general forms: *commodity money*, such as gold and silver, and *credit money*, such as banknotes and loans. These twin forms, in turn, both serve two uses: as a *standard of value* and as a *means of circulation*. The standard of value function is paramount and determines circulation insofar that money circulates because it has value, but it does not have value just because it circulates. Thus, stable money can be invested for longer; devaluing money is passed on faster, and appreciating money is hoarded. Experience shows that the supply of commodity money tends to be countercyclical, which, by definition, frustrates trade, whereas credit monies are typically produced procyclically; they are also characterised by varying degrees of elasticity, and they depend on the growth, development and innovation of the financial economy. In a commodity-based financial system, declines in the price level, i.e. increases in the *price of money*, lead to an expansion in the money supply as the production, say, of gold is stepped-up. This does not tell us whether or not gold will be hoarded given lower prices, but importantly new supply should automatically occur because it has now become more profitable to mine gold. Thus, 'liquidity' in a commodity-based financial system depends on the production of precious metals. This property is self-balancing since the supply of commodity money expands as the price of money rises. In contrast, in a modern debt-based financial system, the supply of liquidity crucially requires the issuance and take-up of new credit. This is often dependent on the prevailing pricing background, because in periods of deflation and falling prices, i.e. increases in the *price of money*, borrowers are more reluctant to borrow and lenders become less willing to lend, since default risks are greater when the real value of debt rises. Here, unlike in commodity-based systems, the new supply of liquidity is procyclical because new credit faces rising costs for the debtor in a deflation, and in contrast becomes cheap in an inflation. Therefore, the supply of credit money contracts as the price of money rises (i.e. price deflation), but it expands when the price of money falls (i.e. price inflation). Movements in the value of the US dollar epitomise these effects in cross-border lending markets, because a stronger (weaker) US dollar exchange rate often has the same effect as a monetary tightening (easing), as we show later in Chapter 8. Such positive feedbacks amplify initial monetary shocks and they can help to explain why monetary inflations and, particularly, monetary deflations lead on to financial crises. Figure 2.4 has already warned us that Global Liquidity often proves fragile. Self-sustaining

and adverse dynamic effects can be set in motion such as those often seen around financial crises. Importantly, experience shows that liquidity is not fungible in crises (i.e. it quickly disappears) and nor can it be properly measured by the level of interest rates.

Despite the importance of Global Liquidity, these days the most visible and most discussed monetary instrument remains the policy interest rate. In the modern economy, this is typically a market-based overnight rate, such as US Fed Funds. This interest rate is widely thought to impact markets through the expectations of investors and credit providers, and so affect long-term yields, consumer and capital spending, cross-border capital flows and the exchange rate. See Bernanke (2008). However, we argue throughout this book that when the economic background is characterised by the need to refinance large outstanding debts, rather than to finance new capital projects, balance sheet capacity, i.e. liquidity, is crucial, and the cost of capital, i.e. interest rates, becomes secondary. Indeed, the 2007–2008 Global Financial Crisis (GFC) and the subsequent policy response evidenced that interest rates are not the main channel of monetary transmission. This period demonstrated unambiguously that setting the short-term interest rate is, by itself, an inadequate monetary policy tool, and that so-called 'forward guidance' on rates,[7] quantitative easing (QE) and quantitative tightening (QT) policies, and changes in banks' regulatory capital/asset ratios matter much more. Using these latter tools, both Central Banks and Financial Regulators can affect the aggregate growth rates of money and credit by slowing or stimulating the expansion of banks' assets and liabilities. Notes and coin, as well as bank deposits, loans and securities all exist in the real world and their rates of growth are affected by these policy decisions. In other words, all money that is anywhere, must be somewhere. Attention has, consequently, refocussed on alternative monetary channels, such as the quantitative effect of these direct supplies of credit and overall capital market funding conditions. By disturbing balance sheet quantities and specifically the balance sheets of financial intermediaries that invest and directly supply credit to the private sector, the policy-makers can affect risk-taking, wealth and collateral values, and, hence, GDP. See Borio and Zhou (2008).

Are Policy-Makers Behind the Curve?

Not surprisingly, Global Liquidity has become a highlight of international policy debates and investor concerns over recent years. In many of the writings by researchers based at the BIS, disruptions to Global Liquidity are

frequently cited as a potential threat. See, for example, BIS (2011): "*Global Liquidity has become a key focus of international policy debates over recent years. This reflects the view that global liquidity and its drivers are of major importance for international financial stability... In a world of high capital mobility, global liquidity cannot be approached as it used to be a few decades ago. It has both an official and a private component...These two concepts both capture one common element, namely the ease of financing*". The European Central Bank (ECB) is even more explicit: writing in its *Financial Stability Review* (December, 2011), the ECB warned that: "*Global Liquidity, both in times of abundance and shortage, has a range of implications for financial stability. Surges in global liquidity may be associated with strong asset price increases, rapidly rising credit growth and – in extreme cases – excessive risk-taking among investors. Shortages of global liquidity may lead to disruptions in the functioning of financial markets and – in extreme cases – depressed investor risk appetite, leading to malfunctioning markets*". Adding later that "*... in the run-up to the financial crisis the level of global liquidity was an important determinant of asset price and consumer price dynamics in several economic regions ... and ... measures of global liquidity are one of the best performing leading indicators of asset price booms and busts*" (ECB 2012). Federal Reserve Board (2012) appears to agree: "*...financial crises create and are then perpetuated by illiquidity...concerns about liquidity rapidly become concerns about solvency ...the evolution of the financial system away from traditional banking [and] towards a system dominated by a complex network of collateralized lending relationships serves only to increase the primacy of liquidity*". Moreover, the role of quantities, i.e. flows is explicitly acknowledged by the Banque de France (2018): *...most of the channels through which QE [monetary policy] might work...are entirely independent of the accompanying level of nominal interest rates*".

Put into context, modern industrial economies are usually dominated by a capital expenditure cycle. Economic growth depends on capital accumulation, which must be financed. A key characteristic of Capitalism is that investment is financed by liquidity and not just through savings. Capital is raised over several years, with funding needing to be *refinanced* several times over the lifetime of a project. This is more-than-ever true today given the large outstanding stock of global debt that needs to constantly refinanced. We know that the refinancing process is a frequent source of weakness: "*... the remote cause of* [the] *commercial tides ... seems to lie in the varying proportion which the capital devoted to permanent and remote investment bears to that which is temporarily invested soon to reproduce itself*".[8] Mismatches between assets and liabilities can occur at different points between gestation and the

project completion, leading cash pay-outs to fall short of cash receipts and, thereby, threaten temporary illiquidity, regardless of long-term solvency. It follows that there are predictable periods of both stable and unstable financing regimes, or much as the economist Hyman Minsky has proposed. In other words, the modern business cycle is increasingly dominated by changes in the broad capital structure, rather than simply by changes in the underlying pace of economic growth. With its complex and towering capital structures, modern capitalism has become far more a *refinancing* system than a *new financing* system.

As we argue in Chapter 6, the problem is that over the past two decades the global financial system has moved from retail bank-based credit provision to wholesale market-based provision, where the source of liquidity is the repo rather than the bank deposit, and where gross funding, i.e. refinancings and debt rollovers, dominates net credit provision, i.e. new financings. Repos require a stable collateral base. Traditionally, this has been provided by 'safe' asset government bonds, i.e. Treasuries. However, the widespread pursuit of austerity policies by several Western governments, and often with the IMF's blessing, has limited the new supply of these safe assets, against a background where the rising debt levels Worldwide require ever-larger balance sheet capacity in order to roll-over these sizeable positions. Consequently, lower quality private sector securities are being used as an alternative source of collateral. But a collateral pool skewed towards flaky private sector debt makes liquidity procyclical and potentially fragile. The solution requires a major injection of safe assets though more government bond issuance, and/or greater Central Bank liquidity. This is not yet happening. In fact, lately we have suffered the very opposite. The credit mechanism is broken and, ironically, despite their homage to the importance of Global Liquidity, the policy-makers seemingly appear not to know how to fix the problem, and, in cases, they are making things worse.

'New' Global Liquidity Shocks

Whereas dislocations in the real economy in the 1960s mostly took the form of wage and labour cost shocks, and in the 1970s oil and commodity price shocks, we now face an entirely different regime characterised by repeating financial shocks. Such international financial instability is frequently driven by wayward fluctuations in Global Liquidity. Market practitioners, such as Barry Riley, writing in the *Financial Times* back in 1990 then caught the mood vividly: "*There is a vast pool of liquidity, much of it borrowed,*

under-pinning share prices and ready to move in on any setback. Only when the credit markets are disrupted … is the buying power undermined. The investment fundamentals now play little role …". Legendary American investor Stanley Druckenmiller summed things up with brilliant clarity in a 1988 *Barron's* interview: *"…the major thing we look at is liquidity … looking at the great bull markets of this century, the best environment is a very dull, slow economy that the Federal Reserve is trying to get going".*

From our experience, the two main independent drivers of Global Liquidity are the US Federal Reserve and, increasingly, the People's Bank of China (PBoC), the main organ of Chinese monetary authority, which, ironically, is still tightly controlled by the Communist Party. By balance sheet size, the PBoC is already one-fifth bigger than America's Federal Reserve. Admittedly, its large size also helps the PBoC stabilise the US dollar-based international system, because China has lately become a major user of dollars, as we show in Chapter 9. Alongside, private liquidity in both economies is increasingly collateral-based, rather than bank-based, and it depends significantly on attitudes towards risk-taking and the, sometimes fuzzy, perceptions as to what constitute 'safe' assets. The rise of non-traditional banks, or what are now termed *shadow banks*, as providers of funding rather than just new credit, has compromised existing methods of monetary control. Expressed differently, financing chains have grown more in length than in number. These shadow banks have been fed by the recent rapidly growing corporate and institutional cash pools (CICPs), that, in turn, largely owe their existence to geopolitical developments, demographics and financial deregulation over the past twenty-five years.

New industrial technologies have been quickly exploited and propagated by these fast-moving flows of Global Liquidity. This has resulted in a growing disconnect between economic textbooks and the practical operation of the economy. The theoretical assumptions,[9] critical for market equilibrium between producers and consumers, are probably absent and the independence between supply and demand, vital for economic stability and for building an academic case in favour of free market capitalism, are being more frequently questioned. What's more, traditional policy tools, such as the Phillips Curve trade-off between inflation and unemployment, no longer seem to work. Widespread technological innovations and the importance for many economies of 'catch-up' growth, following the Fall of the Berlin Wall in 1989, drive increasing returns from production and help underwrite limitless numbers of 'free' web-based products. These forces skew Western economies towards the service industry, but alongside they also intensify the use of debt, widen trade deficits, change the distribution of incomes and alter the pattern of savings. They may help to explain why capital markets have shifted their character from being essentially money-raising mechanisms into becoming more refinancing and capital redistribution mechanisms, dominated by these rapid flows of Global Liquidity.

Our central contention is that the financial system has changed radically over the past three decades, with new players, both from within Emerging Markets and from beyond the traditional banks, essentially reversing the polarity of the circuit. Financial innovation is an important factor behind the more elastic liquidity supply. In the earlier bank-dominated financial World, M2 money supply, defined as the sum of notes, coin and bank deposits,[10] served as a decent measure of the balance sheet size of leveraged lending institutions, but today this ignores increasingly important market-based liabilities, e.g. secured repos and commercial paper, and large-sized corporate deposits. The World is changing. There has been a shift from unsecured funding to secured funding. There has been a shift in the denomination of Global Liquidity towards the US dollar, with much of it now transacted outside of mainland USA. There has been a shift in the benchmark rate for global dollar funding from bank-based LIBOR in the Eurodollar markets to the collateral-based US repo rate. There has also been a shift in credit provision from the balance sheets of global banks to the balance sheets of asset managers and broker-dealers. And, there has been a shift towards alternative monies, such as Bitcoin, XRP, Ethereum and other cryptocurrencies, as well as alternative policies, such as the latest proposal[11] for a 'People's QE', so signalling our growing distrust in the abilities of both global banks and national Central Banks to maintain financial solvency and promote future economic growth.

Unfortunately, policy-makers and many experts have failed to keep up with these shifts. We can better understand these challenges in terms of the three key features of modern economies, namely: (1) the high productivity of industrial capital; (2) the ever-greater elasticity of finance, and (3) the persistent instability of the investment cycle, together with a fourth, namely (4) the economic 'catch-up' of China and the Emerging Market economies. All four find their voices in today's financial markets. Worryingly, instability is becoming more regular, more inclusive and deeper. These crises are systematic, not idiosyncratic. Their roots lie in the progressive maturity of Western capitalism relative to the financial underdevelopment of China and other Emerging Markets, and specifically with the shift from a *capital-raising* to a predominantly *capital distribution*-focussed financial system. This features inventive bankers and rapacious speculators, rather than economist Joseph Schumpeter's emphasis on innovative industrial entrepreneurs, and it is coloured by periodic lurches between ever-greater regulation, followed by periods of sweeping deregulation.

How Do the Academics See It?

Traditional economics and finance have until recently either ignored these liquidity factors entirely or else grudgingly accepted them as annoying frictions. For example, the standard neo-Keynesian economics textbooks (see, for example, Woodford 2003; Galí 2008) argue that output is demand determined in the short run, and monetary policy stimulates aggregate consumption and investment. In this narrow world of economic theory, neither spreads nor risk premia, the very essence of financial markets, play a role. Rather identical individuals act selfishly, singularly, independently, instantaneously without making any obvious error. These individuals are endowed with a unique precocious prophecy and they live forever, seemingly knowing everything about every possible future outcome! In other words, such 'assumptions' remove all those phenomena that should be interesting to economics, e.g. quantity rationing, deep uncertainty, involuntary unemployment, inflexible or 'sticky' prices and balance sheets (since in this World, why hold assets or be required to manage the duration of assets and liabilities?).

A plausible reason why liquidity is shunned in the traditional literature is that it is perceived to be both hard to measure and difficult to define. But just because a task is challenging, there is no reason not to try. Economics is itself often guilty of raising to heights of great importance factors that are easily measured. This fallacy can be colourfully described by the tale of the drunkard searching for lost keys under a streetlamp: not because this is where they were lost, but simply because that is where the light is better! Often economic truths lie in the shadows where they can be hard to see. A compelling real-World example is the economists' worship of foreign trade and current account balances. Why focus so much on trade imbalances, when economic welfare is surely determined more by the sum of exports and imports than by their differences, because the size of total trade governs the division of labour? What's more, many experts simply assert that capital flows passively adjust to balance the corresponding trade surpluses and deficits. Balance of payments 'balance', by definition (the clue is in the name), but, in practice, not only are the size of current accounts often forced to passively adjust to capital movements, these net flows themselves hide a richer and much wider network of gross capital flows, involving the buying and selling of different assets and large-scale borrowing and lending, in turn, involving both foreigners and domestic residents.

This inadequate theoretical structure permits economics to pay infrequent attention to balance sheet analysis. Yet, digging into the detail contained within the international balance sheet reveals that the bulk of cross-border capital movements are speculative portfolio flows and bank financing flows, and not foreign direct investments (FDI). And, although capital appears to be exported from high savings Emerging Market economies to a few advanced economies with relatively slow domestic demand growth, the reality is different as we explain in Chapter 8. Gross balance sheet analysis shows large-scale bank and portfolio flows heading into these risky Emerging Markets, with slightly larger amounts flowing back into the deeper capital markets located in the large money centres of New York, London and Frankfurt, and often in search of 'safe' assets. In other words, risk-seeking capital enters and risk-averse capital leaves. What's more, the former tends to be more long-term in nature than the latter. Modern economics also misses the importance of this gross funding dimension, because it takes every credit as a debt (debit), every debt as a credit: so assets and liabilities must match, and the system always balances to zero, by definition. Thus, it never acknowledges either the character of these flows nor how big these gross numbers are: regardless of how much credit or debt there is in the system, the net figure is always the same. But knowing this fact is akin to scaling the World's longest ladder and promising never to fall off!

When liquidity does appear in academic writings, it tends to be used in one of three senses:

- *Market Depth*[12]: describes the 'liquidity' of an individual investment position and denotes the ease of selling (or buying) the security in size and at short notice, without affecting its 'price'.
- *Money-plus*: a more refined term for the economy's entire money stock, or some characteristic of money, such as broad credit or equally high-powered money (e.g. 1959 UK Radcliffe Report).
- *Risk*: a gauge of the robustness of financial sector balance sheets, or "...*the ability to settle obligations with immediacy. Consequently, a bank is illiquid if it is unable to settle obligations in time*". ECB (WP#1024, March 2009). The Basel Committee's liquidity definition is similar, adding that banks must also "...*unwind or settle positions as they come due*".

Some frustration with the adequacy of these separate definitions of liquidity has spawned a number of recent hybrids that pair up in various combinations. For example, Brunnermeier and Pedersen (2009) embody 'market depth' in their concept of *market liquidity*, which they define as the difference between the transaction price of a security and its fundamental value. They also integrate what we call the 'risk' definition of liquidity with the 'money-plus' notion to describe their *funding liquidity* concept. Funding liquidity risk arises when the net capital of a dealer bank decreases, short-term borrowing availability is reduced, and margin requirements increase, thereby disturbing cash flows. Brunnermeier and Pedersen allow these two concepts to negatively interact and so give rise to so-called downward *liquidity spirals*. For example, heightened market risk from, say, greater realised asset price volatility, leads to higher margin requirements and, hence, tighter funding liquidity, which, in turn, feeds back to reduce market depth and further undermine market liquidity. Similar hybrid measures include empirical risk statistics, such as the recently published Bank of England *financial market liquidity index* and the US Office of Financial Research (OFR) *financial stress index*.[13] These combine 'market depth' measures of liquidity, such as bid/ask spreads in the gilt repo market and LIBOR/OIS spread, with 'risk' measures, such as data on commercial bank funding and the CBOE VIX index of implied volatility on the S&P500, the headline US stock market index.

Not surprisingly, the idea that shocks suffered by the financial sector matter for the real economy has gained significant attention in the wake of the 2007–2008 GFC. There is a large and growing body of academic work supporting this link, with plenty of empirical evidence that financial cycles, and their specific credit and asset price components, are prescient leading indicators of financial crises (e.g. Borio and Drehmann 2009; Schularick and Taylor 2012; Detken et al. 2014). Financial crises typically lead to deep and lengthy recessions, as Jordà et al. (2018) and Adrian et al. (2014) show. A number of studies also suggest that credit booms weaken medium-term industrial output (e.g. Mian et al. 2017; Lombardi et al. 2017; Borio and Zabai 2016). Most of this work focusses on the yield curve, i.e. the spread between longer-dated and short-term Treasury yields. As we have demonstrated elsewhere (see Howell 2017) these conclusions are flaky and more likely to involve other hidden variables. Refreshingly, new work by Borio et al. (2019) shows the greater predictive power of financial flows. They compare the signalling power of the yield curve against measures of the financial cycle for the US, as well as for sixteen other advanced economies and nine Emerging Market economies over the period from 1985 to 2017.

Gerdesmeier et al. (2010) carry out an extensive literature review and conclude that "...*the one robust finding across the different studies is that measures of excessive credit creation are very good leading indicators of the building up of financial imbalances in the economy...*". Their results regarding excessive money creation prove less conclusive than for credit. Alessi and Detken (2011) compare the performance of a large number of global and domestic variables (real and financial) as early warning indicators of (composite) asset price booms. They find that global liquidity measures (based on the aggregate for 18 OECD countries), notably a global private credit gap or a global M1 gap (defined as detrended ratios to GDP) are the best early warning indicators. Borio and Lowe (2002) use a noise-to-signal approach and show that a domestic credit gap is a better early warning indicator of financial crises than a domestic asset price gap, a domestic investment gap (all gaps are defined as detrended ratios to GDP) or domestic real credit growth in a sample of 34 countries. Drehmann et al. (2011) use data for 36 countries and show that a domestic credit gap achieves the lowest noise-to-signal ratio for predicting banking crises, relative to 14 other indicators, including measures based on GDP, M2, property prices and equity prices.

Bierut (2013) shows that global liquidity measures outperform domestic measures as early warning indicators of asset price booms. This study confirms the conclusions of the Committee for Global Financial Stability (BIS, CGFS 2011) that quantity measures are better suited to capture the build-up of potential risks. It notes evidence that Basel III capital, leverage and liquidity rules are likely to reduce traditional bank-based intermediation, in favour of non-banks. This implies that the scope of quantitative measures of liquidity may in the future need to be extended to include non-banks in order to support their early warning properties. Adrian and Shin (2007) were among the first to detail the procyclical amplification mechanisms embedded in the modern financial structure. Parallel work by Miranda-Agrippino and Rey (2019) finds that a single global factor can explain up to a quarter of the variation in World risk asset prices. This commonality is also confirmed by Jordà et al. (2018). In a study of financial cycles across 17 advanced economies over the past 150 years, they find that the co-movements of credit, housing prices and stock markets have hit historical highs during the past three decades. Both sets of research lend weight to the notion of a Global Liquidity cycle. Baks and Kramer (1999) find that global liquidity is negatively correlated with interest rates and positively related to equity returns. The IMF (2010) has examined the linkages between global liquidity expansion, asset prices and capital inflows in emerging economies. This study found that rising global liquidity is associated with rising equity returns and declining real interest rates in 34 'liquidi-ty-receiving' economies. Bruno and Shin (2015) show that a strong dollar is associated with tighter credit conditions Worldwide and emphasise the key role played by US monetary policy in driving global risk premia. Rey (2013) also shows that US monetary policy influences financing conditions even in economies operating with fully flexible exchange rates, such as Canada, Japan, the Eurozone and the UK. This seriously questions whether floating exchange rates really can provide an effective barrier[14] for Emerging Markets against the growing power of global capital?

What precisely comprises these liquidity transmission channels is still hotly debated among academics. When capital market frictions and bal-ance sheets are included, an expansionary monetary policy should lead to an increase in the net worth of borrowers and investors. This feature helps to explain the subsequent expansions in lending and in aggregate demand, or the so-called *credit channel* of monetary policy (see Bernanke and Gertler 1995). Other researchers emphasise instead *the risk-taking channel* of mon-etary policy (see Borio and Zhou 2008; Bruno and Shin 2015; Coimbra and Rey 2019), where financial intermediation plays a key role, and where system-wide monetary expansions relax leverage limits and encourage lend-ers to take additional credit risks. It seems plausible that these two channels often complement and reinforce each another. Indeed, the importance of credit and its role in financial instability are emphasised both by Alessi and Detken (2011): *"... global monetary liquidity measures ... are more informa-tive than real variables in detecting boom and bust cycles"*, and by Schularick and Taylor (2012): *"...with respect to crises, the results of our analysis are clear: credit matters, not money ... financial crises throughout history can be viewed as 'credit booms gone wrong' ... [and] past growth of credit emerges as the single best predictor of future financial instability"*.

Recently, it is argued that Central Bank *quantitative easing* (QE) reduce transactional frictions through a liquidity channel that operates by increas-ing the opportunities for sellers of those securities targeted by the author-ities. Evidence comes from several so-called *event studies*, such as of the Federal Reserve's second QE programme where the liquidity premiums between TIPS yields and inflation swap rates were reduced, implying that QE improved *market liquidity. Market liquidity* is derivative, whereas *fund-ing liquidity* is more fundamental. Here, onshore and offshore wholesale money markets have become central to the supply of funding liquidity. Aligned with this is the demand for 'safe' assets. The supply of safe short-term debt requires collateral as backing. We have noted that this collateral can be Treasuries, as well as privately produced safe debt. Holmstrom and

Tirole (2001)[15] present an asset pricing model that includes a liquidity demand factor. In their model, risk neutral firms willingly pay a premium on 'safe' assets that provide benefits when liquidity is scarce. This premium persists because collateralisable assets are assumed to be in short supply. Gorton et al. (2012) finds around one-third of total assets are 'safe' and, in turn, around one-third of these are government securities. We show in Chapter 6 that private sector financial intermediaries are able to produce additional safe assets and through this channel they can affect asset prices. He and Krishnamurthy (2012), Adrian et al. (2014), Brunnermeier and Sannikov (2014), and Moreira and Savov (2017), among others, all emphasise this supply-side channel. In this new world, we warn in Chapter 11 that the quality mix of collateral in the economy becomes critically important to the supply of liquidity. Too low a stock of outstanding Treasuries results in an increase in privately produced collateral and a credit boom, which likely increases financial fragility. In the previous, retail-based market this was of less concern because the dominant form of safe debt, i.e. demand deposits, was insured by the State. However, the composition of private sector 'safe' assets has since changed with bank deposits now down to 30 from 80% in 1950s. We are in a different place.

The Key: Flow of Funds Analysis

Many of these academic approaches bring together the 'risk' and the 'money-plus' definitions. Some also explore how funding liquidity affects system-wide liquidity, often by using a flow of funds analysis. We strongly favour a flow of funds approach. The methodology was pioneered by Morris Copeland[16] (1952) and first developed in the US where flow of funds accounts have been regularly published by the US Federal Reserve System since 1951. Henry Kaufman popularised flow of funds analysis during the 1970s and 1980s as one way to understand both the credit creation process and the changing position of the interest rate yield curve through the credit cycle. An important contemporary international contribution came from Raymond Goldsmith's *Comparative National Balance Sheets: A Study of Twenty Countries, 1688–1978* (1985). Flow of funds accounts are vital tools, because in standard National Income accounting, income equates with expenditure, but financial assets and debts, and their relationship to current and capital account transactions are all ignored. This may help to explain why financial markets are not integrated into traditional economic analysis, which notionally devalues the importance of finance. Flow of funds accounting, in contrast, links income and expenditure flows to their counterpart changes in stocks of assets and liabilities. They effectively ensure that all money that is anywhere is accounted for somewhere, guaranteeing consistency between stocks and flows, and between different economic sectors and the national and international economies. The stock consequences of flows are incorporated into the flow of funds arithmetic, e.g. government budget constraints are satisfied, and the consequences of runaway government debts are acknowledged. According to Kaufman,[17] flow of funds data capture financial transactions and financial positions of sectors in the economy, and: "...*provides perspective and, like double-entry bookkeeping, contains built-in features that help prevent errors in logic ... the amount of funds supplied must equal the amount demanded because it is impossible to lend money unless someone borrows it ... the function of interest rates is to allocate the funds supplied by lenders among those who want to borrow*".

More recently the German Central Bank has given a ringing endorsement to flow of funds accounting and described how it is used to compile the German national financial accounts: "*Financial accounts (FA) are a part of the national accounts, a macroeconomic statistical accounting system that encompasses the entire economy ... The FA, which are usually compiled by central banks because of their access to primary statistics, thus add to the picture provided by the national accounts focusing on the real economy that are supplied by statistical offices by including transactions in the financial sphere that run in parallel with real transactions. The results show who in an economy is providing or drawing what amount of funds in what form, and the financial intermediaries that are involved in the economy's financial flows. This provides an idea both of the basic structure of the economy's financial flows (i.e. the channels of domestic financial investment and external borrowing) and of financial behaviour, particularly among households and enterprises...The results are used,* inter alia, *to analyse the investment and financing behaviour of enterprises and households, which, in turn, provides information about the monetary policy transmission process. For instance, these analyses focus on studies on shifts in financial structures and on the relationship between lending by domestic banks and other sources of financing (such as capital markets and foreign lenders)...*" (Deutsche Bundesbank 2013).

A major leap forwards in our understanding of the impact of these flows came with Gurley and Shaw's *Money in a Theory of Finance* (1960), which argues that there is a continuum of financial assets and institutions based on their 'liquidity'. This resembles Keynes' use of the term 'liquidity preference' to describe a monetary attribute. Gurley and Shaw saw little difference between the assets of non-bank financial institutions and bank assets. In short, certain non-bank financial institutions (or what we now dub shadow banks) can create liquidity.

Flow of funds analysis has proved useful in untangling the increasingly convoluted nature of the financial markets. Financial crises often result from abrupt 'stops' in funding liquidity that prevent essential projects and asset holdings from being refinanced. Traditional economics focusses, instead, almost exclusively on the uses of funds, rather than fluctuations in their sources. Thus, the economic categories of government spending, retail sales and money supply each represents a different use of funds. Because it highlights sectoral imbalances and balance sheet mismatches, flow of funds data is a far more important tool for assessing financial stability. It gave insights that allowed Kaufman (1986) to foresee upcoming financial turmoil, emanating from the growth of institutional money. Thus, he could warn as early as the mid-1980s that: "*Vast improvements in communications and financial technology have created close linkages within the US credit markets and with markets abroad. Distinctions among institutions have been so blurred that it would be impossible to put Humpty-Dumpty together again. We need to implement the best aspects of deregulation and the best applicable safeguards of regulation. By and large, this will require injecting some friction into the debt creation process – not more lubricants*".

More Capital Ideas?

It is worth setting these ideas about 'liquidity' into a broader context. Recently, investment commentator John Authers[18] reflected on the impact of Peter Bernstein's masterful *Capital Ideas*, a 1992 book that surveyed the achievements of academic finance. Although it focusses much more on equities than on bonds and currencies, *Capital Ideas* serves as a great yardstick. Yet, with due humility and the benefits of much hindsight, four key concepts seem to be missing:

(1) institutional theories of capital markets and savings, including the importance of national currency seigniorage and Central Bank policy, are not covered, and instead the Modigliani and Miller view that (among other things) the structure of financing should not matter permeates the book
(2) inflation/deflation threats seemingly play no explicit role in asset allocation decisions
(3) the role of the interest rate term structure on asset and liability pricing is ignored entirely
(4) risk is wrongly equated with asset price volatility alone.

Arguably, each of these four points contains the common themes of *liability management, duration* and *Global Liquidity* which we put great weight upon. The trailblazer here was Marty Leibowitz, who gets a mention in Peter Bernstein's book, but deserves at least a chapter. Henry Kaufman's seminal contribution to flow of funds analysis and his prescient warnings about future financial instability need to be added. Practical experience also gives a strong hint that *geopolitics* frequently play a key role in finance, which is not surprising since assets are denominated in national currencies, over which policy-makers have legal jurisdiction and some control.

Risk matters when liabilities cannot be properly hedged, which, in turn, should encourage a greater demand for 'safe' assets. We raised the failings of volatility as a measure of risk with Peter at the time. He nonetheless felt it was the most practical definition and many practitioners would still agree. Yet, the subsequent decades have unkindly opened up many more dimensions of risk, most of which arise when liabilities are not properly matched. Several subsequent books, and notably Nassim Taleb's *Black Swan* and Benoit Mandelbrot's *The Mis-Behaviour of Markets*, question the use of volatility as a risk measure and highlight the implicit absurdity of using the Gaussian 'normal' probability distribution (or bell curve) to model risk events.[19]

In addition, Modern Portfolio Theory (MPT) and the Efficient Market Hypothesis (EMH) focus on individual securities, not on the behaviour of the investment crowd or of monetary institutions, such as Central Banks. Yet, while madness is rare in individuals, the philosopher Nietzsche, among others, taught us that it becomes the norm in groups. People go mad in crowds and crowds form because uncertainty, or unquantifiable risk, being the dominant feature of financial markets, forces us to fall back on rules of thumb and consensual thinking. Crowds with money are particularly unstable and they go a long way to explain the roller-coaster swings of financial markets between the extremes of greed and fear. Therefore, we argue that, contrary to the textbooks, investment is fundamentally about risk, return and liquidity.

Frustratingly, the relative importance of each factor, changes over time. For much of the pre-WW2 and immediate post-war years the markets concentrated on the return dimension, with investors largely concerned with growth, value and dividends. By the 1980s, risk management had come into vogue, often paralleling the search for a deeper understanding of what risk really means? More recently and, particularly, with deregulation, changing demographics, the retreat of inflation and other structural changes to the savings markets, including Central Bank large-scale asset purchases (LSAP)—popularly known as *quantitative easing* (QE)—following the 2007–2008 Global Financial Crisis (GFC), the emphasis has switched towards liquidity.

Notes

1. OTC: over the counter.
2. Rather than overall, which defines *solvency*.
3. Lance Taylor, *Notes on Liquidity*, New School for Social Research, April 2008.
4. See Brunnermeier and Pedersen (2009).
5. See https://www.bis.org/statistics/gli.htm.
6. BIS estimates, end-March 2019.
7. Forward guidance refers to setting out a likely future path for policy interest rates, such as expressed by the Federal Reserve's well-known 'dot plot' diagram.
8. William Stanley Jevons, *Investigations in Currency and Finance*, 1884.
9. In technical jargon, these are often thought of as the 'convexity' of underlying consumer preferences and technical production possibilities, which, say, require constant or decreasing returns to scale.
10. Demand, or checking deposits, retail time deposits and money market funds.
11. This policy channels liquidity directly to the general population. It is related to Modern Monetary Theory (MMT), which explicitly subjugates Central Banks to Finance Ministries in order to finance, say, public infrastructure, tax cuts and even universal basic incomes.
12. The associated term 'dark liquidity' refers to hidden order flow increasingly dealt off-exchange via computer-to-computer trades.
13. See https://www.financialresearch.gov/financial-stress-index/.
14. The Canadian Nobel Prize winner Robert Mundell famously identified his eponymous trilemma where only two out of three policy choices between free capital movements, monetary policy independence and stable exchange rates are ever possible.
15. Bengt Holmstrom and Jean Tirole, *LAPM: A Liquidity-Based Asset Pricing Model*, 2001.
16. Morris Copeland, *A Study in Moneyflows in the United States*, 1952.
17. Henry Kaufman, *Interest Rates: The Markets and the New Financial World*, 1986.
18. Bloomberg, April 3, 2019.
19. Benoît Mandelbrot and Richard L. Hudson, *The Misbehavior of Markets: A Fractal View of Financial Turbulence*, 2007. Nassim Nicholas Taleb, *Black Swan*, 2008.

References

Adrian, Tobias, and Hyun Song Shin. 2007. Liquidity and Leverage. BIS Annual Conference, September.

Adrian, Tobias, Erkko Etula, and Tyler Muir. 2014. Financial Intermediaries and the Cross-Section of Asset Returns. *Journal of Finance* 69 (6) (December): 2557–2596.

Alessi, L., and C. Detken. 2011. Quasi Real-Time Early Warning Indicators for Costly Asset Price Boom/Bust Cycles: A Role for Global Liquidity. *European Journal of Political Economy* 27 (3): 520–533.

Bank for International Settlements—Committee on the Global Financial System. 2011. Global Liquidity—Concept, Measurement and Policy Implications. CGFS Paper No. 45, November.

Banque de France. 2018. Financial Stability Review No. 2, April.

Baks, K., and C. Kramer. 1999. Global Liquidity and Asset Prices: Measurement, Implications and Spillovers. IMF Working Paper No. 99/168.

Bernanke, Ben S. 2008. Liquidity Provision by the Federal Reserve. Speech, Board of Governors of the Federal Reserve System, May 13.

Bernanke, Ben S., and Mark Gertler. 1995. Inside the Black Box: The Credit Channel of Monetary Policy Transmission. *The Journal of Economic Perspectives* 9 (4) (Autumn): 27–48.

Bierut, Beata. 2013. Global Liquidity as an Early Warning Indicator of Asset Price Booms: G5 Versus Broader Measures. DNB Working Paper No. 377, May.

Borio, Claudio, and Anna Zabai. 2016. Unconventional Monetary Policies: A Re-appraisal. BIS Working Papers No. 570, July.

Borio, Claudio, and Haibin Zhou. 2008. Capital Regulation, Risk-Taking and Monetary Policy: A Missing Link in the Transmission Mechanism? BIS Working Papers No. 268, December 17.

Borio, Claudio, and Philip Lowe. 2002. Asset Prices, Financial and Monetary Stability: Exploring the Nexus. BIS Working Papers No. 114, July.

Borio, C., and M. Drehmann. 2009. Assessing the Risk of Banking Crises-Revisited. *BIS Quarterly Review*, March, 29–46.

Borio, Claudio, Mathias Drehmann, and Dora Xia. 2019. Predicting Recessions: Financial Cycle Versus Term Spread. BIS Working Papers No. 818, October.

Bruno, Valentina, and Hyun Song Shin. 2015. Capital Flows and the Risk-Taking Channel of Monetary Policy. *Journal of Monetary Economics* 71 (April): 119–132.

Brunnermeier, Markus K., and Lasse Heje Pedersen. 2009. Market Liquidity and Funding Liquidity. *The Review of Financial Studies* 22 (6) (June): 2201–2238.

Brunnermeier, Markus K., and Yuliy Sannikov. 2014. A Macroeconomic Model with a Financial Sector. *American Economic Review* 104 (2): 379–421.

Coimbra, Nuno, and Hélène Rey. 2019. Financial Cycles with Heterogeneous Intermediaries. NBER Working Paper No. 23245 (Revised).

Copeland, Morris. 1952. *A Study of Moneyflows in the United States*. NBER.

Detken, C., O. Weeken, L. Alessi, D. Bonfim, M.M. Boucinha, C. Castro, S. Frontczak, G. Giordana, J. Giese, N. Jahn, J. Kakes, B. Klaus, J. H. Lang, N. Puzanova, and P. Welz. 2014. Operationalizing the Countercyclical Capital Buffer. ESRB Occasional Paper No. 5.

Drehmann, Mathias, Claudio Borio, and Kostas Tsatsaronis. 2011. Anchoring Countercyclical Capital Buffers: The Role of Credit Aggregates. BIS Working Paper, November.

ECB. 2012. Global Liquidity: Concepts, Measurement and Implications from a Monetary Policy Perspective. *ECB Monthly Bulletin*, October.

Federal Reserve Board. 2012. Shadow Banking After the Financial Crisis, Remarks by Daniel K. Tarullo, June.

Galí, Jordi. 2008. *Monetary Policy, Inflation, and the Business Cycle: An Introduction to the New Keynesian Framework and Its Applications*, 2nd ed. Princeton: Princeton University Press.

Gerdesmeier, Dieter, Hans-Eggert Reimers, and Barbara Roffia. 2010. Asset Price Misalignments and the Role of Money and Credit. *International Finance* 13 (3) (December): 377–407.

Gorton, G., S. Lewellen, and A. Metrick. 2012. The Safe Asset Share. *American Economic Review* 102 (3): 101–106.

He, Zhigu, and Arvind Krishnamurthy. 2012. A Model of Capital and Crises. *Review of Economic Studies* 79 (2): 735–777.

Holmstrom, Bengt, and Jean Tirole. 2001. LAPM: A Liquidity-Based Asset Pricing Model. *Journal of Finance* 56 (3) (October): 1837–1867.

Howell, Michael J. 2017. *Further Investigations into the Term Structure of Interest Rates*. London: University of London.

International Monetary Fund. 2010. Global Liquidity Expansion: Effects on 'Receiving' Economies and Policy Response Options. Global Financial Stability Report, April.

Jordà, Òscar, Moritz Schularick, Alan M. Taylor, and Felix Ward. 2018. Global Financial Cycles and Risk Premiums. NBER Working Paper No. 24677, June.

Kaufman, Henry. 1986. *Interest Rates, the Markets and New Financial World*. Time Books.

Lombardi, Marco, Madhusudan Mohanty, and Ilhyock Shim. 2017. The Real Effects of Household Debt in the Short and Long Run. BIS Working Paper No. 607.

Mian, Atif, Amir Sufi, and Emil Verner. 2017. How Do Credit Supply Shocks Affect the Real Economy? Evidence from the United States in the 1980s. NBER Working Paper, August.

Miranda-Agrippino, S., and H. Rey. 2019. US Monetary Policy and the Global Financial Cycle, March 28.

Moreira, Alan, and Alexi Savov. 2017. The Macroeconomics of Shadow Banking. *Journal of Finance* 72 (6) (December): 2381–2432.

Rey, Hélène. 2013. Dilemma Not Trilemma: The Global Financial Cycle and Monetary Policy Independence. Jackson Hole Conference, August 2013.

Schularick, Moritz, and Alan M. Taylor. 2012. Credit Booms Gone Bust: Monetary Policy, Leverage Cycles, and Financial Crises. *1870–2008, American Economic Review* 102 (2): 1029–1061.

Woodford, Michael. 2003. *Interest and Prices: Foundations of a Theory of Monetary Policy*. Princeton: Princeton University Press.

3

Synopsis: A Bigger, More Volatile World

The Economic Earthquake

As the investment World has got bigger, it has become ever more volatile. Financial crises seem to strike with an apparent regularity every eight to ten years. Igniting this explosive background is a battle for supremacy between national capitals, and specifically the intensifying tussle between America and China, with fast-moving financial flows the modern equivalent of shock troops. But once traditional patterns are broken new Worlds emerge. The 1989 fall of the Berlin Wall symbolises the great geopolitical shifts that not only ended Eastern European Communism, but also effectively reversed the polarity of the World financial system by unleashing the new economic forces powering waves of Global Liquidity. In giving access to 2–3 billion new 'producers' (and not the 'consumers' that the billboards promised), this created a 'globalisation' of production through international supply chains,[1] initially led by the US, Germany and Japan, but now increasingly dominated by Chinese manufacturers and logistics companies. Barely a decade after the end of Eastern European Communism, the World economy was stuck by a second shockwave. On 11 December 2001 China joined the World Trade Organisation (WTO). In the next ten years alone, over 200 million Chinese workers, roughly equivalent in headcount to the entire European Union's labour force, shifted from the countryside into the rapidly expanding Eastern coastal cities that dominate China's export economy. For sure, China and the West traded before, but WTO entry saw a huge step-up in the scale and depth of their cross-border trade. 2001 was also a

© The Author(s) 2020
M. J. Howell, *Capital Wars*,
https://doi.org/10.1007/978-3-030-39288-8_3

signal year for China because she won the right to host the 2008 Olympics. This confidence-boosting chase towards ceremonial perfection culminating that August in Beijing was led by a then little-known Party official, named Xi Jinping, since elevated to the Presidency of the People's Republic of China. China had been officially welcomed into the World economy, but, as we explain, her path has been first and foremost a story about economic 'catch-up' hampered by uneven financial development.

Rates of return on capital are ultimately equalised across economies by capital mobility and the reshuffling of investments. Secular movements in real interest rates combine these changes in saving and investment behaviour with fluctuations in the safety and liquidity properties of safe assets, such as Treasury instruments. We argue that both falling industrial profitability and the associated structural shortage of safe assets are key factors behind the long downward slide in World interest rates. Finance affects risk premia through gross liquidity flows and the financial sector's overall balance sheet size. Three charts highlight the visible effect that China has had on Western Capitalism. Figure 3.1 shows the secular declines in the returns from new investments for US, Chinese and German industrial capital. The general decline in marginal returns is plain, but this slide started earlier for US and

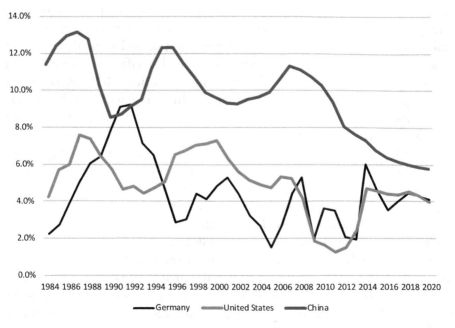

Fig. 3.1 Real marginal returns on industrial capital—US, Germany and China, 1984–2019 (percent) (Source *CrossBorder Capital*)

German firms, with Chinese capital alone enjoying a further boost through the early 2000s. Thus, the gap between Chinese and US marginal profitability, which stood at a less threatening 2.3% in the year 2000, widened to a whopping 8.9% by 2009. As new investment projects became less attractive, the Western industry flipped into a mode of aggressive cost-cutting across their existing capital in order to maintain reported profits. Profits can be boosted both by making new investments in high return projects and by better managing existing businesses. Incentivised by share option schemes, management's new-found devotion to cost-cutting forced plant closures and led to mass job losses, but it raised the average return on American capital, as the visible step-up in average returns in Fig. 3.2 confirms. Between 1984–2001, prior to China's WTO entry, the return on US capital averaged 3.5% in real terms, but through the post-2001 period it topped an average 4.1%. The gap between marginal and average returns closed dramatically as the effect of Chinese competition pulled down marginal returns, while domestic cost-restructuring pushed average returns higher. This narrowing differential can explain the collapse in US capital expenditure back to levels that now barely cover its wear and tear, as Fig. 3.3 suggests. Cash flows consequently rebounded, but corporations either hoarded this cash or spent it on share

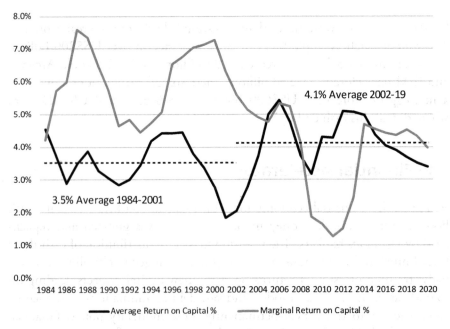

Fig. 3.2 Marginal versus average returns on US industrial capital, 1984–2019 (Source *CrossBorder Capital*)

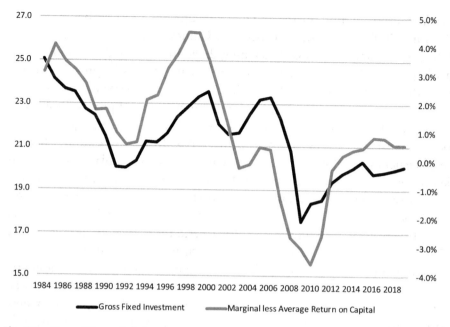

Fig. 3.3 The differential between marginal and average returns on US capital (percent) and US gross fixed investment spending (% of GDP), 1984–2019 (Source *CrossBorder Capital*)

buybacks and takeovers, rather than investing it back into the real economy. The winners such as Apple Inc.'s treasury now sits on over US$200 billion; Microsoft and Google hold circa US$125 billion, while, Facebook, Amazon and IBM have close to US$50 billion. These six US corporations alone own a nest-egg of more than US$600 billion, or 3% of overall US GDP. So, where did all this cash end up?

The Financial Accelerator

As fast as the industrial economy lost out, financial markets won out. Cash flooded into wholesale money markets where it was grabbed and repackaged by rapacious bankers. The resulting massive redistribution of cash flows forced much of World industry to reorganise, both geographically and internally: trashing investment returns on many new capital projects, leading on to both 'asset-lite' business models and vast debt accumulations, and encouraging the US to run a near-permanently loose monetary policy. Financial markets, fuelled by what we later describe as a large and fast-growing *shadow monetary base*, took on a sizeable part of the economic adjustment burden.

This transmission is explained because the new supply chains restricted cost movements and, being largely US dollar based, they also required stable cross-exchange rates between the member economies. This globalisation of manufacturing industry and major consumer brands effectively put a ceiling on wage and price flexibility. It also underpinned structural unemployment and growing wealth divisions within Western economies that have ultimately forced economic growth to rely evermore on further dollops of debt to sustain consumer spending. Unlike traditional capital investment, much of this spending is unproductive and, therefore, not so easily paid back. Hence, these swollen debt burdens need to be refinanced. Defaults occur not necessarily because of insolvency, but far more frequently because of illiquidity. As we will keep stressing, this refinancing pressure makes balance sheet size and, hence, inflows of liquidity much more important than the level of interest rates. Yet, when this liquidity expansion becomes dependent on the uncertain supply of safe assets, sudden stops in funding can heighten systemic risks. The fact that the modern financial system has turned from a *new financing* system to a *refinancing* system that is more than ever dependent on the supply of potentially flaky safe assets to help rollover increasingly flaky debts creates a negative feedback that highlights the inherent dangers in credit markets.

In a World economy characterised by global supply chains, financial markets have become an integral part of the economic adjustment mechanism, resulting in a heightened Global Liquidity cycle and the death of the traditional Phillips Curve trade-off between domestic inflation and unemployment. Think of these Global Liquidity shocks being channelled through changes in exchange rates, not interest rates, as the flow diagram in Fig. 3.4 explains, with private sector liquidity and cross-border flows largely affecting

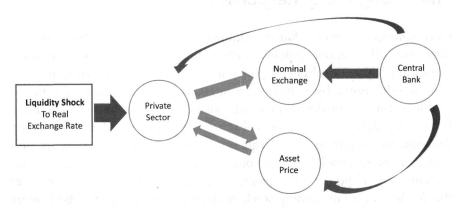

Fig. 3.4 The transmission of Global Liquidity (schematic)

the real exchange rate, and with Central Bank liquidity the more important influence on the nominal exchange rate.

The loose US monetary policy spilled over through cross-border flows into similarly relaxed local monetary conditions across many Emerging Market economies and allowed cash to build up in offshore Eurodollar funding markets. The financial immaturity of China and several other Emerging Markets economies amplified both the domestic and ultimately the aggregated international impact of these cross-border flows on Global Liquidity. Combined with buoyant savings flows, induced by ageing demographics and the 'new rich', these factors encouraged a structural excess demand for (largely US dollar-denominated) 'safe' assets. Large-sized CICPs (corporate and institutional cash pools) increasingly dominate the recycling of the World's surplus savings and they demand secure, collateral-backed short-term instruments. These are provided by fleet-footed wholesale money markets, which now frequently outstrip our traditional and overly regulated, banks in providing vital funding. Put another way, institutional repos now surpass household bank savings accounts as the most popular financial instruments. But the scarcity of good quality collateral, a vital counterpart to these repos, induced by recent government austerity policies and tight Central Banks, disrupts Global Liquidity and means there is insufficient balance sheet capacity available to rollover and refinance the World economy's towering US$250 trillion columns of debt. And, by so heightening default risks and pushing up the odds of systemic risk, this encourages the hoarding of precious 'safe' assets, so further worsening the collateral shortage. See Fig. 3.5.

The Wrong Policy Response?

Governments everywhere fail to acknowledge that debt also has a quality dimension. Their austerity policies, often put in place to balance quantitative easing (QE) and ultra-low policy interest rates, have deprived markets of vital 'safe' assets. By reducing Treasury debt issuance, they have forced private sector intermediaries to search out new investors and to issue more low-quality debt as an inferior collateral substitute, thereby mismatching liabilities and requiring more frequent refinancing. In short, austerity policies that try to avoid 'crowding-out' private sector initiatives simply end up 'crowding-in' poor quality private sector debts. This makes rolling-over the World's huge outstanding stock of debt, shown in Fig. 3.5, both more

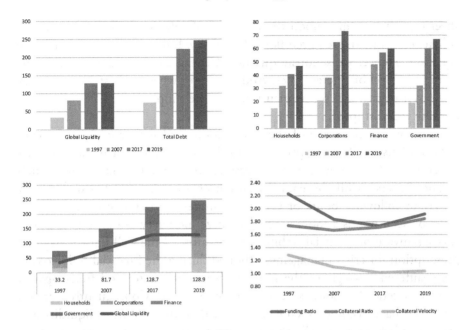

Fig. 3.5 Measures of World debt, Global Liquidity and funding capacity, 1997–2019 (Source *CrossBorder Capital*)

difficult and potentially dangerous. Ironically, the key challenge lies not in the failure of new investments, but rather in our inability to refinance the old ones. It concerns finance, not economics. By expanding the Central Bank balance sheet, QE fills an important funding gap. The large-scale structural changes over the past three decades, described above, have shifted the World's financial markets from acting as a *new capital-raising mechanism* to serving as a *capital distribution and refinancing system*. We alternatively describe this in terms of a reversal in the polarity of the finance, because many former lenders have become borrowers and many previous borrowers have become lenders. This topsy-turvy financial World has consequently become more difficult to read.

The beating heart of a refinancing system is a large and flexible balance sheet that helps to facilitate debt rollovers. Indeed, this is the very reason why the financial system exits! Here the *capacity of capital*, i.e. liquidity, is critical, rather than the *cost of capital*, i.e. interest rates. For example, when maturing home mortgages cannot be easily refinanced, many choose to pay higher interest rates to ensure the roll, rather than face eviction. Balance sheet capacity depends upon the existence of sufficient safe assets to act as collateral against the required flow of liquidity. Interest rates rarely enter the equation. Hence, we seriously question Central Banks' obsession with targeting the level of interest rates. And, more so, when interest rates get very low (even negative) it seems plausible that the supply of new liquidity itself actually gets disrupted.

Therefore, in the wake of the 2007–2008 Global Financial Crisis, with debt burdens swollen and private sector balance sheet capacity significantly lower, it has become even more necessary for Central Banks to grow their balance sheets to fill the gap. The resulting substantial jump in liquidity provision following bouts of QE programmes worries many. However, it must be seen not as a more accommodative monetary policy, but as a necessary bulwark of financial stability policy: after all the well-known Bagehot prescription for crisis management, honed during the financial rollercoaster years suffered throughout the nineteenth century, is to lend freely against good collateral, but always at a high interest rate. Consequently, interest rate levels have become much less relevant than the volume of liquidity and the size of balance sheets. With the international financial system now more procyclical, potentially fragile and with monetary power more concentrated in the hands of the US Federal Reserve and People's Bank of China, finance has also been left looking much like its volatile nineteenth-century predecessor. Policy-makers appear not to understand these changes. They have been forced to fall back on unconventional policies and inevitably they become reactive rather than pre-emptive in their responses to these rising tensions.

The four stages in our argument can be traced through the schematic flow diagram in Fig. 3.6:

- *Productivity Catch-Up*—The 1989 fall of the Berlin Wall and economic enfranchisement of 2–3 billion producers lead to economic 'catch-up' of Emerging Market economies and greater use of the US dollar
- *Globalisation of Production*—China's 2001 entry into WTO and supply chains push adjustment through financial markets and force a loose US monetary policy
- *Nascent China/ EM Financial Sector*—US easing spills over to EM and to China—big US dollar users—and fuels the cash demands of CICPs
- *Lack of Safe Assets*—tight US fiscal policy to balance loose monetary policy restricts the supply of 'safe assets', making the World financial system evermore procyclical and fragile.

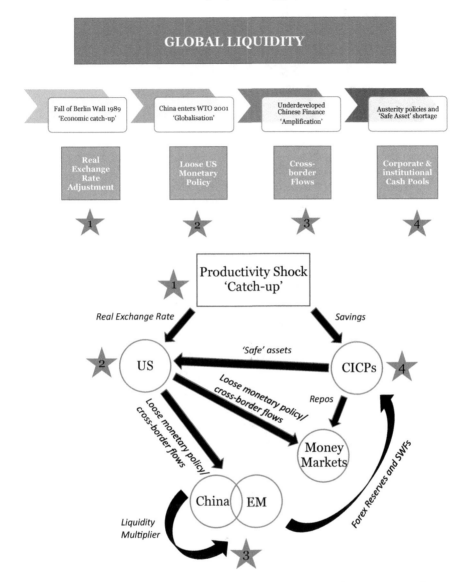

Fig. 3.6 Global Liquidity—schematic showing major issues (*Note* CICPs refers to Corporate and Institutional Cash Pools; SWF denotes Sovereign Wealth Funds, and EM is Emerging Market Economies)

Note

1. Also known as Global Value Chains (GVCs).

4

The Liquidity Model

The Flow of Funds Framework

From the discipline provided by the flow of funds framework, we can represent liquidity algebraically. The standard *budget constraint* allows us to quantify the funding decisions of the private sector. In a technical sense, the private sector is always in balance, because it can both absorb financial assets and issue financial liabilities. In other words, income is either spent or used to accumulate net savings instruments:

$$\text{Income} = \text{spending} + \text{net acquisition of financial assets}$$

$$Y_t = C_t + I_t + \text{NAFA}_t = C_t + I_t + \Delta\text{FA}_t - \Delta\text{FL}_t$$

here NAFA_t denotes the net acquisition of financial assets; FA_t is financial assets and FL_t financial liabilities; Y_t represents income, and C_t and I_t denote consumption spending and investment spending, respectively. Δ is the period difference operator applied at time t.

By definition, the *net acquisition of financial assets*, NAFA_t, equals the *gross acquisition of financial assets*, FA_t, less the *gross acquisition of financial liabilities*, FL_t. Hence, we can rewrite the budget constraint by moving financial liabilities, i.e. borrowings and debt issuance, to the left-hand side of the expression. This now reads:

$$\text{Income} + \text{gross acquisition of financial liabilities}$$

$$= \text{spending} + \text{gross acquisition of financial assets}$$

© The Author(s) 2020
M. J. Howell, *Capital Wars*,
https://doi.org/10.1007/978-3-030-39288-8_4

$$Y_t + \Delta FL_t = C_t + I_t + \Delta FA_t$$

Because savings are defined as income less consumption, by subtracting consumption spending, C_t, from both sides gives:

Saving + gross acquisition of financial liabilities

= fixed investment + gross acquisition of financial assets

$$S_t + \Delta FL_t = I_t + \Delta FA_t$$

We can define liquidity as the sum of savings and 'liquid' financial liabilities. We will ignore 'illiquid' liabilities for convenience, at least for now:

Liquidity = fixed investment + gross acquisition of financial assets

$$L_t = S_t + \Delta FL_t = I_t + \Delta FA_t \tag{4.1}$$

The flow of funds budget constraint has now been rewritten in terms of the *sources* and *uses* of funds, where L_t denotes 'liquidity'. The equation shows that the flow of liquidity can move independently of savings and that it is not the same thing as money. Money, being defined as bank deposits, features on the right-hand side, classified under financial assets. In addition, because of its frequently large credit component and its dependence on collateral, liquidity is both endogenous and highly procyclical.

The changes in financial liabilities and financial assets can, in turn, be broken into their subcomponents:

$$\Delta FL_t = \Delta MB_t + \Delta BSC_t$$
$$\Delta FA_t = A_t \cdot \Delta P_t + \Delta CH_t = I_{f,t} + \Delta CH_t$$

where MB_t is Central Bank Money, but it can also include what we have called the *shadow monetary base*; BSC_t represents bank and shadow bank credit; CH_t denotes cash holdings, including bank deposits; S_t is total savings of households, corporations and foreigners, and A_t is the number of securities or assets in existence.

Defining real (I_t) and financial investments ($I_{f,t}$) as:

$$I_t = P_t \cdot \Delta A_t$$
$$I_{f,t} = A_t \cdot \Delta P_t$$

We can now rewrite this fundamental relationship Eq. (4.1) as follows:

$$L_t = S_t + \Delta \text{MB}_t + \Delta \text{BSC}_t = \Delta \left(P_{f,t} \cdot A_t \right)$$
$$+ \Delta CH_t = I_t + I_{f,t} + \Delta CH_t \tag{4.2}$$

The left-hand side of Eq. (4.2) describes the *sources* of funds and the far right-hand side the *uses*. The middle expression represents the overall change in wealth. In other words, increases in liquidity, i.e. credit and savings, finance increases in wealth, which comprise changes in real investment, financial investment and cash deposits.

In turn, we can further subdivide these sources into public sector liquidity, namely changes in the Central Bank monetary base (CBL = ΔMB), and private sector liquidity, namely savings plus new credit extended by banks and shadow banks (PSL = $S + \Delta$BSC). These divisions are similar to the concepts of *outside money* and *inside money*, respectively, that appear in the literature. We will later explain why they are important, but as a brief introduction, let us initially assume that public sector liquidity moves inversely with policy interest rates, and that private sector liquidity moves positively with the profitability of industrial capital (R). The former statement implies that policy-makers increase the supply of base money in order to reduce short-term interest rates (r) in-line with their policy rate targets. The latter assumption suggests that savings expand with economic activity and the pool of profits, and that credit providers are more willing to make new loans when profitability is good. It follows that forex markets, which are incentivised by average available returns, follow the path of private sector liquidity less Central Bank liquidity ($R + r$): in other words, the mix of liquidity (PSL − CBL). Alongside, domestic financial markets, which are influenced by risk premia, such as the term spread and credit spread ($R - r$) are affected more by the overall flow Central Bank and private sector liquidity (CBL + PSL). In short, risk premia depend on the aggregate quantity of liquidity, whereas exchange rates (and we shall also see credit spreads) depend on the quality mix of liquidity.

An Alternative Decomposition

We can alternatively derive the liquidity framework by recasting it in terms of the standard quantity equation of money. We often refer to liquidity analysis as the 'quality theory' simply because the velocity of money is always changing, either because of regulation, innovation or because of changes in the value of money. High-powered money (MB) times its velocity (v) must equal the value of transactions, i.e. price (P) times volume (T):

$$\mathrm{MB}_t \cdot v_t = P_t \cdot T_t$$

In terms of period-on-period changes:

$$\Delta(\mathrm{MB}_t \cdot v_t) = \Delta(P_t \cdot T_t)$$

Expanding the right-hand side:

$$\Delta(P_t \cdot T_t) = \Delta\mathrm{GDP}_t + A_t \cdot \Delta P_{f,t} + \Delta\mathrm{BD}_t$$

where GDP is economic activity; A is the stock of assets; P_f asset prices and BD bank deposits. Since we can define $\Delta\mathrm{GDP} = I - S$, where I denotes capital spending and S is savings, this can be rewritten as:

$$\Delta(P_t \cdot T_t) = I_t - S_t + A_t \cdot \Delta P_{f,t} + \Delta\mathrm{BD}_t$$

The left-hand side can be expanded into:

$$\Delta(\mathrm{MB}_t \cdot v_t) = v_t \cdot \Delta\mathrm{MB}_t + \mathrm{MB}_t \cdot \Delta v_t$$

Rearranging the expression gives our definition of Liquidity (L):

$$\begin{aligned} L_t &= S_t + v_t \cdot \Delta\mathrm{MB}_t + \mathrm{MB}_t \cdot \Delta v_t \\ &= I_t + A_t \cdot \Delta P_{f,t} + \Delta\mathrm{BD}_t \end{aligned}$$

We can also measure 'Financial Liquidity' as the left-hand side (L) minus real investment (I). This quantifies the flow of funds going into the financial asset economy. It comprises private sector savings (e.g. household savings and corporate profits) changes in the supply of high-powered money and changes in its velocity of circulation. Changes in velocity effectively measure the impact of credit. Velocity is not constant. Rather it fluctuates significantly through the business cycle, and typically also sees a strong upward trend over time because of financial innovation. It is the asset economy that tends to absorb and cushion most of these liquidity swings.

5

Real Exchange Adjustment

The Industrial and Financial Circuits of Money

Traditional economics largely focusses on what John Maynard Keynes in his *Treatise on Money* (1930) describes as the industrial circuit of money. In other words, the so-called *real economy*. While it is important to distinguish the financial economy[1] from the real economy, we must not permanently separate the two. They enjoy a complex interrelationship, with events in both affecting one another, but with finance playing the increasingly dominant role. Henry Thornton in his prescient Paper Credit (1802) recognised these close links: "*The subjects of coin, of paper credit, of the balance of commerce, and of exchanges* […are] *intimately connected to each other*".

The standard textbook model assumes that interest rates can be divided into real and inflation components and into short-term and long-term components. The real interest rate is supposedly determined in the real economy by the savings-investment gap, while inflation results from excess money creation. Imbalances between investment spending (*I*) and savings (*S*), say *S > I*, are redressed through interest rate movements, where greater capital spending is incentivised by lower rates. Short rates are set by the Central Banks, which, in turn, can control long-term interest rates with appropriate 'forward guidance' policies. Yet, from our market experience almost every dimension of this conventional paradigm seems wrong.

Keynes, as we know, argued differently by suggesting that equilibrium is restored and not necessarily at a full-employment level, by changing incomes, rather than interest rates. In other words, excess savings reduce incomes, which, in turn, lower future savings until they match the given rate

© The Author(s) 2020
M. J. Howell, *Capital Wars*,
https://doi.org/10.1007/978-3-030-39288-8_5

of investment spending. Modern macroeconomics can, therefore, be seen, perhaps cynically, as a long debate about why the rate of interest fails as an adjustment mechanism. First, nominal interest rates are strongly affected by risk and term premia, which, in turn, are governed both by future expectations and current beliefs,[2] as well as by access to liquidity, which is a gross flow or balance sheet concept. Interest rates, as well as other financial asset prices, are determined in financial markets by decisions about gross, rather than net, funding. As we showed in Chapter 4, this is because in a modern capitalist economy, investment depends on the total pool of *liquidity* and not just on savings. In other words, thinking in flow of fund terms, net savings (i.e. savings less capital expenditure, $S-I$) represents the net acquisition of financial assets, and it is only one small component of overall funding, i.e. liquidity. The net acquisition of financial assets, in turn, comprises the difference between the change in financial asset holdings and the increase or decrease in financial liabilities. Plainly, there can be many ways of arriving at any given net change: by a large increase in assets; a large fall in liabilities; some moderated combination of the two or even by a huge rise in financial assets alongside a large but lesser rise in financial liabilities. These gross balance sheet changes are independent of the net savings position and by implication of what happens in the real economy. They have been described elsewhere by Raymond Goldsmith (1985) as 'financial deepening' and they explain his belief that the so-called *financial interrelations ratio* rises over time. Similar observations apply to current account balances and the underlying movements in gross capital inflows and gross capital outflows. A narrow focus on net imbalances too easily concludes that Emerging Markets, being economies that typically enjoy net savings surpluses, drive Global Liquidity, e.g. the *savings glut* story. However, the broader concept of gross flows shows that a major force has been the huge increase in foreign liabilities of safe assets and credit issued by the major developed economies, as when global money centre banks feverishly increased their lending ahead of the GFC and investors from Emerging Market economies piled into US Treasuries. It also follows that each asset/liability mix likely has a different implication for financial asset prices. At the same time, globalisation, and particularly our experience of cheap Chinese imports, reinforces the idea that inflation is to a large extent driven by costs, rather than by monetary factors. Consequently, real interest rates must, by definition, also be affected by these same monetary shifts and the implied fluctuations in risk and term premia. Financial history tends to show that short-term policy interest rates follow rather than lead long-term rates, and, in turn, policy rates typically precede inflation[3] and, what's more, they often act in the same direction.

In contrast to flow of funds data, the more widely used National Income Accounts (NIA) report macroeconomic aggregates, such as GDP and consumer spending. These are measures of expenditure that track how money is spent, but they do not explain how spending is financed and therefore they cannot show whether or not it is sustainable. As we have already argued, in Chapter 2, flow of funds statistics give a far more comprehensive picture of financing activity by measuring the net acquisition of financial assets by each economic sector. Unlike spending flows, which once spent disappear, financial flows accumulate and they are ultimately reflected in rising stocks of financial assets and liabilities in sectoral balance sheets. Such high debt and leverage ratios may consequently curtail further new flows. Sustainability depends upon future access to liquidity, which today largely reflects financial intermediation beyond the traditional banking system.

Because investment spending is determined by liquidity and not just by savings. This means that we need to bring in credit, i.e. financial liabilities and financial assets and think more broadly in flow of funds terms. It requires adding a financial circuit of money to our economic models and considering how the balance between the overall sources and uses of funds is maintained and restored? What's more, it tells us that interest rates and other financial asset prices are determined more by gross flows, i.e. the entire financial sector balance sheet, and not solely by net flows. While any monetary imbalances will express themselves through fluctuations in the *price of money*, contrary to conventional thinking, this is not the interest rate. Like every other 'price' it should measure what money can buy: in other words, its terms of trade or exchange rate. The interest rate can be better thought of as the *premium* paid on money when it is borrowed, and these premia can vary by the time horizon and according to the riskiness of the borrower, which again depend on balance sheet factors.

Recognising that liquidity is the sum of savings and credit, there are four adjustment outcomes following a positive liquidity shock:

- Greater real investment (including both what turn out to be productive as well as unproductive schemes)
- Rising value of financial assets
- Falling value of financial liabilities
- Lower national savings.

The first is the most feasible adjustment for an Emerging Market economy that enjoys abundant investment opportunities, but suffers a comparative shortage of domestic savings. It is a less likely path for mature Western economies, and more liquidity is likely to inflate asset values in these cases. It is possible that this ultimately causes a financial bubble, which may then lead, in sequence, to debt write-offs, i.e. lower financial liabilities, and lower savings, possibly in the way Keynes foresaw through reduced income and employment levels. Nonetheless, not only are these adjustments potentially more complex than the traditional narrative suggests because they involve financial markets, but it is far from clear that any adjustment will either restore balance or act particularly quickly. For example, when liquidity exceeds capital spending $(L > I)$, the private sector can accumulate financial assets. Put differently, this likely means that the change in the value of their financial assets exceeds the change in the value of their financial liabilities. In a World where collateral stands as an important element backing new credit supply, this net increase in financial asset values may, in turn, induce a further expansion in financial liabilities, i.e. credit. In other words, these financial imbalances amplify the initial shocks, from which it may take years to restore equilibrium.

Looked at another way, the inclusion of the financial circuit complicates adjustment largely because liquidity has two dimensions—quantitative and qualitative. In Chapter 2, we argued that the qualitative dimension can be thought of as 'moneyness' and this tends to act procyclically to raise the effective quantity of liquidity. In other words, as the cycle extends the effective supply of liquidity naturally expands as more assets are used as money. Similarly, vice versa, so amplifying the initial shocks. This can be seen both as the result of improving risk appetite (which permits greater leverage) and from the enhanced collateral values (which increase the stock of high-powered money). We show later that high-powered monies are assets that can be leveraged, and they include both traditional reserves held at the Central Bank, as well as the collateral used to borrow from money markets and the extra cash available to borrow from offshore money markets. The effective stock of high-powered money consists of traditional Central Bank reserve money plus what we have called the *shadow monetary base*. This, in turn, is fed by the Eurodollar markets and by the increasing substitution of poorer quality private sector collateral for higher quality government bonds. The supply of these genuine 'safe' assets has been limited by recent policies of fiscal rectitude. Consequently, as a result of this qualitative dimension, the volume of Global Liquidity is increasingly procyclical and potentially fragile, resulting in an expanding, but at the same time more volatile World financial system.

Digging deeper into this idea, as additional liquidity is channelled into the financial circuit, default[4] risks decline, risk premia narrow and the term premia associated with 'safe' assets increase in size as demand for them drops. This boosts equity markets, so improving the climate for capital-raising and risk-taking, and through a steepening interest rate yield curve bank profit margins expand, which incentivises greater bank lending. The qualitative dimension of liquidity again holds the key. Money borrowed in a boom or economic upswing, i.e. *means of purchase*, is qualitatively different from money borrowed in a slump or economic downswing, i.e. legal tender or *means of settlement*: the former is used to expand the circuits of money the latter to close the circuits. Central Bank money is unique because it can always take both forms. Private sector liquidity fluctuates in size, in part, because its 'moneyness' changes, i.e. its ability to serve as means of settlement. At these times, the overall volume of liquidity may be enhanced by more Central Bank money. While this is national legal tender, it is not international legal tender and the so extra supplies will likely cause the exchange rate to devalue.

This helps explain why increases in both private and Central Bank liquidity cause national risk premia to narrow (and, therefore, the antithesis 'safe' asset premia to notionally widen), whereas differential changes in private and Central Bank liquidity cause exchange rates to fluctuate. Thus, strong (weak) private sector liquidity and weak (strong) Central Bank liquidity can both strengthen (weaken) national currencies. The intuition comes from thinking about the return on industrial capital and the policy interest rate. Let us assume that private-sector cash flow is positively related to the underlying return on industrial capital (say, R) and Central Bank liquidity is negatively associated with the policy interest rate (say, r). Then, the yield curve slope should be determined by the spread between industrial returns[5] and short-term interest rates (i.e. $R - r$). Similarly, the exchange rate is related to the size of the average returns available from industry and money markets (i.e. $R + r$). This exchange rate channel is worth further study.

The Exchange Rate Channel

Exchange rates are supposed to restore external balance, because an economy experiencing an appreciating currency should expect to suffer lower net exports. In our experience this is rarely so straightforward and particularly in the case of the Emerging Market economies. Rather than dampening economic activity, periods of strong currency appreciation often coincide with similarly strong cross-border capital inflows and buoyant business activity. In practice, exchange rates influence economies through both real as well as financial channels. A net export channel is embedded in standard open-economy macro models,[6] but exchange rate fluctuations and cross-border capital flows also influence the economy through changes in the composition and size of its external balance sheet, or through what has been called the *valuation channel of adjustment*.[7] These financial channels work alongside the standard trade channel to achieve external balance. Gourinchas et al. (2019) find that as much as one-third of adjustment comes from valuation effects alone, compared to 41% coming from trade.

To better understand the financial transmission, we again engage flow of funds analysis. Dislocations in the flow of funds ultimately affect the real economy through the so-called *real exchange rate*. The real exchange rate expresses real purchasing power. Think of it as being determined by the relative productivity performance of two economies. Hence, faster-growing economies should have stronger real exchange rates. Helped by free trade, capital flows and technology transfers, other newly industrialised economies, such as China, enjoy relatively faster productivity growth than America.[8] Over the 1981–2019 period, the US enjoyed real productivity growth averaging 1.5% per annum, compared to 1.4% for Japan; 4.3% for Korea and 7.3% for China.[9] Since 2010, productivity growth has dropped everywhere. In the US it averaged 1.0% per annum; in Japan 0.7%; Korea 2.0% and in China 6.1%. Figure 5.1 highlights the secular decline in the

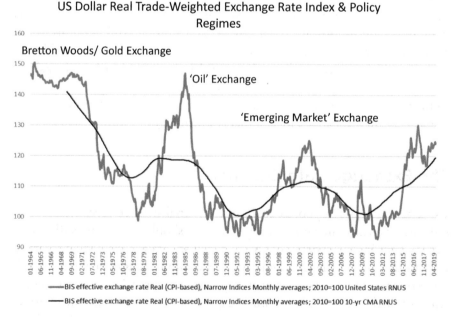

Fig. 5.1 US dollar real trade-weighted exchange rate index, 10-year trend and policy regimes, 1964–2019 (*Source* BIS and *CrossBorder Capital*)

US real trade-weighted exchange rate, as calculated by the BIS (Bank for International Settlements). Fitting a trend line to the data prior to 2016, shows the real US dollar losing roughly ten index points in value each decade, or circa 8%. We have added annotations to describe the three periods (explained in Chapter 1) when a greater demand for dollars halted this slide and allowed the US terms of trade to temporarily improve, sometimes surging by as much as 20% above its downward trend. Latest data since 2016 lends weight to an argument that this long downtrend in relative productivity performance may have ended. While this is possible, the counterargument notes China's still yawning absolute productivity gap with America.

The real exchange rate can be calculated by adjusting the nominal exchange rate for relative price movements, but what exactly comprises these baskets of prices is less straightforward. We take a broad definition that includes traded and non-traded goods and service prices, wages, and asset prices. The degree of flexibility exhibited by these various price types differs considerably. It seems plausible that, in a World economy dominated by large global businesses, asset prices are among the most flexible and traded goods and service prices among the least flexible. There is supporting evidence that shows how prices tend to be rigid in the currency in which they are invoiced (see Gopinath et al. 2018). This means that the choice of invoicing currency determines the response of export and import prices to exchange rate movements. Consequently, the more extensive use of the US dollar in both trade invoicing and trade settlement alters the sensitivity of business activity to changes in the US exchange rate. Global Value Chains (GVC) use US dollars extensively to finance their inventories and their US dollar needs grow disproportionately as these supply chains lengthen. This suggests that the wider role of the dollar in invoicing results in less price flexibility and, correspondingly, greater adjustment through profit margins, supply and trade volumes. According to Gopinath et al. (2018), a generalised 1% US dollar appreciation leads to a 0.6–0.8% decline in the volume of total World trade over a one-year period. A corollary is that this deeper dollarisation of domestic bank deposits forces the national Central Bank to build up precautionary dollar reserves in order to protect the financial system from external shocks.

Liquidity shocks, whether coming externally through net capital inflows or internally from the effects of faster productivity growth on domestic profits, initially impact private sector liquidity and thereby trigger changes to the real exchange rate. A favourable liquidity shock tends to increase the flow of private sector liquidity, and this, in turn, will cause the real exchange rate to appreciate. The specific division between a change in the nominal exchange rate and a change in relative prices is at this stage unclear, but by simultaneously injecting more or less liquidity policy-makers can affect the split. Put another way, if the real exchange rate adjustment is initially channelled through a stronger nominal exchange rate, larger cash injections by the Central Bank will slow this appreciation and potentially force more adjustment on to goods prices and wages. Returning to our previous discussion about the relative responsiveness of different price-types, it may follow that this policy action ultimately fuels rising financial asset prices, when other prices are sticky.

Indeed, this is our experience from Emerging Market investing. Central Bank interventions to suppress upward pressure on their nominal exchange rates, usually against the US dollar, often lead to domestic asset booms in both real estate and equity markets. Late-1980s Japan provides another clear example. Although the Yen rose significantly against the US currency through the prior decade, it did not rise sufficiently to eliminate Japan's huge productivity advantage. The resulting build-up of liquidity from Japan's remarkable export success, which became further boosted through unregulated and leveraged *zaitech* financial products, inflated a huge asset bubble that finally burst in December 1989. Japan's financial markets slumped and equity prices have ever since failed to regain their former dizzy heights.

We believe that under the prevailing *globalisation* regime, policy-makers can therefore effectively choose between the level of asset prices and the nominal exchange rate. Emerging Market economies and other export-focussed economies, such as Japan, Germany and China, tend to favour exchange rate stability against the US dollar. In contrast, policy-makers from economies dominated by large banking sectors and deep financial markets, like the US and the UK, instead aim at preserving or even enhancing the collateral values of domestic assets and they are consequently more willing to accept nominal exchange rate weakness. This may explain the alacrity with which both the UK and US have sacrificed their exchange rates in times of trouble? It may also hint at why the traditional Phillips Curve trade-off between the unemployment rate and high street inflation no longer seems to work? US nominal devaluation policy has a long history, having been used successfully to claw out the economy from the 1930s Depression. Deliberately devaluing money primarily against commodities, rather than assets, in the 1930s can be understood because agriculture was then far more important to the US economy than it is today. Nearly a century on, the modern credit-based economy has a greater need to maintain the value of its collateral. George F. Warren, a key interwar policy advisor, wrote this in a letter to President Roosevelt, 24 April 1933:

There is one and only one way to raise our commodity price level; that is by reducing the amount of gold in the dollar. A rise in prices this week of basic commodities was directly in proportion to the decline in the value of the dollar in foreign exchange....[10]

Although the necessity to export dollars to the Rest of the World does not automatically force the US to run trade or current account deficits,[11] they are likely consequences. This may explain the ongoing *deindustrialisation* of American manufacturing[12] simply because flows of goods adjust more easily to international shocks than services can. The manufacturing sector matters to the extent that it is an important source of future productivity growth, which implies that a smaller industrial base may feed back to further weaken the US real exchange rate. The resulting slide in the real exchange rate may, in turn, justify the US authorities' adoption of a near-permanently loose monetary policy to underpin collateral, which it then balances with a tight fiscal stance. This policy mix channels adjustment through a weaker nominal exchange rate while simultaneously trying to ensure stable domestic financial markets. However, in the process, the US exports her monetary largesse through cross-border flows, which becomes amplified into bigger moves in Global Liquidity. In theory, the widespread adoption of floating exchange rate regimes should prevent these national liquidity shocks from spreading elsewhere, but as Rey (2015) has shown, this tends not to be the case.

Figure 5.2 traces out this financial adjustment mechanism. An initial positive liquidity shock on the left-hand side of the diagram strengthens private sector liquidity, which puts upward pressure on both the nominal exchange rate and asset prices. Moving to the right-hand side of the diagram, the precise division between changes in the exchange rate and asset prices depends on the scale of subsequent Central Bank intervention. By changing the size

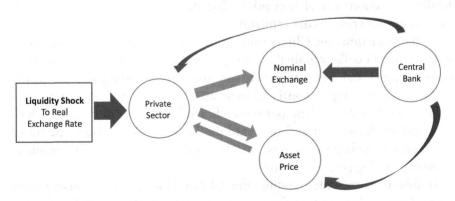

Fig. 5.2 Schematic diagram showing real exchange rate adjustment

of their balance sheets, Central Banks can further fuel private sector liquidity, directly through easing funding terms and indirectly through the effect that rising collateral values have in boosting the willingness of credit providers to lend more. The diagram incorporates a number of positive-feedback effects that explain the liquidity cycle and asset bubbles.

The precise transmission starts from the left-hand side of the diagram, when productivity increases and capital inflows put upward pressure on an economy's *real exchange rate*. Under a targeted nominal exchange rate regime, shown by the diagram's lower path, and assuming that the price levels of traded goods are set internationally and are, therefore, 'sticky', the bulk of the economic adjustment comes through movements in service sector prices and notably asset prices. Therefore, economies with strong productivity growth and net capital inflows often enjoy rising asset prices, especially when their nominal exchange rates are relatively stable. And, because appreciating capital asset prices tend to attract more investors, these moves can be amplified by further capital inflows, thereby, fueling an asset price spiral.

One important nexus can be identified when this diagram is redrawn for America alongside a China equivalent. Under this joint schema, a negative productivity shock to the US—possibly resulting from a shift in market share towards Chinese businesses—leads to downward pressure on the US real exchange rate. (There is an equivalent upward pressure on the real Chinese RMB exchange rate.) This may be met by an easier monetary stance from the Federal Reserve in order to ensure that asset prices remain largely unaffected and, hence, loan collateral values are maintained. The strength of America's domestic banking lobby could help to explain why? Nonetheless, the result is a weaker US dollar. As the US nominal exchange rate devalues, surplus liquidity spills over into offshore funding and investment markets. In addition, the weaker US dollar itself both encourages more cross-border lending and boosts global asset prices. Together, both effects tend to encourage still greater cross-border capital flows.

At the same time, the Chinese authorities will likely resist downward pressure on the US dollar nominal exchange rate against the Yuan by monetising capital inflows and any new export surpluses. The resulting liquidity injections underpin rising domestic Chinese asset prices, and may, in turn, spill over to affect other similarly positioned Emerging Market economies, which then quickly follow suit and monetise the foreign inflows. Thus, the initial US monetary policy easing gets quickly amplified Worldwide as a result of these contrasting policy objectives.

It follows that understanding the Global Liquidity cycle may simply come down to interpreting the motives and actions of the two key Central Banks—the US Federal Reserve and the People's Bank of China—as well as the separate effect that US dollar movements have on boosting cross-border capital flows. These two Central Banks also indirectly exercise control over these capital flows: first, because nominal US dollar movements depend to a large extent on their joint policy actions. And, second, because the ultimate direction of cross-border capital flows is itself often dictated by the tempo of the Chinese economy (see Chapter 9), which, in turn, is, at one remove, determined by PBoC monetary policy. Through this mechanism, whenever the PBoC matches its actions, the US Fed enjoys huge leverage over Global Liquidity conditions.

Testing the Model with Data: US Dollar and EM Currencies

The data reported in Fig. 5.3 are sourced from *CrossBorder Capital* and represent normalised index measures of the expansion of US Central Bank and US private sector liquidity. The index constituents consist of liquidity subcomponents that accord with divisia methods, e.g. separating bank from shadow bank credit, and weighted, in part, using principal components. These indexes are explained in greater detail in Chapter 13. Whereas it is more common in monetary analysis to simply treat the entire money stock as an amorphous whole, this division allows us to incorporate a quality dimension, for many of the reasons given earlier, where more private sector liquidity is 'good' and value-enhancing for the exchange rate, whereas the supply of Central

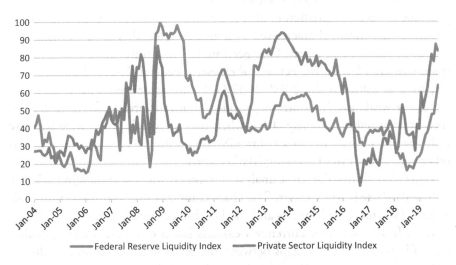

Fig. 5.3 US private sector and US Federal Reserve Liquidity Indexes, 2004–2019 (Source *CrossBorder Capital*)

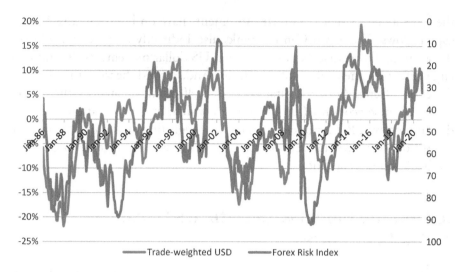

Fig. 5.4 US forex risk index (advanced 12-months) and US trade-weighted exchange rate (percentage deviations from 3-year trend), 1986–2019 (indexes 0–100) (Source *CrossBorder Capital*)

Bank liquidity is 'bad' and likely to weaken the currency. Figure 5.3 reports these two indexes, while Fig. 5.4 takes their difference (private sector less Central Bank liquidity) to create a so-named forex risk index, which is then compared to the US trade-weighted, or effective, exchange rate. The forex risk index is advanced by 12 months and the US effective exchange rate index is shown as percentage deviations away from a trailing three-year trend.

According to the analyses shown in Fig. 5.5 and Table 5.1, the model provides a decent predictor of future US currency movements some 6–12 months ahead, characterised by a high R-squared. The forex risk index also appears to be one-way Granger causal[13] of future movements in the trade-weighted US dollar. Periods of excessive Federal Reserve liquidity supply, such as followed the 2007–2008 GFC, are associated with subsequent US dollar weakness. In contrast, periods of buoyant private sector cash flow, such as occurred in the early 2010s when America's tech giants were strongly cash generative, lead on to a rising US dollar. Similar conclusions apply to other currencies, even Emerging Market units.

Figure 5.6 shows the same analysis for the JPMorgan Emerging Market (US dollar-based) forex index. The chart compares the individual forex risk indexes for Emerging Markets and the US. Higher readings for both indexes warn of future potential currency weakness based of a deteriorating quality mix of liquidity. The two gaps between the series in 2002–2004 and 2012–2015 indicate, respectively, upcoming periods of Emerging Market currency

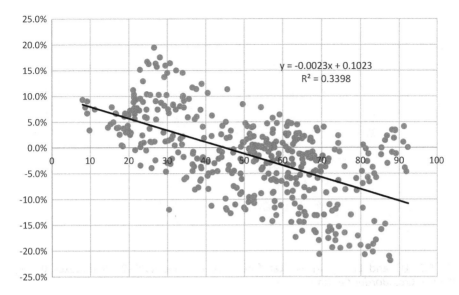

Fig. 5.5 Scatter diagram of US forex risk index (advanced by 12-months) and trade-weighted US dollar, 1986–2019 (Source *CrossBorder Capital*)

strength and weakness. In the first period the Emerging Market forex risk component improved significantly (i.e. it fell in the chart), whereas the US dollar forex risk component deteriorated (i.e. it rose in the chart). In the second period, the reverse situation applied. US forex risk stood at low levels, whereas Emerging Market forex risk began to deteriorate substantially through 2012–2013, and largely, as it turns out, through inappropriately loose domestic monetary policies.

The resulting exchange rate prediction is reported in Fig. 5.7. This compares the Emerging Market less US forex risk indexes to the JPMorgan exchange rate basket index. The JPMorgan index is again drawn as percentage deviations from a trailing three-year trend and the EM less US forex risk index is again advanced by 12 months. The reported results compare

Table 5.1 Pairwise Granger causality tests between US forex risk (US FXRISK) and trade-weighted US dollar (US TW$ %dev)

Sample: 1985M1 2019M12			
Lags: 2			
Null hypothesis	Obs	*F*-statistic	Prob.
US TW$ %dev does not Granger cause US FXRISK	477	0.32421	0.7233
US FXRISK does not Granger cause US TW$ %dev		5.91246	0.0029

Source *CrossBorder Capital*

Fig. 5.6 US and Emerging Market forex risk indexes, 1997–2019 (indexes 0–100) (Source *CrossBorder Capital*)

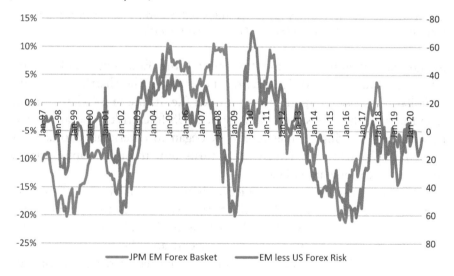

Fig. 5.7 EM less US forex risk indexes (advanced by 12-months) and JPMorgan EM forex basket (percentage deviation from 3-year trend), 1997–2019 (indexes −50 to +50) (Source *CrossBorder Capital*)

well with those for the US dollar. The forex risk data are strongly one-way Granger causal, while the R-squared between the forex risk data and future 12-month ahead movements in the JPMorgan forex basket is sizeable and statistically significant (Fig. 5.8). These analyses add weight to our belief that forex market movements depend crucially on the quality mix of liquidity and capital flows (Table 5.2).

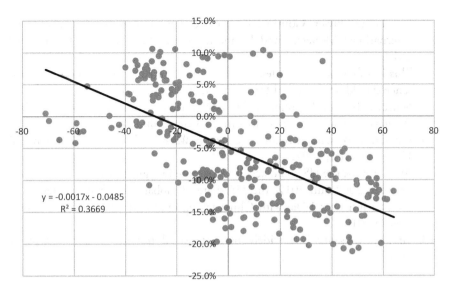

Fig. 5.8 Scatter diagram of EM less US forex risk indexes (advanced by 12-months) and JPMorgan EM forex basket, 1997–2019 (Source *CrossBorder Capital*)

Table 5.2 Pairwise Granger causality tests between EM less US forex risk (EM FXRISK-US FXRISK) and JP Morgan EM forex basket (JPM FX% dev)

Sample: 1997M1 2019M12			
Lags: 2			
Null hypothesis	Obs	F-statistic	Prob.
JPM FX %dev does not Granger cause EM FXRISK-US FXRISK	309	0.34600	0.7078
EM FXRISK-US FXRISK does not Granger cause JPM FX %dev		4.77197	0.0091

Source *CrossBorder Capital*

Notes

1. An associated term is the similar concept of the *asset economy*.
2. Uncertainty in economics cover both the lack of knowledge about the long-term future, as well as a lack of knowledge about how other economic agents are likely to act in the near term. Hence, we develop 'rules of thumb'.
3. See James Bullard, *The Seven Faces of the Peril*, St Louis Fed, 2010.
4. Defaults may recognise underlying insolvency, but they are usually triggered by illiquidity, i.e. an inability to access sufficient funding.
5. Industry tends to fund at longer maturities consistent with its investment horizon, e.g. 10 years.
6. This is the so-called Mundell–Fleming approach.

7. See Pierre-Olivier Gourinchas, Helene Rey and Maxime Sauzet, The International Monetary and Financial System, LBS Working Paper, April 2019.
8. This is, of course, true unless it is not. Thus, an American economic renaissance should drive the real US dollar exchange rate higher.
9. Source IMF World Economic Outlook Database, April 2019, except China. We have estimated productivity directly from Chinese data.
10. Quoted in Bernard F. Stanton, *George F. Warren—Farm Economist*, Cornell University Press, 2007.
11. Alternatively, the US could accumulate more foreign assets.
12. Between 2002 and 2017, the US share of global manufacturing fell from 28% to just over 18%, with China taking over as the World's largest supplier in 2010.
13. Granger causality is a widely used statistical test for a specific type of causality.

References

Goldsmith, Raymond W. 1985. *Comparative National Balance Sheets: A Study of Twenty Countries, 1688–1978*. Chicago: University of Chicago Press.
Gopinath, Gita, and Jeremy C. Stein. 2018. Banking, Trade, and the Making of a Dominant Currency. NBER Working Paper, March.
Gourinchas, Pierre-Olivier, Helene Rey, and Maxime Sauzet. 2019. The International Monetary and Financial System. LBS Working Paper, April (Forthcoming, *Annual Review of Economics*).
Keynes, John Maynard. 1930. *A Treatise on Money*, 2 vols. London: Macmillan.
Rey, Hélène. 2015. IMF Mundell Fleming Lecture.
Thornton, Henry. 1802. *An Enquiry into the Nature and Effects of the Paper Credit of Great Britain*. London.

6

Private Sector (Funding) Liquidity

Funding Liquidity

In Chapter 2, we classified liquidity in two different ways: in terms of a notional buyer's access to cash, which we called *funding liquidity* (i.e. a measure of cash flow), and as a notional seller's access to cash, which is *market liquidity* (i.e. a measure of market depth). Conceptually, these two properties derive, respectively, from the left- and the right-hand sides of the traditional flow of funds equation that matches *sources* to *uses* of funds. Whereas market liquidity is frequently linked to the 'price' and 'size' embodied in bid-ask spreads, funding liquidity can be gauged from the quantity and the quality of the sources of new liquidity, i.e. access to *means of payment* or cash, the ultimate 'safe' asset. In practice, we measure this by the amount of cash on-hand plus the ability to borrow more cash from banking and credit markets.

Liquidity: A Measure of Funding

Liquidity can be split into its private and public components. Public liquidity is measured by the short-term liabilities of the Central Bank and the government e.g. cash in circulation, bank reserves, reverse repos, Treasury bills. Private sector liquidity consists of equivalent short-term private liabilities, e.g. bank and shadow bank credits, repos and commercial bills.

© The Author(s) 2020
M. J. Howell, *Capital Wars*,
https://doi.org/10.1007/978-3-030-39288-8_6

Liquidity has both qualitative and quantitative dimensions, as well as private and public sector ones. Unlike money supply measures, such as the popular M2, liquidity is global and not just national. It is used in wholesale financial markets, as well as in retail markets. It embraces the entire private sector and not just high street banks. It includes access to credit as well as to savings deposits. And, since it measures funding,[1] e.g. the refinancing of existing positions, and not just new credit, it is best measured by gross flows, i.e. changes in the entire balance sheet capacity of the private and public sectors, rather than by net flows, as is more common in economics. The only role for traditional money supply is to serve as one part of this overall liquidity picture.

Although the stock of M2 money, i.e. retail bank deposits, has a long history of representing liquidity, a better and more accurate definition would today include wholesale money markets, such as repos (a form of secured borrowing), commercial paper and Eurodollars (forms of largely unsecured borrowing). This is underlined by Adrian and Shin[2] (2009): "*The money stock is a measure of the liabilities of deposit-taking banks, and so may have been useful before the advent of the market-based financial system. However, the money stock will be of less use in a financial system such as that in the US. More useful may be measures of collateralized borrowing, such as the weekly series of primary dealer repos*".

It is our contention that 'modern money' really starts where conventional definitions of money supply end. In other words, the well-known monetary aggregates,[3] e.g. M0, M1 and M2, are only the tip of a growing iceberg of short-term claims that, as the 2007–2008 GFC shows, can severely disrupt the markets. Traditional money is, therefore, just one of a number of financial assets and high street banks constitute only one of the many types of financial intermediaries, albeit still important ones. M2 money, the broadest official US monetary measure, comprises notes and coins, as well as insured household deposits. It excludes the uninsured claims of institutional money managers, corporations and forex reserve managers, as well as offshore Eurodollar balances. Together this combined broad funding pool stands close to US$26 trillion, easily dwarfing the US$15 trillion that makes up M2 money supply.

Public sector money[4] is very important in supporting this funding hierarchy because the national Central Bank balance sheet is a widely acceptable means of payment within its own jurisdiction, i.e. legal tender, and sometimes beyond. It is fashionable among some academics to argue that the Central Bank and the Treasury or Finance Ministry are essentially the same institution, and that Central Banks can be circumvented by the

Treasury Department simply altering its funding mix between short-term and long-term debt. Such thinking ignores the subtle role played by the Central Banks in setting the terms for credit and controlling leverage, which we address more directly in Chapter 7. For example, during financial crises, Central Bank money is deemed high quality because it represents an unambiguous *means of settlement*[5] for debts. Put another way, the quality mix of the liquidity components matters. This explains why we prefer to think in terms of a *quality theory of money* rather than the more popular *quantity theory of money*. The changing importance attached to private sector and public sector, i.e. Central Bank, liquidity through the business cycle is a good example of fluctuations in this quality dimension.

The quality of liquidity is governed by the degree of substitutability between different monies, such as coins, banknotes and bank demand deposits, bank credit and other financial instruments. The range of 'near monies' includes time deposits, various money market instruments, such as bills of exchange, commercial paper, repos, Treasury bills, shorter-dated Treasury securities, the cash surrender values of life insurance policies, shares in savings and loan associations, saving bonds, building society deposits, postal saving deposits, savings in money market funds and most other credit instruments issued by the financial sector firms in the economy. We include these broader financial instruments in our definition of liquidity when: (1) their prices are relatively stable, and (2) they are easily convertible into legal tender, as and when desired. This means that each asset's liquidity is determined by the speed of conversion into the *means of settlement* at full value and this, in turn, both owes something to the asset's duration[6] and something to its credit quality. Therefore, 'liquidity' strictly has two quality dimensions, not one. A liquid asset has both low *credit risk* and low *duration risk*. In practice, this means is it also equated with being 'safe'. For example, a US dollar bill has zero duration risk. At the same time, it has zero credit risk and serves as legal tender, i.e. cash for residents. A British Government gilt-edged bond has near-zero credit risk, but depending on its maturity it has non-zero duration risk. Because asset duration, itself, should not always be thought of as an absolute concept, but relative to the duration of liabilities, duration risk will vary by institution. Hence, a traditional bank takes on sizeable duration risk given that it holds a large amount of zero duration liabilities as retail deposits. However, a pension fund, which faces liabilities, say, on average ten years hence, should measure its duration risk against a default-free 10-year bond. Thus, this can explain why the 10-year Treasury is the canonical safe asset for many investors.

Figure 6.1 shows our classification of liquidity based on the assets side of the balance sheet of all credit providers, including, for example, traditional high street banks, *shadow banks*, such as wholesale and investment banks, finance houses and other specialist lenders, dealer banks in money markets, mortgage banks and the Central Bank. Balance sheets, by definition, 'balance' with total assets equalling total liabilities, so we could have equally chosen to define liquidity from the liability side. However, in keeping with the sequential distinction implicit in flow of funds accounts between the *sources* and *uses* of funds, and also believing that the decision to borrow is the more active, we prefer to use an asset-based definition.

Table 6.1 provides a detailed breakdown of US Liquidity between traditional banks and the five main types of shadow banking, excluding repo finance. Overall US Liquidity is close to US$26 trillion, sizeably more than both US GDP (US$20 trillion) and traditional US M2 money supply (US$15 trillion), with shadow banking making up just under half (Fig. 6.2). Shadow banking[7] is a term originally coined by analysts at PIMCO to describe banking activities that are either off-balance sheet or outside the

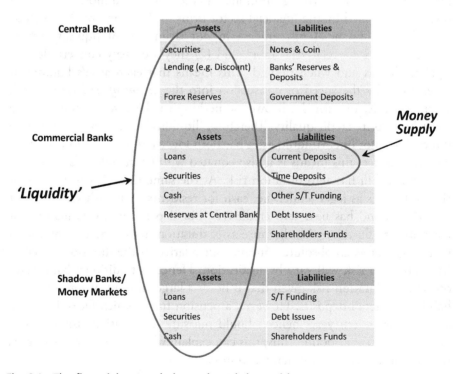

Fig. 6.1 The financial system balance sheet (schematic)

Table 6.1 US bank and shadow bank credit, 1999–2019E (US dollars in billions)

	Total	Shadow banks	Bank credit	Securitisation	Finance Cos.	Other consumer credit	GSEs	US commercial paper
1999	10,313.8	5809.4	4504.4	1503.7	1085.3	394.2	2060.3	1362.8
2000	11,317.9	6452.2	4865.7	1573.1	1273.3	434.7	2275.9	1572.9
2001	12,340.0	7274.3	5065.6	1865.1	1379.8	453.2	2702.2	1437.4
2002	13,424.6	7967.7	5457.0	2055.9	1483.2	464.4	3134.8	1352.3
2003	14,392.8	8603.3	5789.5	2159.6	1610.5	453.0	3615.9	1284.2
2004	15,517.7	9143.4	6374.3	2281.4	1781.2	459.1	3813.0	1403.9
2005	16,787.7	9715.9	7071.8	2318.2	1898.1	494.9	4009.8	1662.2
2006	18,510.1	10,669.7	7840.4	2542.8	2031.7	488.6	4354.3	1983.1
2007	19,749.8	11,175.9	8574.0	2656.1	2069.4	492.4	4992.3	1780.6
2008	20,634.0	11,601.8	9032.2	2932.1	1919.0	504.6	5318.6	1658.7
2009	20,029.3	11,246.2	8783.2	2970.4	1622.4	590.5	5491.2	1148.7
2010	19,190.4	10,207.4	8983.0	2072.6	1518.2	721.5	5388.9	1036.7
2011	19,362.7	10,254.5	9108.2	2167.0	1468.8	855.2	5259.9	937.5
2012	19,947.4	10,321.0	9626.5	2269.3	1399.1	1004.9	5146.6	1009.8
2013	20,148.6	10,320.4	9828.2	2197.8	1413.9	1145.1	5079.4	1039.1
2014	21,026.7	10,486.5	10,540.1	2235.2	1442.2	1290.4	5034.2	1015.8
2015	22,108.3	10,765.1	11,343.2	2462.4	1310.8	1439.4	5041.0	1026.6
2016	23,214.6	11,136.5	12,078.1	2588.0	1274.4	1586.2	5155.7	991.5
2017	24,094.9	11,554.9	12,539.9	2727.7	1253.0	1725.6	5314.1	1045.8
2018	24,973.8	11,904.7	13,069.1	2791.0	1247.2	1872.4	5451.1	1077.8
2019E	25,860.5	12,323.1	13,537.4	2988.6	1262.0	1932.1	5586.7	1110.9
% change 2000–19	128	91	178%	90	–1	344	145	–29
% share	100.0	47.7	52.3	11.6	4.9	7.5	21.6	4.3

E—estimate
Source US Federal Reserve, CrossBorder Capital

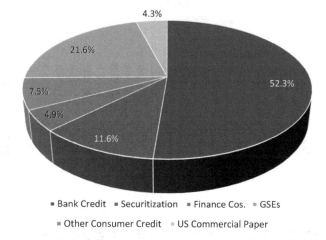

Fig. 6.2 US bank and shadow bank credit, 2019 (percent) (*Source* US Federal Reserve, *CrossBorder Capital*)

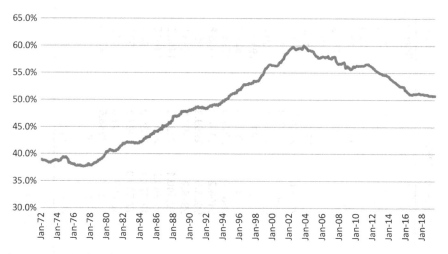

Fig. 6.3 US shadow banking, 1972–2019 (percentage of total private sector liquidity) (Source *CrossBorder Capital*)

scope of traditional bank regulators. Figure 6.3 shows the rise and recent fall in the importance of American shadow banking over a near-five decade span. From providing less than 40% of total liquidity in the 1970s, it expanded rapidly over the next two decades, reaching a peak share of 60% in the early 2000s, before retreating back to settle at around half of total US private liquidity.

The largest component of American shadow banking is the US Government Sponsored Enterprises (GSEs), such as the Federal National

Mortgage Association (FNMA), commonly known as Fannie Mae, and the Federal Home Loan Mortgage Corp (FHLMC), commonly known as Freddie Mac. These institutions provide access to funding for smaller banks, savings and loans, and mortgage companies that grant housing finance loans. Fannie Mae and Freddie Mac buy mortgages from lenders, which they either hold as investments or repackage into mortgage-backed securities (MBS) that may be sold on to others. Lenders use the cash raised from selling mortgages to the GSEs to engage in further mortgage lending. MBS are one example of securitisation, which is the other main type of shadow banking activity. More generally, the securitisation of other loan types is often undertaken by the major money-centre banks themselves, often though off-balance sheet entities. Finance Houses tend to focus on the product finance, hire purchase and consumer credit markets. Commercial paper, which includes asset-backed instruments, hit a peak ahead of the 2007–2008 GFC, but has declined in importance thereafter.

Traditional banks are themselves highly leveraged (e.g. typically around 10 times equity), and because they mainly borrow short-term and lend long-term, they also take on substantial maturity risk. Technically, this is measured by the difference between the duration of assets and the duration of liabilities, which for US banks averages around four years. Duration also serves as a rough measure of their interest rate sensitivity, so that each 100 bp rise in interest rates across the term structure will cause liabilities to increase in value by 4% (= 4 × 100 bp) relative to the value of assets. For banks leveraged at 10:1, their equity return would, consequently, collapse by some 40%. In short, banks should be highly sensitive to interest rates. As a result of their higher leverage and greater exposure to maturity transformation risk, many shadow banks are even more exposed to interest rates.

Since the GFC, regulators have therefore sought to better understand and monitor the shadow banks. The Financial Stability Board[8] (FSB) formally defines shadow banking as "… *credit intermediation involving entities and activities (fully or partially) outside of the regular banking system*". Using their broad classification, we estimate that World shadow banking now exceeds a huge US$210 trillion, or more than 2½ times World GDP, while using a narrow definition covering institutions deemed to be exposed to the most vulnerable business strategies, high-risk shadow banking currently totals around US$60 trillion. These estimates are reported in Figs. 6.4 and 6.5 and Table 6.2. The FSB concludes that broad shadow banking comprised 48% of World financial assets at end-2017. This strikes us as a high estimate when compared to our calculation of around US$13 trillion for the US market, but the FSB figure represents the overall asset size of these institutions rather

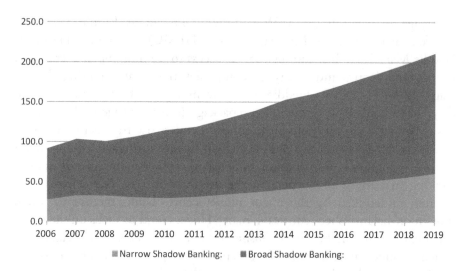

Fig. 6.4 World shadow banking—broad and narrow measures, 2006–2019 (US$ in trillions) (Source *CrossBorder Capital*, FSB)

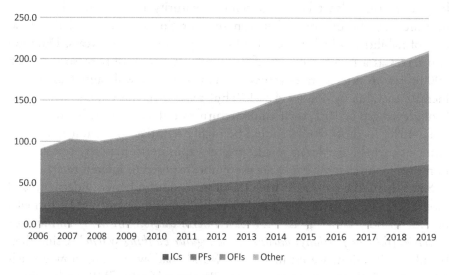

Fig. 6.5 Broad shadow banking by major source 2006–2019 (US$ in trillions) (Source *CrossBorder Capital*, FSB)

than their direct shadow banking activities. It is also a gross measure that includes some double counting (important for financial stability monitoring) because of overlapping exposures. For example, the FSB estimate that the stock of World financial assets stands at around US$400 trillion, whereas

Table 6.2   Broad shadow banking by major source, 2006–2019 (US$ in trillions)

US$ trillions		Components			
	Total	ICs	PFs	OFIs	FAs
2006	91.4	19.6	19.0	51.7	1.1
2007	103.3	20.5	20.0	61.6	1.2
2008	100.6	19.2	18.7	61.6	1.2
2009	106.5	20.8	20.4	63.8	1.5
2010	114.6	22.3	22.4	68.3	1.7
2011	118.7	23.1	23.4	70.6	1.7
2012	128.8	24.8	25.2	77.1	1.8
2013	139.1	26.0	27.0	84.3	1.8
2014	152.8	28.0	28.7	94.2	1.9
2015	160.7	28.9	29.5	100.3	1.9
2016	172.7	30.5	31.4	108.8	2.1
2017	185.0	32.0	33.6	117.0	2.3
2018	197.3	33.7	35.7	125.5	2.4
2019	210.7	35.6	38.0	134.7	2.5
% change 2006–19	130.6	81.6	100.0	160.5	125.0

IC—insurance companies; PF—pension funds; OFIs—other financial institutions; FA—financial auxiliaries
Source FSB, CrossBorder Capital

our calculation, based purely on primary assets and excluding repackaged instruments like mutual funds, is nearer US$225 trillion.

The FSB estimates cover 29 financial jurisdictions and include insurance companies and captive insurance (US$36 trillion), pension funds (US$38 trillion), investment funds (US$46 trillion[9]), money lenders, broker-dealers (US$10 trillion), money market mutual funds (US$6 trillion), hedge funds (US$5 trillion), structured finance vehicles (US$5 trillion), trust companies(US$5 trillion), finance companies (US$5 trillion), real estate investment trusts and funds (US$2½ trillion) and central counterparties (US$1 trillion). They classify high-risk (i.e. narrow) shadow banking activity into categories by assessing their exposures to: (a) liquidity transformation risk; (b) credit risk; (c) maturity risk and (d) leverage. These are reported in Table 6.3. The five categories shown refer, respectively, to: (1) the risk of 'bank' runs; (2) dependence on short-term funding; (3) the intermediaries that provide short-term funding; (4) credit guarantors and (5) securitisation exposed to short-term funding. Taken together this US$60 trillion pool of high-risk functions has grown by 120% since 2006 and is roughly double its size at the time of the 2007–2008 GFC. Moreover, within this total, assets of institutions exposed to 'bank' run risk have worryingly more than tripled since the GFC, largely because of taking on more maturity risk and greater leverage.

Table 6.3   High-risk (narrow) shadow banking by major risk type, 2006–2019 (US$ in trillions)

US$ trillions		By risk type					
	Total	RR	STC	ISTC	CG	SFI	Other
2006	27.6	11.5	3.1	6.9	0.1	5.5	0.6
2007	32.8	14.0	3.3	7.8	0.1	6.7	0.9
2008	32.6	14.2	3.6	6.2	0.1	6.8	1.7
2009	30.4	14.9	3.3	4.0	0.2	6.6	1.3
2010	29.5	15.9	3.4	3.5	0.2	5.2	1.2
2011	31.2	18.1	3.4	3.7	0.2	4.4	1.3
2012	34.3	21.7	2.9	3.8	0.2	4.3	1.3
2013	37.2	24.7	2.9	3.9	0.2	4.3	1.2
2014	40.9	27.7	3.1	4.3	0.2	4.4	1.3
2015	44.0	30.6	3.1	4.1	0.2	4.5	1.5
2016	47.5	33.6	3.3	4.0	0.2	4.5	1.9
2017	51.6	36.7	3.5	4.2	0.2	5.0	2.0
2018	55.8	40.5	3.6	4.2	0.2	5.2	2.1
2019	60.6	44.7	3.7	4.3	0.2	5.5	2.2
% change 2006–19	119.4	288.4	19.4	−37.7	100.0	0.0	266.7

RR—risk of bank run; STC—dependency on short-term credit; ISTC intermediation of short-term credit; CG—credit guarantors; SFI—securitisation of short-term financial credit
Source FSB, CrossBorder Capital

The Impact of Regulation

Two post-GFC regulations driving banks' recent demands for cash-like assets are the liquidity coverage ratio (LCR) and, so-called, resolution plans that form part of the Basel III reforms (http://www.bis.org):

Liquidity Coverage Ratio: LCR creates a standardised minimum daily liquidity requirement for large and internationally active banking organisations. The LCR is a formula-based liquidity metric that requires a bank's HQLA (high quality liquid assets) to be larger than its projected net cash outflows over a 30-day 'stress' period.

The potential net cash outflow estimates how much of the bank's short-term borrowing is unlikely to be rolled over, as well as how many short-term deposits it could lose. Banks publicly disclose details of their LCR calculations each quarter.

Resolution Plans: also known as 'living wills', resolution plans try to ensure large banks can rapidly and orderly resolve immediate liabilities in the event of material financial distress. Part of this resolution ensures that banks have enough short-term liquidity to cover demands from stakeholders and counterparties during these distressed periods.

Banks can demonstrate sufficient liquidity to regulators by reporting the results of internal liquidity stress tests. These internal tests are not public, but one should expect that the more financially interconnected and structurally complex banks will hold more HQLA.

Intermediation Chains and the Growth of Wholesale Money

In general, the credit markets have become both more international and more interconnected, spanned by complex intermediation chains and financed by the increasing use of market-based collateral. Refinancings of existing positions now easily surpass new financing activities. In other words, the dramatic rise in 'funding', or gross credit provision, has been even faster than the still rapid pace of new credit growth. According to the IMF, the shadow banking sector is responsible for some two-thirds of this gross funding, but they still account for less than 15% of new credit provision. What shadow banks essentially do is to transform traditional bank assets and liabilities and to refinance them in longer and more complex intermediation chains, e.g. A lends to B who lends to C, etc. In doing this they provide alternative stores of value, e.g. asset-backed securities, to institutional investors that do not want to hold all of their liquid assets as (uninsured) demand deposits. Therefore, shadow banks largely repackage and recycle existing savings. By lengthening intermediation chains to generate more securities they are involved in large volumes of wholesale funding, without creating much new lending. Shadow banks, therefore, increase the elasticity of the traditional banking system by relaxing banks' capital requirements through, say, selling loans externally to government-sponsored enterprises (GSEs, such as Fanny Mae and Freddie Mac in the USA) or internally to off-balance sheet vehicles, so boosting the credit multiplier. A speculative appetite to borrow likely exists most of the time within the economy and seemingly this is independent of interest rates. Keynes once dubbed this the 'unborrowed fringe'. Admittedly, the shadow banks could not have single handedly started the credit boom that led up to the 2007–2008 GFC, since they themselves ultimately depend on bank credit. Nonetheless, the fragility of this wholesale funding model based on short-term repos has heightened systemic risks, because it is collateral-based, subject to market pricing and highly procyclical. What's more, it frequently threatens to feed back negatively onto the funding, as well as the lending books of high street retail banks.

The growth of shadow banking is also far from being a new economic feature. Writing several decades ago, Gurley and Shaw (1960) correctly foresaw many of these opportunities and their associated risks. They make the key observation that in a growing economy, non-bank financial institutions proliferate, which undermines the effectiveness of conventional monetary policies and threatens financial instability. According to them, the entire financial structure matters for growth and stability, and not just banks: a point also made later by Goldsmith (1985). In fact, under certain circumstances, most commodities, financial claims and accounts receivable can be mobilised to create liquidity. Maintaining financial stability, consequently, becomes more challenging, because many of these nascent financial intermediaries will try to manufacture liquidity by creating, sometimes questionable, liquid claims from the less liquid securities they own. This underscores the important role played by the quality of liquidity. It follows that liquidity frequently serves as a vital barometer of financial stability rather more than it acts as a predictor of future high street inflation, because it reflects the gross balance sheet capacity vital for refinancing debts. This fragile elasticity, alongside often-unbridled financial innovation, explains why the history of finance teaches us that payment systems frequently require a level of liquidity backstopping that no private entity and often only large States can provide. For example, during the 1930s Depression, the monetary economist Frederick Hayek, observed: *"...there exist still other forms of media of exchange which occasionally or permanently do the service of money ... [A]ny increase or decrease of the quantity of these money substitutes will have exactly the same effects as an increase or decrease of the quantity of money proper...[W]e may distinguish these circulating credits from other forms of credit which do not act as substitutes for money is that they give to somebody the means of purchasing goods without at the same time diminishing the money-spending power of somebody else... The characteristic peculiarity of these forms of credit is that they spring up without being subject to any central control, but once they have come into existence their convertibility into other forms of money must be possible if a collapse of credit is to be avoided"* (Hayek 1933, *Prices and Production*).

The specific circumstances that drive this elasticity differ over time, but, deregulation aside, what explains much of the recent rise in shadow banking is the associated rapid growth of wholesale money as alternative funding sources, led by corporate and institutional cash pools (CICPs). Worldwide, these pools may total upwards of US$30 trillion. Their appearance forms part of what we often describe as a switch in the 'polarity' of Western financial systems, where large-scale structural changes have forced many former lenders, e.g. banks, to become borrowers from wholesale markets, and many previous borrowers, e.g. corporations, to become lenders. These corporate and institutional cash pools are made up from uninvested corporate treasury funds, liquid asset holdings of forex reserve managers, the cash holdings of Sovereign Wealth Funds (SWFs) and institutional money managers, and the cash collateral business of derivative markets. High street banks traditionally intermediate funds between household depositors and corporate borrowers, but in the past two decades these flows have reversed direction. One key reason is that heightened competition from Emerging Market producers, noted in Chapter 3, has progressively destroyed the marginal profitability on new capital in the West, so questioning the viability of further investment spending. But simultaneously, it has hastened the drive to extract more cash flow from existing industrial operations, so replenishing corporate treasuries. Uncertainty in the wake of the 1997–1998 Asian Crisis further encouraged many Emerging Market economies to self-insure against exchange rate disruption by accumulating enormous forex reserve balances. As a result, the CICPs have simply outgrown the banking systems. Their typically large deposit size exceeds the threshold for government retail deposit guarantees and lately banks themselves have been further constrained from taking these deposits by new capital and liquidity regulations, e.g. the so-called *liquidity coverage ratios* (LCR) imposed by bank regulators. Thus, the CICPs eager to invest their swelling coffers demand more alternative short-term liquid investment vehicles and they have turned instead to Treasury bills, asset-backed commercial paper (ABCP), repos and other similarly collateralised instruments. According to D'Arista (2009) writing shortly after the 2007–2008 GFC: "*…the short-term funding strategies on which the largest institutions increasingly relied also contributed to the system's vulnerability to an explosion of global liquidity as assets were monetized through their use as collateral for borrowing to buy more assets. The liquidity that resulted from rising leverage exacerbated the inherent pro-cyclicality of the system, expanding credit over the course of the boom years and leading to a rapid contraction as the downturn developed*".

Sovereign Wealth Funds (SWF)

A Sovereign Wealth Fund is a State-owned investment fund that invests globally across real and financial assets for the benefit of the nation. They are typically funded from commodity revenues, such as oil, or large foreign exchange reserve holdings. Latest estimates suggest that SWFs directly control US$8.1 trillion of assets, but this total exceeds US$20 trillion if pension reserves and development funds (US$7 trillion) and forex reserve funds (US$8 trillion) are included. The largest SWF is the Norwegian Government Pension Fund (US$ 1.1 trillion), followed by the China Investment Corporation (CIC, US$941 billion); the Abu Dhabi Investment Authority (ADIA, US$697 billion); the Kuwait Investment Authority (KIA, US$592billion) and the investment fund of the Hong Kong Monetary Authority (US$509 billion).

Helped by the rise of these CICPs, the wholesale money markets have taken on huge importance in recent decades. In fact, we think of the wholesale money markets as the 'engine room' behind Global Liquidity. Although these markets have seen a gentler expansion since the 2007–2008 GFC, Fig. 6.6 underlines their prior dramatic US expansion to nearly US$10 trillion and the imposing role played within these markets by the US Federal Reserve. The wholesale markets increasingly supplement retail bank deposits and now fund a rising proportion of US and international credit and liquidity. US broker/dealers alone saw their financial liabilities more than double to US$5 trillion between 2004 and 2008. According to the New York Federal Reserve[10]: *".... we saw during the recent financial crisis [that] the tri-party repo market was overly reliant on massive extensions of intraday credit, driven by the timing between the daily unwind and renewal of repo transactions. Estimates suggest that by 2007, the repo market had grown to $10 trillion—the same order of magnitude as the total assets in the U.S. commercial banking sector—and intraday credit to any particular broker/dealer might approach*

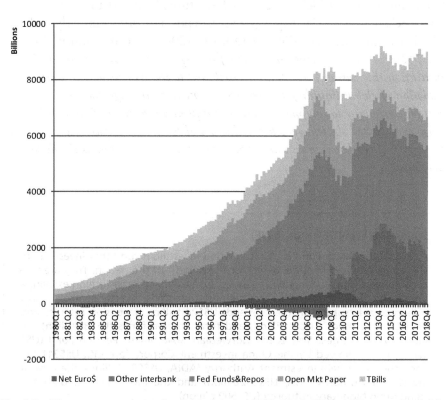

Fig. 6.6 US money markets—by instrument, 1980–2018 (US$ billions, quarterly) (Source *CrossBorder Capital*)

$100 billion. And ... risk was under-priced with low repo 'haircuts'— a haircut being a demand by a depositor for collateral valued higher than the value of the deposit".

Collateral and the Rise of the Repo

The linkages between the wholesale money markets, the shadow banks and the traditional high street banks have become more complex over the past twenty-five years. In fact, in many cases, shadow banks are subsidiaries and sometimes off-balance sheet vehicles owned by the traditional banks themselves. This is partly because financial innovation and deregulation has blurred the distinction between, say, banks, insurance companies and hedge funds, and partly because of structural changes in capital flows which have encouraged the rise of the previously discussed CICPs (corporate and institutional cash pools). The schematic diagram in Fig. 6.7 identifies the notional inflows and outflows from the US money markets. The CICPs need secure short-term liquid assets, which in the absence of the high street banks and the State (e.g. Central Bank reverse repos and Treasury bills) are now provided by the non-bank private sector, largely in the form of repos and asset-backed commercial paper. Eager for safe liquid instruments, these cash

Fig. 6.7 Wholesale money markets (schematic)

pools frequently engage in sale and repurchase agreements, i.e. repos, with the shadow banks. The credit system increasingly operates through these repo markets (see box), and often with active Central Bank participation.

Repo: A Definition

A repo (sale and repurchase agreement) is a financial transaction in which one party sells an asset to another party with a promise to repurchase the asset at some pre-specified later date. A repo resembles a collateralized loan but its treatment under bankruptcy law tends to favour cash investors: in the event of bankruptcy, repo investors can typically sell their collateral, rather than be subject to an automatic stay, as would be the case for a collateralized loan. A reverse repo is simply the antithesis of a repo that equates to a withdrawal of liquidity.

Repurchase agreements, or 'repos' are a means of short-term borrowing. They are essentially a form of collateralised interbank borrowing that has grown to eclipse in size the pre-2008 uncollateralised interbank loan market and, in fact, embeds the latter because participants now prefer secured lending, even between banks. Because it not restricted to traditional banks, the repo market has become the primary monetary policy conduit for Central Banks. However, unlike the Fed Funds market, repos are highly leveraged, which makes the policy-makers' task much harder, demanding more frequent interventions and, when the banks hoard precautionary cash, often needing 'big' liquidity injections to backstop the market. The repo market transacts funds between all types of financial institutions, such as banks, broker-dealers, insurance companies, pension funds, hedge funds and mutual funds, as well as major corporations and government agencies. Traditional banks may no longer be the biggest source of lending, but they still intermediate the vast bulk of these transactions. The increasing use of repos, carry trades and currency swaps underscores the importance of the balance sheet capacity of the financial sector. The repo mechanism bundles together 'safe' assets as collateral, e.g. government bonds, foreign exchange and high-grade corporate debt, and uses these as security against which to borrow. Depending on market conditions and the type of asset offered, the lenders will 'haircut' the value of the collateral to provide themselves with a safety margin. In practice, US Treasuries and German bunds dominate the market in top-quality or 'pristine' collateral. The borrowing party in the repo puts up collateral, such as a quality-rated bond, and they are paid for the value of that asset on the promise to buy it back later (i.e. repurchase) at a higher price. The loan period can be overnight, 7 days, 14 days, 90 days or sometimes longer. Often this collateral is lent out again (re-hypothecated), so generating a supply of credit outside of traditional fractional-reserve high street banking. Today this international repo market is huge, representing some US$8-10 trillion of collateral, with non-bank lenders often holding more assets than traditional banks. US repo market activity is shown in Fig. 6.8. This saw a sharp expansion in the run-up to the GFC, with gross transactions (i.e. purchases plus sales) peaking at over US$7 trillion and net flows testing US$1.6 trillion in 2008. Both have since fallen back, with net flows currently running at around a US$500 billion clip.

Collateralised loans protect the lender against a borrower's default. The dominance of the CICPs has resulted in a considerable increase in the use of collateral and the associated development of rehypothecation agreements, which allow its further reuse in other transactions.[11] Reusing pledged collateral allows credit to be created in a way that is analogous to the textbook money-creation process involving the deposit-loan multiplier and governed by Central Bank reserves. The collateral represents the high-powered money component; the collateral haircut corresponds to the banks' reserve ratio, and the length of the collateral chain, i.e. the number of times collateral is re-pledged, is equivalent to the traditional money multiplier. Yet, trust, i.e. counterparty risk, and the risk appetite of lenders clearly play bigger roles in the modern credit system compared to the textbook model, where government regulation, e.g. statutory reserve requirements, lender of the last resort

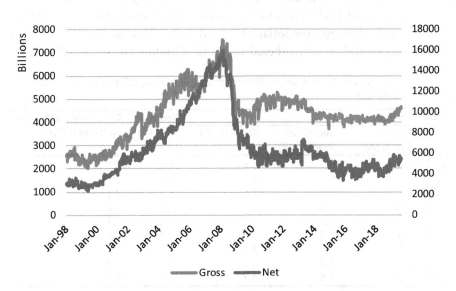

Fig. 6.8 US repo market—net and gross transactions, 1998–2019 (weekly, US$ in billions) (*Source* Federal Reserve Bank of New York)

and insured deposits, are key factors. The collateral multiplier is also endoge-nous, market-determined and sensitive to investors' risk appetite, as captured, for example, by fluctuations in the CBoE VIX index, or so-called *price of risk*.

The more intensive use of collateral through rehypothecation means that the same bonds can be repo'ed several times over. According to IMF estimates (Singh 2019), this so-called *collateral multiplier* stood as high as 3 times in 2007 and although it trended lower following the GFC, it has recently rebounded back to around 2 times. This is shown in the data reported in Table 6.4. Rehypothecation stretches existing collateral, making funding liquidity more elastic. Yet, the continual re-pledging of collateral has limits, because *haircuts* progressively reduce the credit-raising potential of the underlying asset. These collateral 'haircuts' inversely determine the maximum leverage, with a 2% haircut allowing leverage up to 50 times. They parallel the lending terms that apply to traditional loans, are adversely affected by volatility and rate hikes, and, in practice, fluctuate wildly. What's more, because several agents are counting on this same collateral as backup in case things go wrong, rehypothecation also risks excessive leverage and, given the interlocking nature of intermediaries' balance sheets, it heightens systemic risk. At critical times, this risk may encourage precautionary hoard-ing of collateral as well as of cash, so leading to a potentially greater collapse in liquidity when *fungibility* disappears, which it inevitably does during cri-ses. For example, collateral haircuts on US Treasuries jumped from 0.25 to 3% in the lead-up to the GFC between April and August 2007, while hair-cuts on ABS (asset-backed securities) soared from around 4% to nearly 60%. Consequently, leverage potential collapsed from 25:1 to barely 1.7:1. In addition, it should be remembered that while holding collateral will help to

Table 6.4 Pledged collateral and collateral multiplier, 2007, 2010–2017 (US dollars in trillions and times)

Year	Sources			Pledged collateral (C)	Collateral multiplier (velocity C/(A+B))
	Hedge funds (A)	Securities lending (B)	Total (A+B)		
2007	1.7	1.7	3.4	10.0	3.0
2010	1.3	1.1	2.4	6.0	2.5
2011	1.4	1.05	2.5	6.3	2.5
2012	1.8	1.0	2.8	6.1	2.2
2013	1.85	1.0	2.85	6.0	2.1
2014	1.9	1.1	3.0	6.1	2.0
2015	2.0	1.1	3.1	5.8	1.9
2016	2.1	1.2	3.3	6.1	1.8
2017	2.2	1.5	3.7	7.5	2.0

Source Singh (2019)

some extent in mitigating credit risk, maturity transformation risk remains, e.g. the gap between the duration of assets and the duration of liabilities, and it is highly dependent on being able to rollover or refinance positions.

It also follows that the bigger the size of the wholesale money markets, the greater the demands for collateral. The resulting hunt for collateral encourages the issuance of high-grade bonds, which, in turn, by creating more space in the capital stack, allows greater lower-grade bond issuance. Thus, Central Bank QE policies which focus on the money markets likely explain part of the recent ballooning in size of the US corporate credit markets since, excluding the 2007–2008 GFC, the stock of US corporate debt outstanding has averaged a fairly stable 50–60% of the size of the money markets.

The Liquidity Multiplier

The expansion of private-sector liquidity can be thought of in terms of a multiple of certain key assets, which are frequently dubbed 'safe' assets and sometimes high-powered money. This is shown schematically in Fig. 6.9, where balance sheet expansion requires a proportional increase in holdings

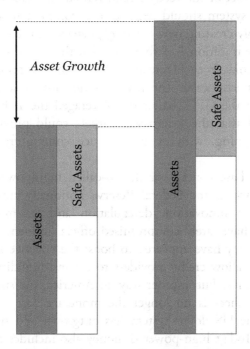

Fig. 6.9 Safe assets and balance sheet expansion (schematic)

of these safe assets. In practice, there are probably twin, overlapping multiplier relationships between the traditional monetary base and the available pool of collateral, which together impose both regulatory and prudent risk limits on balance sheet expansion. By itself, the traditional money multiplier model, popular in textbooks, is no longer a valid description of liquidity creation in a modern economy. First, it only covers the traditional high street banks, which as we have argued are increasing eclipsed by other credit providers, such as shadow banks. Second, it ignores the role of collateral, which, as we have seen, has become more important as credit providers increasingly fund themselves from wholesale money markets. Third, bank lending is, in practice, neither constrained by the lack of deposits nor the Central Bank's supply of reserves. Not only is alternative funding often readily available from domestic and offshore wholesale money markets, but banks typically lend first and then subsequently search for the necessary funding. This sets traditional banks apart from all other financial institutions because they can issue their own liabilities, e.g. demand deposits, that serve the non-bank sector as *means of payment*. Consequently, traditional banks, at least in theory, should face fewer funding constraints than other financial intermediaries, so making their lending more elastic. For as long as capital and regulatory requirements are met or indirectly circumvented via shadow banks, the traditional banking system should be able to accommodate additional credit demands by simply creating new *means of payment* in the process of making new loans. In the traditional textbook model, these banks are backstopped by the Central Banks, in their role as lenders of the last resort, and by State-organised deposit insurance. The reality is not always so straightforward. In the lead-up to the GFC, banks over-leveraged themselves because they wrongly assumed that the interbank markets could provide even greater liquidity backstopping, with extra insurance coming from CDS (credit default swaps).

The monetary base consists of the so-called high-powered money that Central Banks such as the Federal Reserve notionally create and control. However, financial innovation, deregulation and fast-moving cross-border capital flows have lately compromised official influence. New forms of high-powered money have appeared to boost the effective size of the monetary base and so allow credit providers to expand liquidity independently of the Central Banks. Put another way, in America, the size of the Federal Reserve's balance sheet is no longer the monetary base of the US dollar credit system. The US dollar system has outgrown and surpassed Federal Reserve control. Today, high-powered money also includes offshore pools of US dollar deposits, such as the Eurodollar Markets, that can be borrowed by any commercial banks that are short of reserves. In addition, we have seen how credit can be created by shadow banks, formally outside of Federal Reserve control, in the money markets by offering collateral. These assets can be repo'ed to attract funds from large corporate and institutional cash pools (CICPs), which, in turn, can be on-lent to traditional banks for extra funding. Admittedly, the US authorities have been trying to wrestle back control over the US monetary base ever since the GFC, by embracing non-bank credit providers and, more recently, by altering the US tax code to try to reduce the pool of cash available to offshore Eurodollar Markets.

The hierarchy of Global Liquidity is drawn up in Fig. 6.10. The wider expansion of private sector liquidity at the top of the inverted pyramid rests on a narrower base of high-powered money that includes the balance sheet of the Central Bank (i.e. the traditional *monetary base*), as well as: (1) off-shore wholesale markets and (2) the available pool of private sector collateral. These two additional sources of high-powered money, that lie beyond the traditional definition of the monetary base, can be thought of as the *shadow monetary base*.

In the traditional finance model, high street banks use a leveraged balance sheet to recycle savings. An increase in the monetary base is subsequently associated with a greater stock of bank loans. Extra reserves allow banks to proportionately expand their deposit bases and, hence, to make more loans.

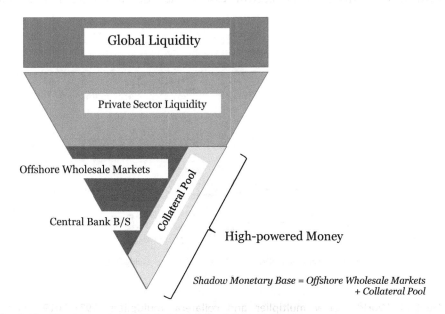

Fig. 6.10 The hierarchy of Global Liquidity (schematic)

As we have noted, wholesale money markets now take on a large part of this role, with a collateral/loan multiplier replacing the previous reserve/deposit multiplier. This transmission channel may still require a larger Central Bank balance sheet, i.e. traditional monetary base, when it involves increased repo activity (i.e. the purchase and sale of Treasury notes) between the Central Bank and the dealer banks in the money markets, which allows them to increase their leverage. Assuming that the Central Bank, say, injects funds through repos. This will increase the cash resources of a money market dealer, who will pay away the short-term financing but will keep the coupon payment on the bond, less some margin. This enables the dealer to purchase more bonds in the open market, and potentially to repo them again. This, in turn, should encourage more risk-taking elsewhere in financial markets, including greater demand for loans. Loan supply could be further stimulated by second-round effects as the value of collateral itself climbs higher. Some experts have worried that this transmission mechanism may be compromised because Central Bank repo activity, by definition, removes precious collateral from the private sector. However, this negative drag seems, from experience, to be more than offset by the subsequent increases in collateral values.

Figure 6.11 estimates the World money multiplier (i.e. the ratio of total liquidity to base money) and the corresponding narrow and broad collateral multipliers (i.e. the ratio of total liquidity to safe assets). Safe assets are defined, respectively, in the 'narrow' case as the stock of government bonds

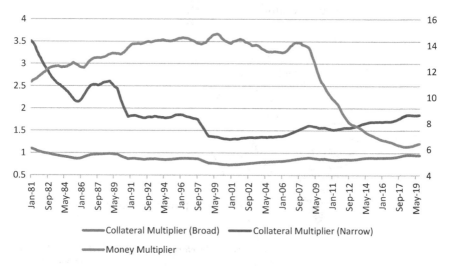

Fig. 6.11 World money multiplier and collateral multipliers, 1981–2019 (times) (Source *CrossBorder Capital*)

issued by developed economies, and in the 'broad' case with the addition of all liquid assets, such as bank deposits and money market funds, in both developed and Emerging Markets.[12] The data show a rise in the money multiplier to peaks in the late 1990s, at close to 15 times, and again to a smaller peak just before the GFC, followed by a collapse in the wake of the crisis as Central Banks ploughed in cash support. The broad and narrow collateral multipliers both show far greater recent stability and highlight generally smoother increases towards one and two times, respectively, since the year 2000. In other words, private sector liquidity rises *pair passu* with increases in collateral values. Collateral was likely a less important constraint compared to Central Bank money prior to the millennium, but it has since risen to prominence. The size of the narrow collateral multiplier reported here is in a similar ballpark to the IMF estimates shown in Table 6.4. If more collateral is important for future liquidity growth then the prevailing fiscal austerity policies currently engaged by many governments around the World may be indirectly depleting financial markets of a precious source of safe asset collateral.

Refinancing Risks?

In summary, *liquidity* should be is seen as a gross funding concept that represents the size of financial balance sheets. We choose to define liquidity broadly to include 'global' or cross-border effects, and deeply, insofar that it extends beyond the traditional retail banking sector, to include corporate cash flows, and repo and wholesale money markets. Today, most credits take the form of collateralised loans that derive from wholesale money markets, not banks; ultimately sourced from corporate and institutional cash pools (CICPs), and which are used mainly for funding, i.e. refinancing of existing positions, rather than borrowings for new investments. In a World dominated by funding the rollover of huge outstanding debts, rather than the financing of large-scale new capital projects, balance sheet capacity, i.e. liquidity, is more important than the level of interest rates, i.e. the cost of capital. Liquidity has both private sector and Central Bank dimensions, with the private sector dependent on being able to bundle up good quality, longer horizon securities as collateral and the Central Bank acting as a liquidity backstop in emergencies. The need to continually *refinance* our towering debts means that crises can occur when funding stops or slows, which, in turn, may arise because of a lack of sufficient good-quality collateral and/ or the withdrawal of Central Bank liquidity support. When both combine, such as in 2007–2008, a significant crisis can unfold. The conclusion is that

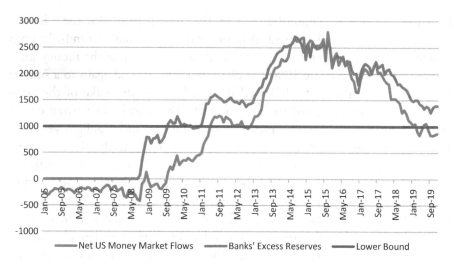

Fig. 6.12 US net money market flows and US banks' excess reserves', 2005–2019 (US$ in billions) (*Source* US Federal Reserve, *CrossBorder Capital*)

QT and public sector austerity policies that diminish the supply of government bonds create a dangerous mix that threatens severe and persistent financial market volatility.

These risks are evidenced in Fig. 6.12, which reports more recent data on the close co-movement between US banks' excess reserve holdings (i.e. surplus to statutory requirements) and US money market flows. The chart highlights the 2013 so-called 'taper tantrum', when hints of policy tightening by the Fed triggered a market sell-off, and the September 2019 surge in repo rates to 10%, or well above the then prevailing Fed Funds rate of 2.14%. Both events coincided with brief dips in money market flows below the critical threshold of US$1 trillion and banks' excess reserves consequently falling below US$1.5 trillion, a hurdle raised sizeably since the GFC by Basel III regulations. These thresholds may prove the liquidity danger lines that the US monetary authorities dare not in future cross?

Notes

1. We often use the generic term *funding* to describe the supply of *gross credit.*
2. Adrian and Shin, *Money, Liquidity and Monetary Policy*, New York Fed Staff Papers, January 2009.
3. The traditional monetary aggregates are liability-based definitions and typically referred to by the abbreviations M0 (Central Bank money); M1 (notes

and coin plus bank demand deposits); M2 (M1 plus bank time deposits and certain money market funds), etc.

4. The national Monetary Authority may comprise the Central Bank, as well as other official bodies. For example, in Japan the list includes the Trust Fund Bureau, which manages the postal savings system. In China, SAFE, the manager of the country's foreign exchange reserves, and even arguably the SOBs (State-owned banks) should be included.

5. Equivalent to *means of payment.*

6. Duration is a specialist concept in finance. It essentially measures the timing of the average cash payment (or pay-out for a liability).

7. In the early 1970s, there was a similar, so-called, 'fringe' banking boom in the UK.

8. The FSB coordinates the work of national financial authorities. See www.fsb.org and their latest *Global Monitoring Report on Non-Bank Financial Intermediation*, February 2019.

9. End-2017 estimate.

10. New York Federal Reserve, February 2014.

11. Manmohan Singh and Peter Stella, *The (Other) Deleveraging: What Economists Need to Know About the Modern Money-Creation Process*, CEPR VOX, 2 July 2012.

12. Of course, not all of these assets will be used as collateral at any one time. Rather, they represent potential collateral.

References

Adrian, Tobias, and Hyun Song Shin. 2009. Money, Liquidity and Monetary Policy. New York Fed Staff Papers, January.

D'Arista, Jane. 2009. Rebuilding the Framework for Financial Regulation. Economic Policy Institute. Briefing Paper No. 231, May.

Goldsmith, Raymond W. 1985. *Comparative National Balance Sheets: A Study of Twenty Countries, 1688–1978*. Chicago: University of Chicago Press.

Gurley, J., and E. Shaw. 1960. *Money in a Theory of Finance*. Washington, DC: Brookings.

Hayek, Frederick von. 1933. *Prices and Production*. London: Mises Institute.

Singh, Manmohan, and Rohit Goel. 2019. Pledged Collateral Market's Role in Transmission to Short-Term Market Rates. IMF Working Paper No. 19/106, May.

7

The Central Banks: Don't Fight the Fed, Don't Upset the ECB and Don't Mess with the PBoC

What Do Central Banks Do?

Whipsawed by the roller-coaster financial markets of Victorian London, Walter Bagehot was among the first to formally outline a proactive role for Central Banking. Writing in *Lombard Street* (1873), he warned that: "*Money does not manage itself, and Lombard Street has a great deal of money to manage*". Yet, looking ahead from a century and a half later, we can see how private sector innovation, the freeing up of international capital flows and the rise of dynamic new economies, such as China, have progressively diluted the traditional powers of the Central Banks. Not surprisingly, the two key debates in monetary economics surround alternative monies, e.g. cryptocurrencies, and alternative forms of policy stimulus, e.g. People's QE and MMT (Modern Monetary Theory). Nonetheless, Central Banks continue to play a crucial, albeit controversial role. Whereas the British banker Francis Baring[1] saw the Bank of England as: "*...the centre or pivot for enabling every part of the monetary and credit machine to move...*". Ben Bernanke, former Federal Reserve Chairman, more cynically suggests that: "*Monetary policy is 98% talk and only 2% action*".

This chapter deliberately avoids many of the subtleties and technical nuances of Federal Reserve, ECB, Bank of Japan and People's Bank of China monetary policies. It also steers clear of recent philosophical questions surrounding their *unelected power*. Nor does it judge the various and sometimes well-known celebrity Central Bankers, such as Paul Volcker, Yasushi Mieno, Alan Greenspan and Mario Draghi, who have held high office. Rather we try

© The Author(s) 2020
M. J. Howell, *Capital Wars*,
https://doi.org/10.1007/978-3-030-39288-8_7

to understand the effect that Central Banks have on the financial system. We argue that, in practice, Central Banks still have considerable tangible power, but they increasingly lack control. They enjoy a privileged status because they can supply as much liquidity, at a fixed policy rate, as they deem necessary for the efficient functioning of the financial system through their monetary operations. Broadly these can be summarised in terms of two operating[2] channels:

- Interest rate and 'forward guidance' policies
- Changes to the size and composition of the Central Bank's balance sheet.

Notwithstanding, there is a sizeable disconnect between the theory and practice of Central Banking. Lower expected interest rates are thought to lead to faster economic activity, helping to satisfy policy-makers' mandates for price stability and high employment. However, it is increasingly being questioned whether lowering interest rates unambiguously ease monetary conditions.[3] These doubts have arisen because of adverse supply and demand effects, such as the drag that low or negative interest rates can have on bank profitability and the functioning of the repo markets, and the second-round effects that ultra-low policy rates may have on reducing inflation expectations and raising investors' precautionary demands for 'safe' assets. Brunnermeier and Koby (2019), for example,[4] introduce the notion of a *reversal rate*. This defines an effective lower bound on policy rates since below this threshold lower rates are contractionary. It operates through banks' net worth and capital adequacy because they face a two-way pull on profitability from lower interest margins on new business versus larger capital gains on bond positions. Some argue that QE could raise the medium-term level of the reversal rate by reducing the potential for capital gains. A more persuasive argument could be made with regard to a threshold for financial stability rather than policy stimulus. Hence, below that threshold, systematic risks may escalate.

Despite their claims otherwise, in practice Central Banks exercise little effective control over the term structure of interest rates and at times they can be relatively powerless to determine the volume of liquidity, notably in the face of large and often volatile international capital flows, or when bankers refuse to lend (e.g. the 2019 US repo market tensions) and debtors are reluctant to borrow. A prescient cartoon drawn by David Low and published in the London Evening Standard newspaper (24 October 1932) highlights how similar fears about the impotency of conventional Central Bank policies haunted the 1930s. It depicts London bankers futilely running around and around a safe (i.e. strongbox) containing 'locked-up capital', led by a hopeful-looking

Montague Norman, the then Governor of the Bank of England. Interest rates on UK Treasury bills had just collapsed from 5.26% in 1929 to 1.49% in 1932, but Central Bank liquidity was simply not circulating.

It is worth considering how liquidity is created in a modern credit-money system, and indeed ponder how this might change in the future following the wider adoption of electronic and digital monies? Currently, a Central Bank guarantees the access of regulated banks to its discount window and in the US, the Federal Reserve, through the FDIC (Federal Deposit Insurance Corporation), underwrites the first US$250,000 (the equivalents in the EU are €100,000 and UK £85,000) of losses per bank depositor. Thereafter, bank customers are covered on a 'first loss' basis up to the banks' equity capital. Banks can leverage their balance sheets subject to access to funding and, where applicable, subject to holding sufficient statutory reserves and capital. The State's guarantee means that a deposit at, say, Citibank is equivalent to a deposit at, say, Wells Fargo, and this assurance allows deposits to be transferred between banks at parity as means of settlement for debts. In other words, a dollar credit from Citibank is worth the same as a dollar credit from Wells Fargo, making a notional Citibank dollar the same as a Wells Fargo dollar and indistinguishable from a Federal Reserve dollar. Transfers are made through clearing houses where interbank payments are netted: one of the first systems operated regularly, during the 1770s, from a room in the Five Bells tavern off London's Lombard Street. It is worth briefly speculating on what might happen in an electronic or e-money system based on an integrated national ledger, owned and maintained by the national Central Bank, because this breaks the traditional credit creation mechanism by removing the ability of high street banks to manufacture means of payment and so automatically fund themselves. Assuming the Central Bank operates the nation's digital ledger, its balance sheet would immediately multiply in size, following the inclusion of high street bank deposits. These might attract a low, zero or even a negative interest rate, as an extreme monetary policy tool. However, the Central Bank balance sheet would no longer represent high powered money and there would no longer be a conventional credit multiplier. Rather collateral would take on a bigger role to mitigate credit risk, and traditional banks would in future likely develop into specialist lenders. They could be funded through trying to bid away deposits using higher interest rates. However, these 'unguaranteed' deposits would be subject to greater credit risk and so fluctuate in unit price like a conventional security. Traditional banks could no longer create and circulate means of payment, so in this giro-like system the Central Bank would have to arrange to expand the supply of e-money at some agreed rate determined by the needs of the economy. The difference between an e-money and a digital money can be seen in terms of the trust placed in the centralised ledger. Digital monies, which may be encrypted, notionally contain undisputed 'intrinsic' value that can be transferred person-to-person as a decentralised bearer instrument without the need for clearing and settlement. On this basis they appear opposite to centralised electronic money, but in terms of elasticity and new credit creation they face exactly the same problem.

The necessity of recycling funds and the need for an elastic means of payment are persistent challenges for all monetary systems. History shows how policy-makers are often forced to be reactive and especially inventive in crises:

> We lent if by every possible means, and in modes we had never adopted before, we took in stock as security, we purchased exchequer bills, we made advances on exchequer bills, we not only discounted outright, but we made advances on deposits of bills of exchange to an immense amount; in short by every possible means consistent with the safety of the Bank; and we were not upon some occasions over nice; seeing the dreadful state in which the public were, we rendered every assistance in our power. Jeremiah Harman, Report from the Secret Committee of the Bank Resuming Cash Payments, Bank of England (1819)

This seems a long way from the calm textbook model of the Central Banker as the cool-headed engineer periodically pausing to polish the burnished hood of a Cadillac-like policy machine. Implicit in the orthodox theory is the idea that by controlling the level and expected future path of short-term policy interest rates, Central Banks can progressively spread their influence along the yield curve. Movements in long-term rates affect capital spending and by influencing business cycle fluctuations, so the story goes, this also changes the inflation rate. There are several suspect links in this causal chain. First, short-term and long-term rates frequently diverge because of highly erratic bond term premia.[5] Second, it is far from clear that long-term interest rates influence the capital spending cycle. Third, the idea that the business cycle determines inflation is based on the increasingly discredited Phillips Curve model. Contrary to the prevailing dichotomy in economics, we see inflation and deflation more as real economy phenomena (e.g. the result of low Chinese wage rates), rather than a monetary or financial feature, and likewise we see real interest rates largely determined in financial markets by fluctuating bond term premia and credit risk premia, rather than driven solely by the real economy. We can possibly draw parallel evidence from the late nineteenth century to show the disconnect between asset prices and liquidity, on the one hand, and high street inflation, on the other. Despite a huge jump in 'global liquidity' following soaring South African gold production, technological advances and better logistics often resulted in falling high street prices (average 10-year US CPI inflation stayed below 4% until 1918) and led to a two-and-a-half-fold leap in Wall Street stock prices between 1896 and 1912. Therefore, to claim that Central Banks have reached the highest degree of policy precision, where, by tinkering with short-term policy rates, they can choose a desired inflation rate is surely fanciful?

But why do Central Banks predominantly focus on inflation targets? Although many Central Banks originated as the government's banker, most typically evolved a financial and currency stability role, before more recently being given the task of controlling inflation. We earlier questioned the popular assertion that inflation is always a monetary phenomenon, not least because low inflation has almost certainly been strongly influenced by cheap Chinese imports over the past two decades. Trying to hit an impossible target, may come at the cost of greater financial instability. Concurrently, many experts question whether Central Banks' quantitative actions are any different from Treasury debt issuance? After all, in America, for example, the Fed with its circa US$4 trillion balance sheet is far smaller than the US$23 trillion stock of outstanding US Treasury debt, which itself has been recently expanding at a US$1.5 trillion annual clip. Both divisions of government are involved in monetary policy and both are involved in fiscal policy, so in truth, a continuum exists between them. Both supply 'safe' assets, but the Fed is more focussed on the banking and money markets, with the US Treasury dealing with the longer-term capital markets.

The supply of safe assets serves a critical function because they support financial sector balance sheets and allow them to expand. Big balance sheet capacity matters far more in a World where large debts have to be refinanced, than in regimes characterised by the need to finance new investment, when interest rates and the cost of capital matter. This funding backdrop is too often ignored, and it is the importance of funding that makes the size and composition of the Central Bank balance sheet vital. We can measure the efficacy of monetary transmission in terms of the multiplicative change to overall liquidity that derives from an increase in *high-powered money*. This is shown in Fig. 7.1 which reports the annual movements, measured in US dollars, in Global Liquidity and World Central Bank money. Even though the link between the Central Banks and Global Liquidity is clearly not one-to-one, the chart still reveals a close linkage.

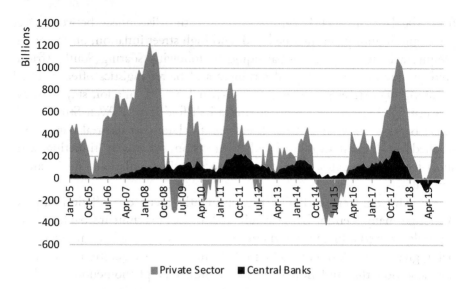

Fig. 7.1 World Central Bank liquidity provision and Global Liquidity, 2005–2019 (US dollars in billions, 12-month changes) (Source *CrossBorder Capital*)

This has become more noticeable since the 2007–2008 GFC. Here, swings in Central Bank money result in far bigger moves in Global Liquidity, and periods of slow Central Bank money growth seemingly precede collapses and often absolute contractions in Global Liquidity.

Funding depends on many dimensions. The effective availability of collateral (i.e. taking into account the variable haircuts applied by lenders) and the ability to source funds internationally through the Eurodollar and swap markets all need to be included. This effectively broadens the monetary base beyond the size of the Central Bank balance sheet by introducing new sources of high-powered money. These new sources, or what we describe as the *shadow monetary base*, typically display a different character. Market-based wholesale funding tends to be both pro-cyclical and often short-term, or much different from the earlier model of dependable retail deposit funding. Moreover, the ability of many Central Banks to discipline their monetary systems is often compromised by their comparatively small size, and their narrow focus on selected domestic institutions, such as the high street banks. These balance sheet policies were traditionally described as *open market operations*, but they are now more colourfully dubbed *quantitative easing* (QE), or *large-scale asset purchases* (LSAP), and their counterpart *quantitative tightening* (QT). The standard textbook model assumes that banks are entirely funded by retail deposits; it is assumed that credit is created from these deposits, subject to reserve-backing, and shortages of reserves are priced at the policy interest rate set by the Central Bank. In practice, liquidity is not fungible and, particularly, during crises, banks are more frequently funding constrained than reserve constrained. Funding is now available from many sources, but less reliable and more capricious wholesale sources rather than retail sources are becoming increasingly important. For example, an important structural change in the financial markets is that many industrial corporations have become providers of wholesale funds to banks rather than net borrowers. As a result, although the Central Banks unequivocally set policy rates, market rates will differ because of potentially large fluctuations in risk premia.

The monetary policy measures that several Central Banks adopted in the wake of the GFC were originally regarded as *unconventional*. Now, more than a decade on, they have become commonplace. Many consider that this development is risky. Although we accept that the impact of unconventional monetary policy measures on the real economy may be subject to diminishing returns, they must be set against conventional interest rate policy which, as noted earlier, may produce zero or even negative benefits, particularly when interest rates fall to very low or negative levels. Moreover, the real worth of many of these unconventional policies is specifically felt in the financial sector itself in terms of improving financial stability.

Unconventional monetary policies can be thought of more broadly as quantitative policies, where Central Banks use their balance sheets to affect asset prices and financial conditions, beyond simply moving short-term interest rates. Large-scale asset purchases (LSAP), or equivalently quantitative easing (QE), is an example of *unconventional* monetary policy. These balance sheet policies differ conceptually and practically from interest rate policies, not least because the level of the short-term policy interest rate can be set independently of the volume of bank reserves in the system. The main transmission channel operates by altering the composition of private sector balance sheets. Assuming that the targeted assets are not perfect substitutes, then by altering the mix and risk profile of private portfolios, say, through the purchase of risky assets, the Central Bank[6] can reduce yields and ease funding conditions. This suggests that high street banks' statutory reserves are less significant than widely perceived. Rather the types of assets that the Central Bank buys or sells, and the credit it directs are more important.

In terms of definitions, we should point out that the Central Bank is not necessarily the Monetary Authority for each economy. Consequently, *high-powered money* is not always synonymous with what is known variously as reserve money and Central Bank money.[7] Reserve money itself is made up of currency in circulation plus regulated banks' reserves held at the Central Bank. This total largely covers the size of the national Central Bank balance sheet, but it should also include the balance sheets of all connected institutions that are part of the Monetary Authority. The difference between this overall balance sheet and reserve money is mainly accounted for by holdings of non-financial assets, such as real estate, and by non-private sector liabilities, such as holdings of public sector deposits. The Monetary Authority is a broader concept than the Central Bank, covering the entire apparatus of State control over the monetary system and it can include institutions beyond the Central Bank. Therefore, policy decisions likely involve a number of official bodies and operate across both interest rate setting and the volumes and types of financial assets bought and sold in the markets. Frequently, the Finance Ministry exercises control over the exchange rate, even though its policies may be implemented by the national Central Bank. In China, for example, it seems appropriate to include SAFE, the *State Administration of Foreign Exchange*. In Japan, the huge *Trust Fund Bureau*—the manager of the postal savings system and at one point in the early 1990s the largest financial institution in the World—is often included in the definition of the Monetary Authority. More generally, every government's funding policy will also affect their national monetary conditions, whether this involves the decisions about how much debt to sell, the specific maturities offered, its use as collateral and whether Treasury balances held at the Central Bank should be deliberately built-up or run-off?

Looking ahead and aided by the lessons policy-makers learned from the 2007–2008 GFC, the global funding system, in some ways, faces lower future risks, because: (1) banks have more capital; (2) regulators have become more vigilant and follow more rigorous macro-prudential analyses; (3) the size of swap lines is bigger and more IMF funding is available; (4) there are shorter, higher quality and better understood intermediation chains, with the more extreme forms of shadow banks all but gone, and (5) a larger and more active role is now being played by the public sector, through changes in the size and composition of Central Bank balance sheets and the provision of an adequate supply of high-quality 'safe' assets collateral. But major inequalities remain, notably a heavy reliance on the US dollar and the politicisation of the decision to grant foreigners access to Fed swap lines, notably following the 2010 US Dodd–Frank Act. Who sits in the White House now matters more? Future risks will also be different given that the high street banks have been effectively regulated out of a lot of credit provision and now essentially operate as quasi-savings and loan organisations (i.e. building societies or mortgage banks). Instead, the money and capital markets have become the crucial conduits for funds and the key determinants of the cycle of liquidity flows and the frequency of crises. Large sections of these markets lie beyond regulators' grasp. The money and capital markets are linked through the wholesale funding system. While the supply of high-quality collateral is unquestionably important for wholesale funding, recent evidence—a fact apparently underlined by Fig. 7.1—shows that modern financial systems struggle to operate without large Central Bank balance sheets. A recent speech[8] by Andrew Hauser of the Bank of England confirmed that: "...*judged by historical standards, big balance sheets are here to stay.... [W]e have a bigger responsibility than we did to provide liquidity to the system ...*".

It is true that Central Banks have an outsized-effect in deregulated financial systems, where retail deposits are no longer the sole funding source, because what matters most is the ability to refinance positions and ultimately the Central Banks are the marginal suppliers of liquidity. To better understand this transmission, we need to think of Western financial systems as essentially *capital refinancing and distribution mechanisms* that are used extensively to roll-over existing positions, rather than simply *capital-raising mechanisms* used to obtain new finance. The large volume of global debt that currently needs to be refinanced and the prevailing huge overhang of derivative instruments, together require large balance sheet capacity from robust and dependable institutions. This refinancing role means that the *capacity of capital*, i.e. the quantity of liquidity, matters more than the *cost of capital*, i.e. interest rates. Not surprisingly, the relationship between interest rates and the supply of liquidity is rarely one-to-one: a fact that has been especially true in the post-GFC period. It also means that funding (gross claims) is distinct from and far larger than the new credit provision (net claims). We have already argued that this wholesale funding is highly pro-cyclical, to a degree that is still not well understood. Assuming a high and steady level of refinancing needs, then: (1) the inherent cyclicality of private sector money market flows; (2) the uneven distribution of liquidity and (3) the fact that liquidity is never *fungible* in crises, the very times that it matters most, together force the Central Banks to frequently step in. Central Bank interventions into the money markets significantly affect the elasticity of the financial system through the volume of *funding liquidity* and, sometimes directly, the depth of *market liquidity*. This link between, say, the Federal Reserve's quantitative easing operations and the US money markets might be thought of as paralleling the historical link between the Central Bank and the high street banks, at times when statutory reserve requirements mattered.

Nonetheless, this remains a controversial area. Prior to the 2007–2008 Global Financial Crisis, Central Banks mainly conducted monetary policy through two instruments. First, and mainly via the short-term policy rate, e.g. the US Fed Funds target rate. Second, by influencing expectations about the future path of policy rates through its official communications, or what is termed 'forward guidance'. But as this policy rate approaches zero, it becomes increasingly less able to provide stimulus and arguably even becomes counter-productive because it can actually hamper credit supply. Consequently, once the US Fed Funds target rate reached the zero lower-bound in December 2008, in the immediate wake of the GFC, US policy-makers conducted three rounds of LSAPs, the eponymous QE1, QE2 and QE3, over the following five years:

- On November 25, 2008, the FOMC announced a QE1: The Fed proposed to buy up to US$100 billion of Fannie Mae and Freddie Mac debt, and an additional US$500 billion of agency MBS. The program was extended and expanded in March 2009, and, by the end of QE1 in March 2010, the Fed had bought US$1.25 trillion in MBS, US$175 billion in federal agency debt, and US$300 billion in U.S. Treasury securities.
- In August 2010, the FOMC signalled the start of a second round of quantitative easing (QE2), which was implemented from November 2010. QE2 consisted of a total purchase of US$600 billion of long-term US Treasury securities.
- The FOMC announced a third round of quantitative easing (QE3) in September 2012, consisting of monthly purchases of US$40 billion of agency MBS and, from January 2013, a further US$45 billion of U.S. Treasury securities.

Some argue that quantitative easing is ineffective in boosting the economy and rather than stabilising the financial system, it actually creates new risks. According to the academic literature, QE policies can affect the real economy through numerous prospective transmission channels, such as:

(a) *Yields*: QE directly impacts the yields of Treasury and mortgage-backed securities, although the effect varied across the different rounds of QE. Krishnamurthy and Vissing-Jorgensen (2011, 2013) find that QE1 and QE3 decreased MBS and Treasury yields. They show that MBS yields were more strongly affected (across both rounds) and that QE3's effect on MBS yields was much smaller than that of QE1. Moreover, QE2, which consisted only of Treasury purchases, had a limited effect on yields.

(b) *Mortgage refinancing*: Di Maggio et al. (2018) show that when the Fed bought MBS during QE1, it led to a boom in the refinancing of existing mortgages, in particular those types of mortgages that are eligible for purchase by the Fed. Refinancing an existing mortgage at a lower interest rate increases each household's net worth as its debt burden is decreased, which, in turn, allows them to increase consumption. QE can thus stimulate aggregate demand by making mortgage refinancing more attractive, assuming that households maintain positive home equity.

(c) *Bank lending*: Darmouni and Rodnyansky (2017) study the impact of QE on bank lending. They find that banks that owned more MBS prior to QE enjoyed faster loan growth than banks that had little or no MBS holdings. Thus, by purchasing MBS, the Fed was able to generate additional credit provision by banks. Acting like a conventional interest rate cut, QE can encourage additional bank lending, which in turn generates faster economic activity.

Instead, we can divide these and other impulses between two broader transmission channels: (1) a *credit channel* and (2) a *risk-taking channel*. Both, in part, likely overlap. The credit channel refers to all actions that alter the volume of system-wide liquidity, such as deliberate policy easings, but not restricted only to QE policies; cross-border inflows; exchange rate changes and collateral effects. Earlier, in Chapters 1 and 5, we emphasised the importance of the exchange rate and cross-border flow dimensions. They are further analysed in Chapter 8. The risk-taking channel, includes portfolio effects, and describes actions that alter the ratio between holdings of risk assets and holdings of safe assets. The risk-taking channel is studied more closely in Chapter 10. It might indirectly result from more Central Bank QE; from perceptions about the changing business climate; geopolitical shocks and they also include the effect of, say, lower market volatility and the 'feel good' impact from rising collateral values.

The event study literature, in particular, underplays the effect of QE both in pushing asset duration below target and on risk appetite because it focuses on its impact on asset prices during very short duration time windows. Consequently, it may only capture instantaneous effects that are later swamped by far bigger long-term changes in risk-taking. This appears to be the case because many of the examples cited in these studies turn out to be both ephemeral and often more than reversed months later. Consider, for example, the impact effects of QE1, QE2 and QE3 on US Treasury and corporate bond yields. In every case, persistent QE policies ultimately pushed term premia higher and tightened credit spreads. Figure 7.2 shows the (inflation and volatility adjusted) US 10-year Treasury term premium over the 2007–2015 period. The shaded bars denote the QE phases. It seems plausible that when liquidity is abundant, the odds of default reduce and

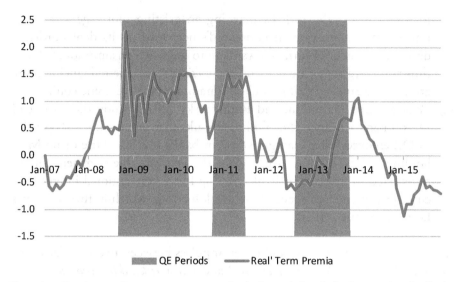

Fig. 7.2 US 10-year Treasury term premia (adjusted for inflation and volatility), 2007–2015 (percent, QE periods shaded) (*Source* Federal Reserve Bank of New York, *CrossBorder Capital*)

systemic risks fall, so incentivising investors to move out along the risk curve by switching from 'safe' assets, such as government bonds, into riskier assets, like equities, corporate credits and new capital projects. This also encourages credit providers to move out of Treasuries, so pushing up their yields, and into loans, attracted by their higher margins. The rise in Treasury yields is largely down to fatter term premia. Similarly, as levels of liquidity sink, so the process reverses as investors and credit providers scramble for safety, so ending up with slimmer or even negative term premia and lower government yields. Therefore, rather than reducing bond yields QE policies tend to increase them, both in absolute terms (by an average of 134 bp across the three US QE phases) and also relative to short-term policy rates.

Yet, many academic and Central Bank researchers remain sceptical about the true size of these balance sheet effects. We return to this paradox again in Chapter 10, but consensus opinion, for example, still believes that the entire US QE programme since the 2007–2008 GFC probably reduced bond yields by around 50–100 basis points,[9] rather than increase them. On the other hand, these same experts failed to see how the subsequent adoption of QT policies in 2015 and again from 2017 would cause market interest rates and term premia to collapse in the way that liquidity analysis predicted through changes in risk appetite. An early foretaste of trouble came with the May 2013 'taper tantrum' when a reduction in the pace of QE by the Federal Reserve caused investors to panic. Renewed tensions recently forced the

Federal Reserve to reconfirm the crucial stabilisation role played by QE, and despite the slated 'normalisation' of the Fed's balance sheet, they insisted that policy would remain flexible: [if] "*...any aspect of our normalization plans was somehow interfering with our achievement of our statutory goals, we wouldn't hesitate to change it and that would include the balance sheet...*" [Chairman Powell, January 2019]. And, to emphasise the point, other FOMC colleagues followed this lead: "*...we will not hesitate to make changes [to]... the ongoing program of balance sheet normalization...*" [Vice Chairman Clarida, January 2019] "*...so, I wouldn't rule out doing something with the balance sheet*" [Boston Fed President Rosengren, January 2019]. Therefore, "*...making adjustments in this balance sheet run-off if we need to...*" [Dallas Fed President Kaplan, January 2019]. Later events in 2019 made them keep their word!

What does the latest Federal Reserve balance sheet look like? Table 7.1 reports the Fed's balance sheet as of mid-August 2019. The US monetary

Table 7.1   Federal Reserve balance sheet, 21 August 2019 (US dollars in millions)

	Assets		Liabilities
Reserve Bank credit	3,725,869	Monetary base	3,269,085
Securities held outright	3,591,937	Currency in circulation	1,751,265
U.S. Treasury securities	2,088,920	Reserve balances with Federal Reserve Banks	1,517,820
Bills	3001	Reverse repurchase agreements	301,218
Notes and bonds, nominal	1,945,599	Other deposits with Federal Reserve Banks	198,466
Notes and bonds, inflation-indexed	116,545	Of which: US Treasury General account	131,447
Inflation compensation	23,775		
Federal agency debt securities	2347	Other liabilities	44,377
Mortgage-backed securities	1,500,670		
Credit	358		
Gold and forex reserves	37,070		
Other assets	183,781		
Total assets	3,813,146	Total liabilities	3,813,146
Memo: Securities held in custody			
Marketable U.S. Treasury securities	3,030,813		
Federal agency debt and MBS	358,293		
Other securities	80,656		
Securities lent to dealers	21,407		
Total	3,469,762		

Source Federal Reserve Banks, US Department of the Treasury base comprises 86% of the near-US$4 trillion balance sheet. Foreign assets account for barely 1% of the balance sheet, largely because the US dollar is the international means of settlement. Correspondingly, the Federal Reserve holds US$3.5 trillion in official reserve assets of other governments representing 91% of its total assets in custody as an off-balance sheet item. A US monetary expansion that boosts the foreign exchange reserves of, say, Emerging Market economies may be traced both through the initial expansion of the US monetary base, but also through the secondary, local impact on these Emerging Markets. Assuming that many of these economies shadow the US unit, the implied increase in their foreign exchange reserves will not only be monetised domestically, but may also show up as an increase in US dollars held in official custody at the Federal Reserve.[10] Adding the US monetary base to this pool of official US dollar assets held in custody give what we think of as the *US dollar monetary base*. This serves as a crude measure of the monetary base of those economies that either use or shadow the US dollar. Some use this US$7.5 trillion hybrid as a proxy for the US$130 trillion pool of Global Liquidity. That it isn't, being far too small, but it may still be a useful aggregate to monitor for other reasons.

Global Liquidity is dominated by private credit money, but because it is largely denominated in dollars the Federal Reserve has to serve as the de facto international *lender of last resort* (LoLR[11]), even though its legal authority is national. The Fed acts essentially as a hybrid between a national Central Bank and an international bankers' bank. During the 2007–2008 GFC this LoLR facility was implemented through a network US dollar liquidity swaps between the Federal Reserve and selected national Central Banks, who acquired dollar funding for their domestic banks. Forensic research by Adam Tooze (2018) has recently uncovered how the Federal Reserve provided some US$10.1 trillion (or US$4.45 trillion on standardised measures) from December 2007 to August 2010, largely to European banks. Operating alongside, the foreign exchange swap market has since grown to provide extra, largely US dollar, liquidity. However, several experts remain worried that this system of cross-currency basis swaps not only disobeys the theoretical covered interest parity (CIP), but deviations away from CIP appear to be positively correlated with the strength of the US dollar exchange rate. This premium can be explained by frictions, but, as we note in Chapter 8, its systematic movements suggest that it reflects a US dollar scarcity created either by a lack of balance sheet capacity and/or by the greater demand for hedging strategies.

As a result, these foreign exchange reserve movements have a significant impact on both the monetary base and the growth of total liquidity.

US dollar denomination and dominance means that any shift in foreign exchange markets, whether through a change in reserves or in parities, will affect Global Liquidity. A simple regression analysis between the annual growth rate of World forex reserves and World Central Bank money since 1981 reveals an R-squared[12] statistic of 39.9% (correlation coefficient 0.63). Regressing Global Liquidity on to World forex reserves instead, gives an R-squared of 49.3%. The same calculations for the Emerging Market economies, excluding China, yield figures of 38.4 and 39.4%, respectively. Similar results apply even when the sample length is narrowed to begin from 2005. However, when the same analysis is applied to China alone the correlations lately plunge, indicating that forex reserves are no longer the sole factor driving Chinese liquidity. For example, over the 2005–2016 period that covers the years of her large forex reserve accumulation, China's forex reserves and her monetary base (total liquidity) were linked with an R-squared of 40.9% (29.7%), but since then (2017–2019) the statistic has fallen to only 2.2% (5.4%). These results not only provide a foretaste of the importance of the US Federal Reserve and the US dollar in international financial markets, but they also signal the growing need to watch the increasingly independent moves of the People's Bank of China (PBoC).

World Central Bank Money

Figures 7.3, 7.4 and Table 7.2 detail developments in aggregate World Central Bank liquidity and the breakdown across the key national policy-makers. Overall, the period since Year 2000 has seen a more than six-fold increase in Central Bank money to over US$20 trillion, with roughly US$14 trillion coming from, so-called QE (quantitative easing), since the 2007–2008 GFC. At first sight, Developed and Emerging Market Central Banks engineered roughly similar rates of increase in their balance sheets over the period. However, closer examination shows standout increases by the Swiss National Bank (3002%); the Bank of England (1460%) and the People's Bank of China (932%). The expansion of the US Federal Reserve's balance sheet looks modest in comparison. Whereas the US Federal Reserve was the largest Central Bank by balance sheet size in Year 2000, it has since been eclipsed in magnitude by both the Bank of Japan (BoJ) and the People's Bank of China (PBoC). In fact, from 2010 to 2018, the PBoC unambiguously held the title of the World's biggest Central Bank, but it has just been pipped by the BoJ, largely because of recent adverse currency movements.

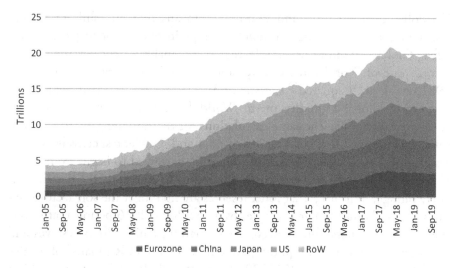

Fig. 7.3 World Central Bank money—by region and major Central Banks, 2005–2019 (US$ in trillions) (Source *CrossBorder Capital*)

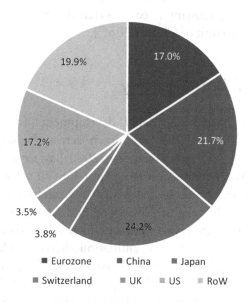

Fig. 7.4 World Central Bank money—by region and major Central Banks, 2019 (annual percent) (Source *CrossBorder Capital*)

Figure 7.5 depicts the distribution of Central Bank power, based on balance sheet size, using a block-map technique. Four Central Banks—US Federal Reserve, People's Bank of China (PBoC), European Central Bank (ECB) and Bank of Japan (BoJ)—dominate, with the aggregate balance

Table 7.2 Central Bank money—by region and major Central Banks, 2000–2019E (US$ in trillions)

Major Central Banks	World	Developed	Emerging	ECB	PBoC	BoJ	SNB	BoE	Fed
2000	2.70	1.85	0.86	0.45	0.44	0.59	0.02	0.05	0.64
2001	2.74	1.82	0.92	0.38	0.48	0.60	0.03	0.05	0.69
2002	3.27	2.22	1.04	0.50	0.55	0.79	0.03	0.05	0.76
2003	3.94	2.69	1.25	0.69	0.64	1.00	0.04	0.07	0.81
2004	4.37	2.94	1.43	0.83	0.71	1.08	0.04	0.08	0.84
2005	4.41	2.81	1.59	0.82	0.80	0.96	0.04	0.07	0.87
2006	4.91	2.89	2.00	1.02	1.00	0.76	0.04	0.12	0.90
2007	6.15	3.46	2.67	1.23	1.38	0.81	0.05	0.14	0.91
2008	7.71	4.61	3.08	1.60	1.89	1.02	0.08	0.14	1.62
2009	8.86	5.36	3.48	1.51	2.11	1.04	0.09	0.32	2.16
2010	9.85	5.41	4.41	1.44	2.79	1.28	0.10	0.30	2.09
2011	12.23	7.02	5.19	1.73	3.55	1.53	0.25	0.34	2.67
2012	13.57	7.68	5.86	2.15	4.01	1.53	0.37	0.54	2.73
2013	15.02	8.62	6.37	1.65	4.43	1.84	0.43	0.60	3.75
2014	15.54	8.86	6.64	1.44	4.80	2.24	0.40	0.57	3.96
2015	15.86	9.76	6.06	2.00	4.29	2.88	0.48	0.56	3.85
2016	17.12	10.82	6.25	2.57	4.47	3.65	0.54	0.55	3.53
2017	20.22	13.04	7.12	3.66	4.88	4.21	0.63	0.73	3.85
2018	19.90	12.80	7.04	3.60	4.81	4.52	0.69	0.72	3.42
2019E	20.08	13.16	6.86	3.57	4.55	4.76	0.72	0.71	3.45
% change	643%	613%	700%	694%	932%	706%	3002%	1460%	436%

E—Estimate based on data to 30 June 2019
Note ECB—European Central Bank; PBoC—People's Bank of China; BoJ—Bank of Japan; SNB—Swiss National Bank; BoE—Bank of England; Fed—US Federal Reserve
Source CrossBorder Capital

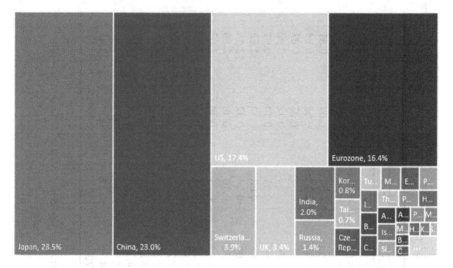

Fig. 7.5 Which are the biggest Central Banks? end-2019 (percent) (Source *CrossBorder Capital*)

sheets of all other World Central Banks roughly adding up in size to the equivalent of another US Fed. Although it is fashionable to measure Central Bank money as a percentage of GDP,[13] we consider this to be a meaningless statistic because its importance depends on the maturity, sophistication and regulatory background of the national financial system more than anything else. More interesting is the relationship between broad liquidity and the monetary base. The size of these implied *liquidity multipliers* that act on Central Bank money is reported in Table 7.3. In the year 2000, each US$1 of World Central Bank money created over US$14 of Global Liquidity, but by mid-2019 this multiplier had skidded to barely US$6½ times, suggesting a large drop in the efficiency of the international credit system. We explained earlier in Chapter 6 why the US liquidity multiplier apparently fell so dramatically over the period by introducing the concept of a *shadow monetary base*. The *shadow monetary base* comprises 'safe' (or leverage-able) assets: for example, assets that enjoy low 'haircuts' and have high rates of re-hypothecation, such as high-quality public and private sector debts and offshore pools of cash. In other words, the conventional US monetary base was enlarged in the early 2000s by access to new sources of high-powered money, such as collateral and offshore US dollar deposits. However, Table 7.3 shows that this collapse in the liquidity multiplier is general and not just limited to the US. This suggests that other factors aside from financial innovation may also play a role. In addition, the data reveal that China has, uniquely, enjoyed a flat to

Table 7.3 Liquidity multipliers—by region and major Central Banks, 2000–2019E (times reserve money stock)

	World	Developed	Emerging	ECB	PBoC	BoJ	Fed
2000	14.04	17.60	6.38	26.95	5.50	8.48	20.78
2001	13.89	17.89	6.07	30.89	5.57	7.17	21.98
2002	13.78	17.40	6.09	30.61	5.56	5.96	21.40
2003	13.15	16.54	5.90	27.12	5.48	5.17	19.08
2004	13.14	16.68	5.91	25.30	5.51	4.85	18.15
2005	13.58	17.80	6.18	25.89	5.82	4.83	18.32
2006	13.79	19.41	5.74	23.99	5.42	5.72	15.75
2007	13.28	19.23	5.61	25.46	5.12	6.11	11.41
2008	10.69	14.38	5.21	18.61	4.59	5.96	14.20
2009	10.10	13.04	5.61	21.56	5.10	5.70	10.81
2010	9.51	12.83	5.46	22.21	4.92	5.10	9.46
2011	8.18	10.25	5.40	18.34	4.73	4.76	8.05
2012	7.69	9.44	5.40	15.11	4.86	4.08	7.26
2013	7.15	8.32	5.58	18.49	5.24	3.44	7.16
2014	6.74	7.53	5.70	17.44	5.40	2.78	8.18
2015	6.69	6.87	6.42	12.34	6.42	2.36	9.10
2016	6.58	6.54	6.64	9.95	6.54	2.22	9.28
2017	6.36	6.10	6.85	8.47	7.09	2.10	7.77
2018	6.42	6.09	7.00	8.05	7.32	2.03	8.04
2019E	6.42	5.97	7.29	8.02	7.82	1.98	7.80

E—Estimate based on data to 30 June 2019
Note ECB—European Central Bank; PBoC—People's Bank of China; BoJ—Bank of Japan; SNB—Swiss National Bank; BoE—Bank of England; Fed—US Federal Reserve
Source *CrossBorder Capital*

moderately rising liquidity multiplier. Put another way, the Chinese monetary system demonstrates a remarkable stability according to this measure.

The charts shown in Figs. 7.6 and 7.7 demonstrate how the comparative stability in China's liquidity multiplier (and by association the Emerging Market multiplier of which it is the dominant part) contrasts with the visible collapse in the multipliers for the large Developed economies, notably the US, the Eurozone and Japan in the wake of the Y2K Bubble and the 2007–2008 GFC.

Digging Deeper into US Federal Reserve Actions

Janet Yellen's chairmanship of the US Federal Reserve was notable in that it popularised, so-called, forward guidance policies. These relatively new tools, which have effectively become part of the US policy armoury since the 2007–2008 GFC, signal the likely future path of interest rates. In the

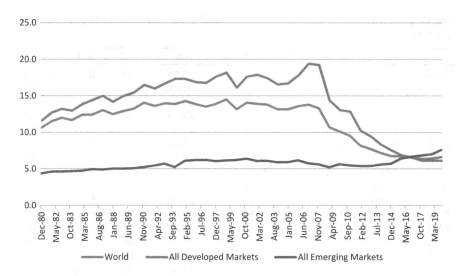

Fig. 7.6 Liquidity multiplier—World, developed and Emerging Market economies, 1980–2019 (times) (Source *CrossBorder Capital*)

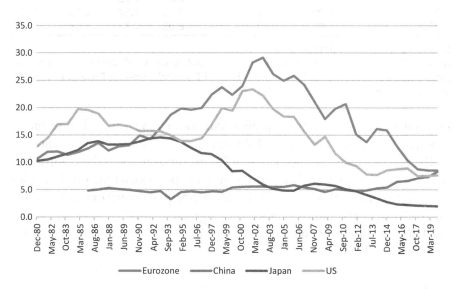

Fig. 7.7 Liquidity multiplier—PBoC, ECB, BoJ and Federal Reserve, 1980–2019 (times) (Source *CrossBorder Capital*)

US, they are epitomised in the so-called 'dot plot' diagram, where FOMC[14] members visually depict their expected future interest rate targets. Many Central Bank policy-makers often insist that interest rates are their sole focus and that quantities do not matter because the Central Bank can simply supply liquidity to meet whatever demand exists. However, this misses two important points. First, in financial crises when access to liquidity matters most, liquidity is rarely fungible, because it gets quickly hoarded. Second, the size of the Central Bank balance sheet which determines these volumes of liquidity, also matters because it represents the ability of the Central Bank to share risks with the private sector and it may also signal to markets the Fed's possible intention to tighten or loosen overall monetary policy more aggressively. A smaller-sized balance policy is therefore an implicitly riskier policy-decision.

The mechanism of interest rate setting is well-covered in existing economics textbooks and is of less concern to us here. In brief outline, the Federal Reserve, like many other Central Banks, tries to maintain its policy interest rate within a corridor by setting boundaries. The floor is the Fed's 'borrowing' rate, which can be set, say, by the premium paid for deposits held by regulated banks at the Fed. In the US, following the 2007–2008 GFC, the floor is the IOER (interest rate paid on excess reserves of banks). The notional ceiling is the Fed's 'lending rate' to the market, which tends to be moved by the rate paid for Central Bank's repo operations and/or the official discount rate (ODR), the premium at which the Fed will lend against certain collateral. Federal Funds[15] and, for example, Treasury bill rates should generally trade within this corridor. Other market-driven rates and rates paid by intermediaries without preferential access to the Fed's balance sheet will likely trade above this corridor. However, unlike other Central Banks that operate interest rate corridors, such as the ECB, the Fed's ceiling rate is far from automatic. This upper limit on the US rate corridor is a notional or loose constraint and dependent on the speedy reaction of policy-makers. Many banks prove, in extremis, unwilling to borrow from the Fed's discount window in case it signals to the market a greater distress, and in the event the Fed is often too slow to prevent upward spikes in repo and Fed Funds rates. Hence, the recent demands for the Federal Reserve to put in place a standing repo facility.

In practice, the vast volumes of reserves currently held by American banks means that their demand for liquidity is likely to be, at times, very interest rate elastic and so less affected by discount rate changes or by open market operations, but when banks are close to their effective minimum reserve levels their demand curves become highly inelastic. Even in other operating systems, these interest rate targeting systems are not always straightforward, largely because the floors and ceilings tend to 'leak'. Moreover, as Marcia Stigum argues in the *Money Market* (1987), traditional economic theory cannot convincingly explain how the Fed gets traction over the US economy: *"… from long experience, Fed technicians knew that the Fed could not control money supply with the precision envisioned in textbooks"*. Like Henry Kaufman (1986), Stigum believes in the importance of credit: *"Much of the macro-theory that links money supply to the price level depends on concepts that have little relevance to the workings of a modern financial system, but … [n]o comparable macroeconomic theory for credit aggregates yet exists"*.

In our experience, the composition of the Central Bank balance sheet makes a significant difference. The assets-side of the balance sheet essentially consists of three active components: (1) gold and foreign exchange reserves; (2) directed lending programmes and (3) securities' holdings. The liabilities-side, in turn, consists of another four key entries: (1) cash-in-circulation; (2) banks' reserves held at the Central Bank; (3) reverse repos (in the US case, these are also held by foreign Central Banks), and (4) Treasury balances. Assuming that cash-in-circulation responds passively to retail demands for notes and coin, then movements in any of the other six categories will define a change in national monetary conditions.

Typically, in the more mature financial systems that span the Developed economies, movements in gold and foreign exchange holdings are not considered to affect monetary conditions because their movements are, supposedly, *sterilised* by active Central Bank operations. However, sterilisation is an imprecise term. In practice, there are often spill-over effects and we noted earlier the remarkably close correlation between World forex reserves and Global Liquidity. Sterilisation refers to the intention that any changes in the value of the foreign reserves do not subsequently affect the domestic money supply. Yet, it is unclear whether this means money on the Central Bank balance sheet; money in the broader banking system, or the liquidity of the wider wholesale markets? Sterilisation has even been used to describe the smoothing out of interest rate fluctuations. When we refer to Central Bank money, sterilisation requires that changes in the foreign reserves, say, are exactly offset in their effect on the monetary base by equivalent changes to other balance sheet categories, such as holdings of securities, Treasury balances and, in cases, statutory reserve requirements.

Security holdings represent assets such as Treasury bonds, notes and bills and some private sector bills. Movements in these totals are termed open market operations. In most economies, these transactions are restricted to secondary markets, with subscription to government new issues, or so-called *monetisation*, usually ruled out for prudential reasons.[16] Following the 2007–2008 GFC, the buying of securities by the Federal Reserve have been re-labelled *large-scale asset purchases* (LSAP), and more popularly known as QE (*quantitative easing*). Directed lending policies allow policy-makers to target troubled institutions, such as through traditional lender of the last resort facilities, the Primary Dealer Credit Facility (PDCF) and other similar credit programmes[17] enacted by the Federal Reserve in the wake of the GFC. Their effects can be wider, such as the Bank of Japan's window guidance policies in the 1970s and 1980s which encouraged the commercial banks to favour certain industries with loans, and, more, recently the directed loans made by China's policy banks.

The Fed focuses on the Treasury repo[18] market and uses this to control the Fed Funds market (even though they are not direct participants), which is the market for reserves held at the Fed. Repos make up a large and growing part of Central Bank operations. A repo, in this context, is a collateralised loan made by the Central Bank for a specific time period, say, 7 or 14 days. The transaction involves the purchase of qualifying security, such as a 10-year Treasury note, from a private sector institution, such as a money dealer. The institution is contracted to buy the security back at the end of the period. The opposite operation, termed a reverse repo, occurs on the liabilities side of the Central Bank's balance sheet. Here, the Central Bank sells a bond into the markets, with an agreement to buy it back on contract expiry. Central Bank repo operations increase liquidity, whereas reverse repos (also dubbed 'reverses') reduce liquidity.

Central Bank operations differ both by their maturity spectrum, and by their size and scope through the cycle. For example, the Bank of England (BoE) largely focuses on the short-term 3-month trade bill, a fact explained by Britain's historic foreign trading roots. Hence, the BoE traditionally provided LoLR[19] facilities to (now defunct) discount houses sufficient to maintain the 'marketability' of bills, whereas the US Fed's Treasury repo operations seek to maintain the 'marketability' of long-term securities. Although the Federal Reserve is only a small player in the General Collateral market, it still wields big influence. However, the Fed is not directly involved in the offshore Eurodollar markets, the World's most liquid short-term dollar market and a ready alternative source for Fed Funds. In both the wider repo and Eurodollar markets the private sector is largely outside of Fed control and hence a source of potentially greater elasticity in liquidity for both money and capital markets. But in crises liquidity loses fungibility and often gets hoarded, and, however hard the Central Banks push, funding liquidity is not easily transformed into the required market liquidity.

Treasury deposits are the working balances that the government holds at the Central Bank. They are the difference between payments made by government departments and receipts from taxes and security issuance. Reserve requirements refer to the amounts that designated, regulated commercial banks are forced to hold as reserves at the Central Bank. Historically, they are measured as a percentage of specified deposits, sometimes with rates varying for different deposit types, and often, and particularly since the 2007–2008 GFC, the banks hold reserves above this minimum. In the US, reservable liabilities consist of net transaction accounts, non-household time deposits and Eurocurrency liabilities. From end-1990, household time deposits and Eurocurrency liabilities have had a reserve ratio of zero. The UK, Australia, Canada and New Zealand are among those economies that no longer impose reserve requirements. Nonetheless, following the 2007–2008 GFC, many Western banks have held substantial excess reserves, largely because of the additional regulations and liquidity demands placed on them by policy-makers.

The deregulation of financial markets has progressively led to greater emphasis on bank capital requirements (e.g. Basel I, II and III) and solvency checks than on reserve requirements and the management of liquidity. Ahead of the 2007–2008 GFC, this encouraged financial innovators to try to sidestep these regulations by effectively splitting financing activity into the three distinct functions: (1) *liquidity* to facilitate refinancing and enable trade e.g. the supply of notes and coin and cheque clearing functions; (2) *maturity transformation* to allow long-term lending (e.g. borrow short/lend long) and (3) *credit enhancement* to boost risk taking. The assets that Central Banks hold on their balance sheets can be broken down to reflect their support for these three dimensions. In the case of the US Federal Reserve it is possible to broadly align each function, respectively, to the aspirations of the eponymous QE1, QE2 and QE3 quantitative easing phases, which helps to better understand the Federal Reserve's crisis response. Whereas the US Fed has operated, at different times, along all three channels, the Bank of England (BoE) generally replaced maturity transformation with liquidity provision; the European Central Bank (ECB) focussed more on credit enhancement and the Bank of Japan (BoJ) on maturity transformation. To illustrate this, Table 7.4 shows the Fed's balance sheet as of end-2014, or roughly when the QE3 programme ended, broken down into the main categories of assets and liabilities. This balance sheet is a less-detailed version of Table 7.1, but this decomposition may better explain the Federal Reserve's new operating channels, as outlined in a February 2009 speech by former Fed Chairman Ben Bernanke.[20] For example, the LSAP not only substantially increased the size of the Fed's balance sheet, it also altered its composition by replacing Treasury bill holdings entirely with long-dated Treasuries and adding sizeable holdings of mortgage-backed securities and agency debt.

Table 7.4 disaggregates the Fed balance sheet by activity, denoting as 'liquidity provision' those assets that contribute to the stock of reserve money; 'maturity transformation' those assets, such as holdings of

Table 7.4 US Federal Reserve balance sheet—reported and reallocated by function, end-2014

US$ billions	Assets			Liabilities
(a) Reported				
Bills	0	Currency		1342
Bonds and notes	2461	Reverse repos		346
MBS and agencies	1777	Reserves		2575
Other	305	Other		280
Total	4543	Total		4543

US$ billions	Assets		Liabilities	
(b) Reallocated by function				
Notional bills/ wholesale funds	4263	Currency, repos and reserves	4263	Liquidity provision (50.1%)
Bonds and notes	2461	Notional bills/ wholesale funds	2461	Maturity transfor- mation (28.9%)
MBS and agencies	1777	Bonds and notes	1777	Credit enhance- ment (20.9%)
Total	8501	Total	8501	

Source US Federal Reserve, *CrossBorder Capital*

long-dated Treasuries, that absorb duration[21] from the market, and 'credit enhancement' those assets that reduce outstanding credit risk for the private sector. Examples of the latter are purchases of mortgage-backed securities (MBS) and support for the bonds of Government Sponsored Enterprises (GSEs), namely Fannie Mae (Federal National Mortgage Association) and Freddie Mac (Federal Home Loan Mortgage Corporation); cash injections into the American International Group (AIG) and the various associated transactions. Mortgage-backed securities are instruments, which securitise mortgage pools and are engineered to have high credit ratings. In 2008, this made them repo-able and eligible to collateralise other securities, such as asset-backed commercial paper (ABCP), which are, in turn, additionally backed by credit lines from banks. Before the 2008 Crisis these securities were often held in the off-balance-sheet subsidiaries of major banks from where they could sidestep capital requirements, but readily attract funding. By divorcing credit funding from credit risk, the financial system created a new class of triple-A rated securities that were deemed as 'safe' as US Treasuries, even though their cash flows attracted no Government guarantee and their marketability was ultimately never as good. Yet, they proved popular and satisfied the rising new demand for 'safe' assets from what we earlier described as CICPs (corporate and institutional cash pools).

The first two tiers of the reconstructed Fed balance sheet in Table 7.4 are balanced by introducing notional 'wholesale' finance. There is inevitably some double-counting in this presentation, but the three-way division

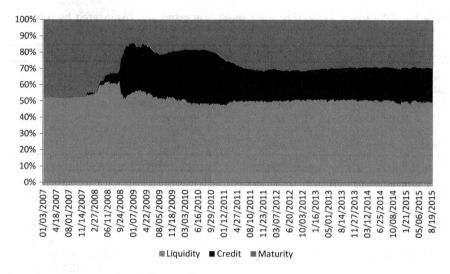

Fig. 7.8 Percentage breakdown of gross Federal Reserve balance sheet by pro-gramme, 2007–2015 (weekly) (*Source* US Federal Reserve, *CrossBorder Capital*)

derived from the Federal Reserve's H4 release and shown in Fig. 7.8 as per-centages of the gross balance sheet over time can provide more detail about the character of Federal Reserve policy than the aggregate LSAP, by itself. This split is motivated by Singh (2013), who explores the significance of collateral for credit expansion, dividing it into three tiers according to qual-ity: 'D' comprises bank deposits at the Central Bank; 'C1' represents 'good' collateral that can be easily converted into D, without any 'haircuts', and 'C2' describes collateral that is only 'good' in certain market circumstances. Singh argues that only specific pre-authorised banks are able to convert C1 to D overnight. He defines 'ultimate' liquidity as D+C1. His framework shows how some Central Banks (e.g. Bank of England) substituted between these collateral types in the wake of the Financial Crisis, whereas the Federal Reserve increased all three in absolute terms: *liquidity provision* (e.g. D); *maturity transformation* (e.g. C1) and *credit enhancement* (e.g. C2).[22]

Economic theory offers some insight as to how these channels may affect risk premia between so-called safe assets (e.g. cash and government bonds) and risky assets (e.g. equities, corporate debt and commodities):

- The *liquidity provision channel* should improve the general re-financing climate within the economy, enabling credit spreads and bid-ask spreads to tighten. We assume that the Federal Reserve receives notional three-month bill rates and pays-out overnight rates for these activities. More liquidity should therefore directly tighten overnight swap/money market spreads. By facilitating funding and helping to stimulate business activity it may also act to reduce default rates. More illiquid and more risky instruments should benefit more than safe and liquid instruments, such as Treasuries. Treasuries may also partially lose their *safety premium* as liquidity increases.

- The *maturity transformation channel* can operate in two ways. First, according to theory, the prices of long duration securities are more sensitive than short dated securities to changes in interest rates (*duration risk*). Therefore, by removing these risky assets from the market, overall risk should diminish. Second, assuming there are *preferred habitat* investors, the removal of specific maturities from the market will create a scarcity and reduce their term premia. We assume that the Federal Reserve receives long maturity returns and notionally pays-out short-term bill rates. More activity through the maturity channel should narrow this yield spread or term spread.

- Similarly, the *credit enhancement channel* acts to remove high credit risk securities from the market. This should reduce overall risk. The Federal Reserve takes in credit returns and pays-out risk-free long maturity yields. Larger holdings of credit should tighten these spreads. A specific risk associated with mortgages is pre-payment risk and by purchasing MBS this risk may also be reduced for investors.

Although all three channels are important, the Federal Reserve itself emphasises the credit channel:

Our approach—which could be described as "credit easing"—resembles quantitative easing in one respect: It involves an expansion of the central bank's balance sheet. However, in a pure QE regime, the focus of policy is the quantity of bank reserves, which are liabilities of the central bank; the composition of loans and securities on the asset side of the central bank's balance sheet is incidental. Indeed, although the Bank of Japan's policy approach during the QE period was quite multifaceted, the overall stance of its policy was gauged primarily in terms of its target for bank reserves. In contrast, the Federal Reserve's credit easing approach focuses on the mix of loans and securities that it holds and on how this composition of assets affects credit conditions for households and businesses. Former Fed Chairman Ben Bernanke, speech January 2009

Figure 7.8 confirms that, prior to the Financial Crisis, the Federal Reserve's activities divided roughly equally between *liquidity provision* (52.3%) and *maturity transformation* (47.7%).[23] After the Crisis broke, the Fed undertook significant *credit enhancement* operations (23.1%),[24] largely conducted through the purchases of mortgage-backed securities (MBS). At their peak, these operations made-up around one-third of the Federal Reserve's gross balance sheet, amounting to US$1.8 trillion of asset purchases. These balance sheet movements indicate that the Federal Reserve's response to the 2007–2008 GFC was continuous and multi-faceted. Its reported balance sheet grew from less than US$0.9 trillion before September 2008 to US$2.2 trillion by 2010; US$2.7 trillion by 2011 and hit a peak of US$4.3 trillion in early 2014. Policy deliberately involved pre-announcements of planned Treasury and MBS purchases, but it did not exclusively rely on them. The physical act of buying different assets was also important. Using the above breakdown of the Fed's balance sheet, we can show the impact of actual transactions on the average real term premia of US Treasuries (TP_t) across 1-year through 10-year Treasuries from a simple partial adjustment model estimated using linear regression, with Newey–West adjusted standard errors:

$$\Delta_m TP_{t+m} = \beta_0 + \beta_1 LP_t + \beta_2 MT_t + \beta_3 CE_t + \beta_4 TP_t + \varepsilon_t$$

LP_t, MT_t and CE_t refer, respectively, to the liquidity provision, maturity transformation and credit enhancement factors. β_i are estimated loadings. The period difference, m, is set at 13 weeks. Taking weekly data that start from the beginning of 2007 and end in August 2015, a sample of 438 observations, the R-squared statistic is 0.347. The results show three things[25]:

- the loading on *liquidity provision* is statistically significant at the 1% level, with a positive sign. Each US$1 trillion of extra liquidity increases the average term premium by 56 bp
- the loading on *credit enhancement* is insignificant at the 5% level
- the *maturity transformation* loading is significant at the 1% level, but it has a negative sign. Each US$1 trillion channelled into maturity transformation reduces the average real term premium by 142 bp.

According to our estimates, QE1 added around US$1.1 trillion through the *liquidity channel*; nothing through the *maturity channel* and US$1.5 trillion through the *credit channel*. Based on the estimated loadings, US term premia should have risen by around 60 bp through QE1. QE2 added a further US$0.7 trillion through the *liquidity channel* (+40 bp); US$0.9 trillion through the *maturity channel* (−125 bp) and actually reduced the *credit channel* by US$0.5 trillion. Together this should have reduced term premia by around 85 bp. The much later QE3[26] added a further US$1.5 trillion through the *liquidity channel*; US$1 trillion through the *maturity channel* and US$0.7 trillion through the *credit channel*, implicitly reducing real term premia by an estimated net 60 bp.

Intuitively, an increase in the maturity channel should, in general, lower term premia. In contrast, the liquidity and credit channels are likely to indirectly raise term premia to the extent that they reduce default risks in the broader economy and encourage a shift of funds out of *safe assets*, such as Treasuries, and into risky assets, namely equities and corporate debt. These are important questions that we will return to again in Chapter 10. Overall, these latter effects appear to be low when compared to the effect of the maturity channel. The insignificance of the credit enhancement channel may be explained because this effect operates indirectly and is unlikely to be instantaneous. Moreover, the Fed was not the only source of credit support to the mortgage market since both Fannie Mae and Freddie Mac were taken into conservatorship by the Treasury in September 2008, effectively becoming part of the US Government balance sheet. In a further test we compared the spread between single-B rated corporate debt and Aaa investment grade rated debt and the size of the Federal Reserve's *credit enhancement* channel. The results appear plausible with an intuitive negative sign and significance at the 1% level. The loading shows that each US$1 trillion of credit support reduces the B-Aaa corporate spread by 415 bp. At its peak in 2008, this spread hit 1670 bp, and based on the estimated impact of this credit channel, LSAP should have reduced these credit spreads by around 700 bp in total. Given that the spread has averaged around 400–450 bp since the early 2000s, the size of this impact is not unreasonable.

Fed actions and responses to alter the size and composition of its balance sheet seem to be important drivers of risk premia. Duration and liquidity effects appear to be significant for Treasury term premia and the credit channel may affect the risk premia on corporate bonds. Figure 7.9 shows the weblink to an interactive map of US dollar funding flows produced by the US Federal Reserve. The programme traces though the sources and uses of funds involved in the onshore and offshore US dollar funding markets, and shows how the Federal Reserve interacts with the private sector at different levels.

The People's Bank of China

The current operating framework of the People's Bank of China (PBoC) sits somewhere between its historic position as the monopoly lender in the pre-Deng period and a modern Central Bank, like the Federal Reserve.

Mapping U.S. Dollar Funding Flows

This interactive map shows how various institutions generally engage with one another, and with the Federal Reserve's balance sheet, in the course of borrowing and lending U.S. dollar instruments in the money markets.

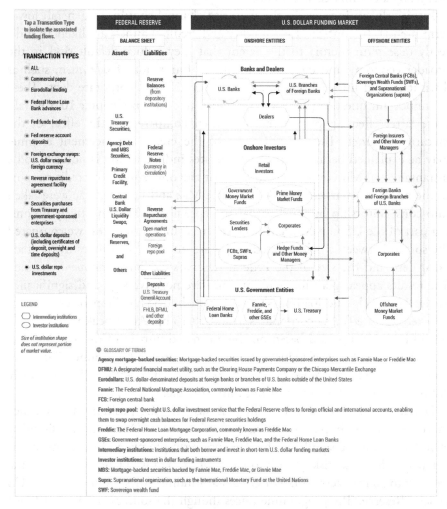

Fig. 7.9 Mapping US dollar funding flows (Reproduced with permission from the Federal Reserve Bank of New York. Original source can be accessed at https://www.newyorkfed.org/research/blog/2019_LSE_Markets_Interactive_afonso)

Quantitative policies and lending directives remain important, but the PBoC is progressively moving towards a system that will allow it to target money market interest rates within some corridor. This has already meant financial de-regulation and led to the removal of many previously fixed rates for savers. Notwithstanding, the major SOEs (State-owned industries) and SOBs (State-owned banks) retain their privileged positions and still benefit from easier access to cheap credit than other institutions.

The PBoC's main monetary tools consist of: (1) open market operations, (2) reserve requirements, (3) a medium-term lending facility and (4) directed lending by the policy banks. Prior to 2014, PBoC operations were largely passive, because the Central Bank balance sheet automatically expanded to reflect China's swelling foreign currency reserves, this being the corollary of the Yuan shadowing movements in the US dollar. Since 2000 and largely coincident with her WTO membership, China's stock of foreign exchange reserves jumped by 20-fold or roughly double the 10-fold increase over the same period in the monetary base. The multiplier between the stock of overall liquidity and the monetary base remained remarkably stable through the period at around 5–6 times, which means that this entire primary monetary expansion fed through to boost overall Chinese credit by a comparable whopping 12-fold multiple. However, the large draw-down in forex reserves through 2014 and 2015 during Premier Xi Jinping's anti-corruption drive,[27] led to a major shift in monetary operations. Figure 7.10 charts the profile of Chinese foreign exchange reserve holdings. These peaked at around US$4 trillion in 2014 and have since fallen and stabilised at close to US$3 trillion. The latest flat-lining partly reflects slower net inflows into China, but also suggests a shift in official policy away from accumulating further US dollar Treasury securities.

Initially, the fall in reserves tightened domestic monetary conditions. This was offset by a step-up in the scale of domestic monetary operations. Reserve requirements, which had been used to contain the effect of rising forex reserves on bank liquidity, were now reduced, and open market operations, notably repos with primary dealers, increased to improve money market liquidity. A medium-term lending facility (MTLF) was introduced in 2014. This allows the PBoC to provide funds at longer maturities, ranging from three to twelve months, but typically at a premium to repo rates. Currently, the MTLF stands at between RMB3½ and 4 trillion (circa US$500 billion) out of a RMB36 trillion balance sheet. More recently, there has also been a step-up in lending by China's policy banks via SAFE. China's policy banks include such institutions as the *China Development Bank*, the *Agricultural Development Bank of China* and the *Export-Import Bank of China*. They can engage in direct project finance and have lately proved to be a useful

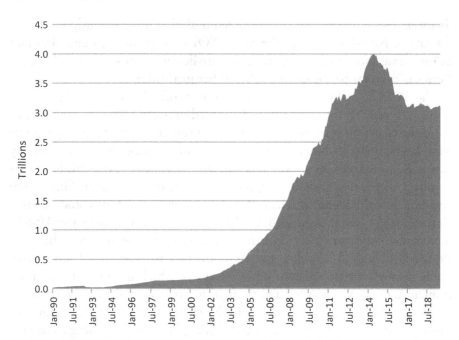

Fig. 7.10 Chinese foreign exchange reserves, 1990–2019 (US$ in trillions) (Source *CrossBorder Capital*, SAFE)

way to channel funds into *Belt and Road Initiative* schemes. According to Germany's Kiel Institute,[28] the PBoC has acquired sizeable external bond claims and may be responsible for a large part of the estimated US$5 trillion of Chinese foreign lending, much of which is undisclosed in official data.

Figure 7.11 plots data on Chinese Central Bank money, along with estimates of the contributions from foreign exchange and domestic asset purchases. The fall-off in the forex contribution is plain to see, as is the subsequent deliberate step-up in domestic asset purchases from late 2015. The People's Bank (PBoC) tightened Chinese monetary conditions sharply from late 2015, to temper capital outflows, and again in late 2018, to protect the Yuan in the face of escalating trade tensions with the USA. Table 7.5 reports the PBoC balance sheet as of mid-2019 and highlights how much its composition has changed: between end-2013 and mid-2019, while reserve money remained fairly stable at around 85% of the balance sheet, foreign reserves fell to 60% of assets from their prior sizeable 86%. Direct loans to Chinese banks rose through this period from 4% to a substantial 28% of assets.

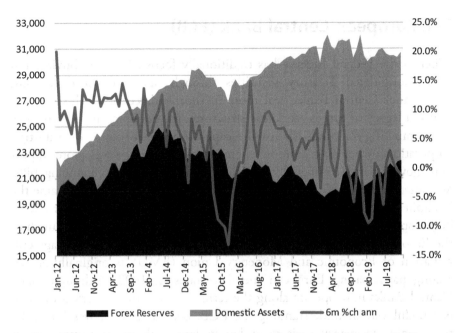

Fig. 7.11 People's Bank of China (PBoC) monetary base—breakdown by foreign and domestic components, 2012–2019 (monthly, RMB in billions) (Source *CrossBorder Capital, People's Bank*)

Table 7.5 Balance sheet of Chinese monetary authority (end-June, 2019)

RMB billions			
Foreign assets	21,852	Reserve money	31,309
Foreign exchange	21,246	Currency issue	7824
Monetary gold	278	Deposits of financial corporations	22,182
Other foreign assets	328	Deposits of other depository corporations	22,182
Claims on government	1525	Deposits of other financial corporations	0
Of which: central government	1525	Deposits of non-financial Institutions	1303
Claims on other depository corporations	10,186	Deposits excluded from reserve money	424
Claims on other financial corporations	484	Bond issue	74
Claims on non-financial sector	0	Foreign liabilities	90
Other assets	2312	Deposits of government	3568
		Own capital	22
		Other liabilities	873
Total assets	36,360	Total liabilities	36,360

Source *CrossBorder Capital, People's Bank*

The European Central Bank (ECB)

Whereas the Federal Reserve has traditionally focussed on the buying and selling long-dated Treasury securities through open market operations, many other Central Banks deal more in shorter dated bills. This convention is a legacy of earlier economic structures, for example, the US Treasury was competing for funds against the capital investment needs of industrial corporations, whereas in Europe where cross-border trade was more important, governments competed against short-term trade and financing bills. We noted, for example, how the 3-month trade bill on London became the linchpin of nineteenth century finance. The European Central Bank (ECB) began operations on 1st June, 1998, or a few months ahead of the launch of the Euro currency unit on 1st January, 1999. This was the third stage culmination of Economic and Monetary Union (EMU) as originally agreed among participating European member states in 1992. Although many Central Banks now operate along the term structure this historical division is a useful way of understanding the ECB, because until it was forced by the ongoing monetary crisis to undertake large-scale security purchases, it more typically operated policy through the short-term repo markets. A system of collateralised borrowing through repos is also used by the US Federal Reserve, but the Fed also traditionally undertakes more direct purchases of financial assets than the ECB. Europe's banks effectively borrow cash short-term from the ECB at a sufficiently short duration that allows interest rates to be continually adjusted. When the repos come due, the participating banks then bid again for funds. An increase or decrease in the quantity of notes offered at auction changes liquidity in the Eurozone economy. The fifteen hundred or so eligible banks in the Euro-system periodically bid for term liquidity[29] in ECB auctions, but they must provide satisfactory collateral against which to borrow. The collateral demanded by the ECB is typically high-quality public and private sector debt instruments. This can be the public debt of member states, but since the GFC an increasingly wide range of private securities are also now accepted. The criteria for determining the *high-quality* grade for public debt are incorporated in the pre-conditions for membership of the European Union's monetary system: total debt must not be too large in relation to gross domestic product (GDP), for example, and fiscal deficits in any given year must not become too large. Yet, in practice, a number of clever accounting techniques have been used to hide the truth about fiscal solvency, e.g. allegedly in Greece.

From late 2009 several individual Eurozone economies faced the prospect of being unable both to repay their Euro-denominated government debts and to finance further bailouts of troubled national banking systems. We touched on the Eurozone's structural problems in Chapter 5 and will return to them again in Chapter 12. However, the essential issue is that the Euro mechanism, like all fixed exchange rate systems makes the rich regions, richer and the poor, poorer. As a side-note, these divergences do not seem to affect those economic neighbours, such as the US and Canada; Australia and New Zealand, or Norway and Sweden, that float their currencies against each other. But in fixed exchange rate systems, such as the Eurozone, without appropriate-sized fiscal transfers, assets will shift from low productivity to high productivity economies, thereby undermining the precious collateral required by local banks. From the outset of the Euro-system in 1999, speculative capital flows from Germany and other richer Northern economies, rather than productivity-boosting FDI, flooded into feed the appetites of Southern European consumers. Paradoxically, intra-European FDI flows headed towards Eastern Europe and into economies, such as Poland, Czech Republic and Hungary, that still floated their currencies against the Euro. Eurozone banks took the strain of these consumer debts.

What is now known as the 2010–2012 *Eurozone Banking Crisis* was triggered by the decision of Greece's newly elected left-wing government to own up to the full extent of her indebtedness and publicly warn of her impending sovereign default. These fears widened to embrace other vulnerable borrowers, notably other Mediterranean and the Irish economies. Sovereign bond yields across several Eurozone countries rose sharply, as a result. A key flaw in the Eurozone is that the 'safe' asset in the system is not the Euro, but the German Bund. Thus, the more these peripheral sovereign bonds yields rose, the more likely was the threat of default, and, so the more that these sovereign yields spreads against Bunds continued to widen.

Financial panic in 2010 was exacerbated by the inability of the European monetary authorities to support their sovereign bond markets. This arose, first, because the ECB's legal framework then disallowed the purchase of sovereign bonds (i.e. Article 123). This prevented the Central Bank from immediately copying the QE policies of the Federal Reserve. Second, credit quality for a Eurozone sovereign bond to be eligible as collateral in the ECB's open market operations had been previously set at an optimistically high minimum credit rating of BBB-minus back in 2005. This meant that whenever the private rating agencies downgraded a sovereign bond below this threshold, the investing banks could suddenly become illiquid because they would quickly lose vital access to ECB refinancing operations. This hastened the rush into safe German Bunds, so setting up a 'doom loop' between banks and their sovereign issuers. In the face of these regulatory constraints, the ECB was initially reluctant to intervene to calm turbulent financial markets in 2010, despite the unfolding crises in Greece, Portugal, Spain and Italy and widening interest rate spreads against the German Bund.

To tackle these problems, in early May 2010 the ECB launched the *Securities Market Programme* (SMP). This allowed discretionary purchases of Eurozone sovereign securities in secondary markets, alongside the European Financial Stabilisation Mechanism (EFSM), which would serve as a crisis fighting fund to safeguard the Euro area from future sovereign debt crises. Although the SMP injected additional liquidity into financial markets, these injections were sterilised elsewhere on the ECB balance sheet, so that the SMP was supposedly neutral when measured in conventional money supply terms. However, by November 2010 it had become plain that Ireland could not afford to bail out her failing banks. The Anglo-Irish Banking Group alone needed upwards of €30 billion, a sum the Irish Government neither had and nor could easily borrow from financial markets given that Irish bond yields traded near to distressed Greek bonds. Cleverly, but controversially, the Irish Government issued a €31 billion promissory note, a form of IOU, to the by now nationalised Anglo-Irish Bank, and, in turn, the bank used the promissory note as collateral for the Central Bank of Ireland (CBI), so it could access emergency liquidity assistance (ELA).

Longer term refinancing operations (LTRO) were introduced from December 2011, under the new and more enlightened ECB presidency of Mario Draghi. Eurozone government securities, mortgage-backed securities and other commercial paper of a sufficiently high credit rating became acceptable collateral. These 1% interest rate loans with a three-year term were extensively used by Eurozone banks, particularly by hard-pressed banks in Greece, Ireland, Italy and Spain. In February 2012, the ECB undertook a second 3-year auction, or so-called LTRO2, to provide around 800 Eurozone banks with over €½ trillion in low-interest loans. The critical shift occurred in July 2012, when renewed fears over Eurozone sovereign default prompted Draghi to leapfrog the prevailing political stalemate and make his now famous commitment that the ECB *"…is ready to do whatever it takes to preserve the Euro. And believe me, it will be enough"*. This watershed statement led Eurozone bond yields to tumble, notably in hard-pressed Spain, Italy and France. In August 2012, the ECB announced that it would undertake *outright open market operations* of a size adequate to reach its objective of ensuring an *"…. appropriate monetary policy transmission and the singleness of the monetary policy"*. The Outright Monetary Transactions programme

(OMT) began in September and replaced the exiting Securities Markets Programme (SMP). Unlike the temporary SMP, the OMT has no prior limits placed on either its duration or its size. It was, however, conditional on the adherence of each beneficiary country to an appropriate adjustment programme. Although Eurozone sovereign debt tensions had eased by 2014, the ECB now faced a new deflation challenge prompted by the persistent slide in the Eurozone's inflation rate. The September 2014 policy response led to the launch of two bond purchase programmes: (1) the Covered Bond Purchasing Programme (CBPP3) and (2) the Asset-Backed Securities Programme (ABSPP). These were extended the following January into a more conventional QE programme, involving the purchase of sovereign bonds of up to €60 billion per month. An initial series of Targeted Longer-Term Financing Operations (TLTROs) was launched in June 2014, a second series (TLTRO II) followed in March 2016, and a third series (TLTRO III) from March 2019. These open market operations helped to finance Eurozone credit institutions. By offering banks long-term funding at attractive conditions, linked to their loans to non-financial corporations and households, they were designed to encourage banks to lend.

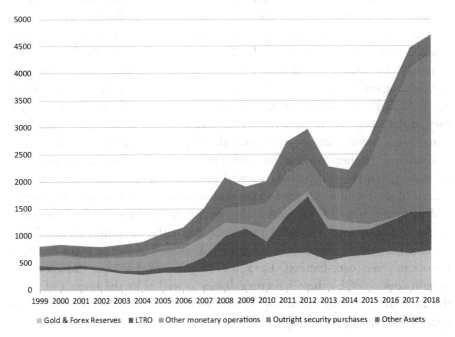

Fig. 7.12 Asset composition of ECB consolidated balance sheet, 1999–2018 (end-period, Euros in billions) (Source *CrossBorder Capital*, ECB)

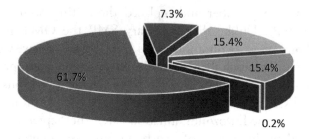

Fig. 7.13 Asset composition of ECB consolidated balance sheet, end-2018 (end-period, percent) (Source *CrossBorder Capital*, ECB)

The progressive scale and depth of these ECB operations now extends into assets that lie outside of what many other Central Banks, notably the US Fed, consider both desirable and feasible. The resulting ECB balance sheet expansion is summarised in Figs. 7.12 and 7.13, which highlight the main sources of liquidity creation. The balance sheet increased from €806 billion in 1999 to €4.7 trillion by end-2018. By far the biggest contribution to liquidity has come through Eurozone security purchases, which jumped from around 2–3% of the ECB balance sheet in 1999 to a huge near-62% by end-2018. As at late 2019, the ECB balance sheet is expanding once again thanks to Draghi's commitment to restart QE, as his 'final' act as ECB President. The debate within the ECB has focussed on the efficacy of their negative interest rate policy. Meanwhile, their experts somehow remain convinced that negative rates do not detract from Eurozone bank profitability. Higher commercial bank profits appear to be their central policy goal, given the still parlous state of private bank balance sheets and the ECB's likely inability to easily facilitate another bank bailout programme and muster future IMF support. The persistence of Europe's banking woes point to deep-seated structural problems about the operation of the Euro-system that we later explore in Chapter 12, as well as to the plain fact that European's are 'over-banked' by a too fragmented banking industry. We remain concerned by these structural issues as well as by the impact of negative rates on Eurozone credit supply, and so we are convinced that still more quantitative easing is coming to Europe.

Notes

1. *Observations*, 1796: quoted by Paul Tucker, *Unelected Power*, Princeton, 2019.
2. 'Operating' as distinguished from 'transmission' channels.
3. See *12 Reasons Why Negative Rates Will Devastate the World*, Zero Hedge, 19/089/2019.
4. Markus K. Brunnermeier and Yann Koby, *The Reversal Interest Rate*, Princeton University Discussion Paper, January 2019.
5. The extra yield investors require to hold long-dated bonds, compared to the expected return from short-term rates rolled period-by-period over the same investment horizon.
6. Strictly speaking, the Treasury can also affect markets through similar asset purchases.
7. It can also be known as *outside money* (i.e. external to the private sector), the *monetary base* and, sometimes, *narrow money*.
8. BoE Speeches, July 2019.
9. See the comprehensive survey by J. Gagnon, *Quantitative Easing: An Underappreciated Success*, PIIE Policy Brief 16-4, Washington DC, 2016.
10. This US$3½ trillion pot represents around one-third of World forex reserves and nearly two-thirds of all US dollar reserves.
11. This official lending facility was pioneered by British banker Francis Baring.
12. R-squared is a 'goodness of fit' statistic that lies between zero and one and tells us the proportion of variation that is jointly common to the variables. It is the square of the correlation coefficient.
13. For the record, World Central Bank money is roughly 25% of World GDP.
14. Federal Open Market Committee.
15. Federal Funds rate is the overnight interest paid between banks and certain other institutions to borrow reserves.
16. In the case of the Bank of Japan, monetization is forbidden under the BoJ Law, because this was the mechanism used by Japan's Imperial Government to provide finance for the war effort in the 1930s and 1940s.
17. In 2007–2008 the 'rescue' acronyms abounded, such as the Fed's TAF (Term Auction Facility) and TSLF (Term Securities Lending Facility), and the US Treasury's TARP (Troubled Asset Relief Programme).
18. Repo—a sale and repurchase agreement.
19. Lender of the Last Resort.
20. *Federal Reserve Policies to Ease Credit and Their Implications for the Fed's Balance Sheet*, National Press Club, February 18, 2009.
21. Think of this as *effective maturity*.
22. We suggest that there may also be a fourth channel involving foreign exchange support through Central Banks swaps (C3).

23. 2007–2008 weekly averages.
24. 2009–2015 weekly averages.
25. Admittedly, the MT and CE variables are highly correlated and there is evidence of strong positive autocorrelation in the regression and of long-horizon effects, but splitting the data sample into sub-periods makes no significant difference to the loadings according to structural change tests. Moreover, the standard errors on the liquidity and maturity variables are relatively low.
26. Commenced September 13, 2012 and ended October 29, 2014.
27. China was simultaneously negotiating with the IMF to make the Yuan a reserve currency and become part of the SDR basket. This required removing certain capital controls, so making the balance of payments vulnerable to sudden outflows.
28. See Sebastian Horn, Carmen Reinhart, and Christoph Trebesch, China's Overseas Lending, Kiel WP #2312, June 2019.
29. Typically between 14 days and 3 months maturity.

References

Bagehot, Walter. 1873. *Lombard Street*. London: Henry S. King & Co.
Brunnermeier, Markus K., and Yann Koby. 2019. The Reversal Interest Rate. Princeton Working Paper, January.
Darmouni, Olivier M., and Alexander Rodnyansky. 2017. The Effects of Quantitative Easing on Bank Lending Behavior. *The Review of Financial Studies* 30 (11) (November): 3858–3887.
Di Maggio, Marco, Amir Kermani, and Christopher J. Palmer. 2018. How Quantitative Easing Works: Evidence on the Refinancing Channel. MIT Working Paper, June.
Harman, Jeremiah. 1819. Report from the Secret Committee of the Bank Resuming Cash Payments. Bank of England.
Kaufman, Henry. 1986. *Interest Rates, the Markets and New Financial World*. Time Books.
Krishnamurthy, Arvind, and Annette Vissing-Jorgensen. 2011. The Effects of Quantitative Easing on Interest Rates: Channels and Implications for Policy. Brookings Papers.
Krishnamurthy, Arvind, and Annette Vissing-Jorgensen. 2013. The Ins and Outs of LSAPs. Jackson Hole Economic Symposium.
Singh, Manmohan. 2013. Collateral and Monetary Policy. IMF Working Paper No. 13/186, August.
Stigum, Marcia L. 1987. *Money Market*, Rev. ed. New York: McGraw-Hill.
Tooze, Adam. 2018. *Crashed*. London: Penguin.

8

Cross-Border Capital Flows

Dollar Supremacy

International investment is big, procyclical and volatile. Throughout history, the internationalisation of finance has frequently paralleled the globalisation of trade because open economies need to diversify their asset bases more widely to hedge against external shocks, such as imported inflation. The large volumes of trade invoiced and transacted in US dollars explain why trading nations hold dollar-denominated assets. Alongside, firms with large dollar-denominated liabilities should invoice their sales in US dollars in order to reduce the currency mismatch between their revenues and their out-goings. In the memorable words of Watergate informant Deep Throat,[1] we 'follow the money'. Recent data show that the rise in Global Liquidity has been paced by still faster growth in cross-border capital flows. These have grown rapidly, expanding at a notably breathless pace from the early 1990s. In the wake of the 2007–2008 GFC, finance suffered from an anti-globalisation backlash involving tighter regulations, such as those imposed on international banks. At first sight, measured by the ratio of foreign assets to GDP the importance of international capital appears undented. However, a more thorough analysis confirms that not only have gross flows slumped since the GFC, but both the composition and the direction of cross-border capital movements have also markedly changed. China has muscled forward in importance; digital cross-border payments have established a foothold; offshore, low-tax financial centres, such as the Cayman Islands and Channel Islands have been forced to limit their activities, and the more stable and more economically vital flows

© The Author(s) 2020
M. J. Howell, *Capital Wars*,
https://doi.org/10.1007/978-3-030-39288-8_8

of foreign direct investments (FDI) that help spread latest technologies now comprise a larger share of international capital movements.

According to recent data reported in Fig. 8.1, America's international assets have settled at close to 125% of GDP, but they have been higher. Indeed, they soared in the period between the Y2K Bubble and the 2007–2008 GFC. International assets and liabilities often move closely together with similar trends. Yet, America's liabilities to foreigners have even outpaced the growth of her foreign assets, peaking at over 180% of GDP. Drilling into this balance sheet data, some have even compared America's international activity to the operations of a giant hedge fund that is 'short' cash and 'long' foreign risk assets. This confirms America's unique position because the dominance of the US dollar in World markets allows her to issue predominantly 'safe' assets in the form of US currency and Treasury securities, which she produces, and which are in high demand by foreign official and foreign private sectors. Americans then use these inflows to purchase risky international assets, such as stocks, foreign bonds and to accumulate FDI though the purchase of foreign businesses. The US dollar's continued dominance may originate from trade finance and hedging activity because it is widely used as an invoicing currency in international trade. Many Emerging Market economies invoice 70–80% of their trade in US dollars, but only export around 10–15% of their trade directly to the US. Similarly, around half of Japanese and nearly one-quarter

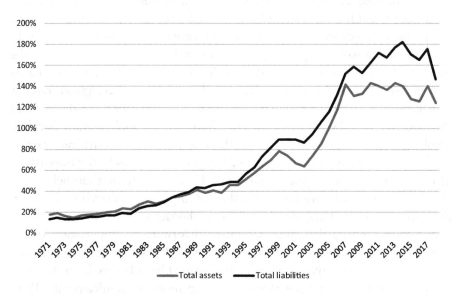

Fig. 8.1 US stock of foreign assets and liabilities, 1971–2018 (percent of US GDP) (*Source* IMF)

of European trade are US dollar denominated, but direct sales to the US make-up under one quarter and less than one tenth of their total exports, respectively.[2] This 'first-mover' advantage for the US unit is reinforced by large and still growing network effects that lower its transaction costs. The widespread use of the US dollar in trade invoicing and its dominance in international banking and finance are self-reinforcing. A consequence of the dollar's international role in transactions is that the global banking system also runs on dollars, making US assets the preferred 'safe haven'.

America's ability to issue these 'safe' assets spills over into other realms, such as the large amounts of private debt issued in US dollars in international markets; the large share of trade invoiced in US dollars and the huge volumes of foreign exchange intermediated through the US unit. Based on the latest triennial survey from the Bank for International Settlements (BIS 2019), the US dollar is now involved in 44.2% of all settlements in the US$6.6 trillion daily market in foreign exchange, with the Euro the second most transacted currency at 16.2%. The dollar is the unit of account in debt contracts insofar that cross-border borrowers usually borrow in dollars and cross-border lenders frequently lend in dollars, irrespective of whether the borrower or lender is a US resident. According to Goldberg and Lerman (2019), 63% of global foreign exchange reserves and 40% of non-US trade are, respectively, held and invoiced in dollars; 49% of debt is issued in dollars and 48% of cross-border claims are dollar denominated.[3] The Bank of England[4] recently calculated that the US dollar is the currency of choice for more than half of international trade invoices; two-thirds of Emerging Markets' external debt is US dollar denominated, and it serves as the monetary anchor for economies that make-up a still growing 70% share of World GDP, with around half of these currency units explicitly US dollar-pegged. These facts are summarised in Fig. 8.2. Taken overall, somewhere around half of the entire World GDP is directly or indirectly dollar denominated. Although the Bretton Woods system officially ended in 1971 when the link between the US dollar and gold was broken, the US unit has remained the undisputed World's anchor and main reserve currency ever since. In fact, despite the falling share of US GDP, the dominance of the dollar has increased, not decreased over time. Ironically, many experts, were quick to point out the US economy's secular slide, but they completely missed the US currency's increasing monetary dominance. This dominance shapes the transmission of US monetary policy throughout the World economy by affecting the prices and volumes of World trade; by changing the balance sheets, funding and risk-seeking activities of multinational financial

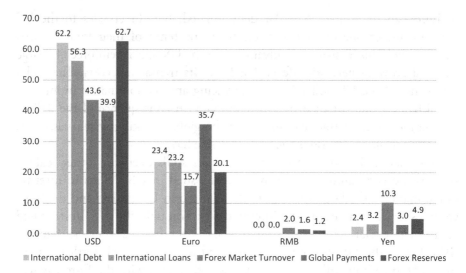

Fig. 8.2 The dominance of the American dollar in 2018 (percent) (*Source* ECB, *CrossBorder Capital*)

institutions, and through the greater synchronisation of Global Liquidity and financial cycles.

Yet, the US dollar's rise has not always been straightforward. We think in terms of three development phases: (1) the Gold Exchange Standard (1945–1971); (2) the Oil Exchange Standard (1974–1989), and (3) the Emerging Market Exchange Standard (1990–date). But, in between, the US currency sometimes devalued sharply and on occasions through political whim, such as following the decision by President Nixon to break the link to gold on 15 August 1971, and again in the late 1970s when 'open mouth operations' were used by the Carter Administration to talk the dollar down. The first development phase is well-described in popular textbooks as the practical implementation of the 1944 Bretton Woods Agreement following the end of WW2. The next phase started around July 1974 when US Treasury Secretary William Simon secretly agreed with Saudi Arabia, and later with OPEC that, in future, crude oil would be priced solely in US dollars. A corollary was that Saudi's subsequent large-scale purchases of US Treasury debt went undisclosed. By a stroke of the pen, America had cleverly created a new demand for US dollars.

The third phase of US dollar supremacy had less clandestine beginnings. The Fall of the Berlin Wall in 1989 and subsequent break-up of the Soviet Empire, together with Chinese Premier Deng Xiaoping's ongoing reforms fostered the rise of the Emerging Market economies. The competition for international capital among these fast-growing countries encouraged further economic reforms, market openness and disciplined currency management that extended far beyond Eastern Europe into the rest of Asia and Latin America. The US dollar was quickly established as the benchmark foreign currency of choice, even being used internally within these economies when doubts grew about the integrity and sustainability of their domestic currency units. China's entry into the WTO in 2001 gave dollar usage yet another boost, because the burgeoning Chinese-led supply chains and logistics were nearly always US dollar denominated. The deliberate targeting of the US dollar by foreign exchange managers required large US dollar reserve holdings. Therefore, possibly more by chance, the US dollar so discovered yet another new source of demand. Its influence could even keep growing: Emerging Market economies already account for some two-thirds of World GDP, up from less than one-third in the early 1980s, and look set to command a three-quarter share within the next decade. Add to this the fall-out from the 2010–2012 Eurozone banking crisis, and the region's associated need for external support from both the IMF and the US Fed. This reinforced the US dollar's dominance by questioning the long-term stability of the Euro unit. Research by economic historian Adam Tooze (2018) shows that the use of Central Bank swap-lines has made the Federal Reserve de facto international *lender of the last resort* by providing a whopping US$10.1 trillion (or US$4.45 trillion on standardised measures) from December 2007 to August 2010, with much it cementing fragile European banks.

Since the GFC, these US dollar swap lines have become more politicised. Not only has the US historically favoured 'friendly' nations with swap arrangements, but according to Adam Tooze the decision now rests ultimately with who sits in the White House.[5] Pointedly, China, the World's biggest US dollar user, and other Emerging Markets are not on this list. This gap matters because, although non-US banks can, in theory, tap stable US dollar deposit funding through their US subsidiaries, US regulations now confine the use of these funds to US-beneficial activities, so they cannot be deployed at a global level. Consequently, China is trying to develop its own network of Yuan swap lines, possibly to tap into the permanent dollar pool, e.g. the recent RMB 350 billion (US$50 billion) agreement with the ECB. Other sources of US dollar funding, obtained through US bank branches and in international capital and credit markets, can be deployed outside the US, but these are mostly wholesale, short term and, consequently, more volatile, and they face sizable refinancing risk, especially in stressful times.

This key role played by the US dollar in cross-border capital markets underscores the importance and power of the US Federal Reserve, but the 2007–2008 GFC also warns that the US authorities do not always exercise full control. Put another way, the monetary base of the US dollar monetary system has, at times, outgrown the Federal Reserve's balance sheet. This *shadow* monetary system, with its focus on collateral and cross-border pools of offshore currency, such as Eurodollars, remains an increasingly important source of global liquidity, but it has often stood outside official control. Essentially, there exists an equivalent *shadow monetary base* that comprises 'safe' (or leverage-able) assets, that is assets that enjoy low 'haircuts' and have high rates of re-hypothecation, such as high-quality public and private sector debts and offshore pools of cash. In the wake of the 2007–2008 GFC, the World's monetary authorities have consequently sought to tighten regulations on bank capital and liquidity requirements, as well as widening the reach of their liquidity operations into these darker shadows.

Global Value Chains

Around 35% of World trade is financed by banks. In turn, some 80% of total bank originated trade financing is US dollar denominated, reflecting the prevalence of dollar invoicing. Given the widespread use of US dollar credit in supporting international trade, factors that influence credit conditions and the supply of dollar lending by banks play a key role in supporting supply chain[6] activity. Figure 8.3 highlights the recent concentration and centralisation of trade and capital around Chinese-led supply chains and logistic businesses. Building and sustaining these supply chains are highly finance-intensive activities that make heavy demands both on the working capital resources of firms and on supplies of short-term bank credit. Global value chains (GVCs) incur large financing requirements because the underlying businesses need to carry sizeable inventories of intermediate goods and maintain 'accounts receivable' on their balance sheets when selling to other firms along the supply chain. Both have to be financed somehow. As supply chains grow longer and the time period between shipments becomes more extended, the marginal financing needs grow at an ever-increasing rate, so that far-reaching GVCs are only viable if they can access highly elastic funding sources. Among the many indicators of the availability of dollar-denominated bank credit, the US dollar exchange rate plays a particularly important role as a barometer of the dollar credit conditions faced by firms. Lending in dollars tends to grow faster when the US dollar is weak, and lending in

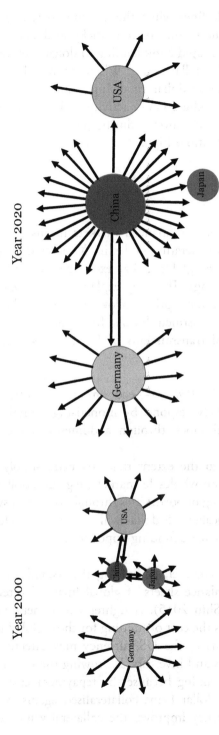

Fig. 8.3 The changing network structure of global supply chains, 2000 and 2020 (Adapted from *Global Value Chain Development Report 2019*, World Trade Organization)

dollars is subdued or declines when the US unit is strong. Invoicing can also affect trade when the invoice price is sticky in dollar terms. There is a striking contrast between rapid bank lending in dollars before the GFC, and subdued bank lending in dollars since. When combined with the fact that supply chain activity tracks dollar financing conditions, a stronger dollar is also associated with subdued GVC activity and, therefore, a lower ratio between trade and GDP. In contrast, during periods when the US dollar is weak, the trade-to-GDP ratio is high.

The Dollar Cycle

Its dominance of cross-border financial markets means that the US dollar plays the central role in generating cycles in World trade and international finance, with a weak (strong) US dollar exchange rate acting much like a monetary easing (tightening). This may explain why the pass-through from US dollar-denominated import prices following currency shocks tends to be high, so channelling the adjustment burden from imports through to exports.

Cross-border financial transmissions of US dollar shocks involve three main factors:

1. *Emerging Market Policy Response*—economies that target the US dollar exchange rate will likely respond by monetising capital inflows and so amplifying the initial shock through a domestic monetary expansion. Similarly, vice versa.
2. *Offshore Borrowing*—to the extent that any extra supply of US dollars is deposited in offshore wholesale markets, e.g. Eurodollar markets, this should improve funding opportunities through loans and swaps
3. *Collateral Effect*—a weaker US dollar will improve the value of local currency collateral and increase funding opportunities.

An international credit channel, embracing the second and third factors, operates through the balance sheets of global financial intermediaries (see Rey 2013; Bruno and Shin 2015). A tighter US monetary policy reduces the availability and raises the cost of funding for those global banks that lend cross-border. Fluctuations in the US currency may directly affect the risk appetites of both lenders and investors. Borrowing the US currency is more attractive when it is devaluing because the repayment cost falls. Similarly, when lenders offer US dollar loans collateralised against a local currency asset, a weaker US currency improves the collateral value. This also works in reverse, so that a strong US unit decreases the dollar value of the borrower's local currency-denominated risky assets, thereby reducing collateral and causing adverse balance sheet effects. As a result, the international economy can suffer weaker credit growth and possibly recession. It follows that the cycles in World trade and global finance are in large part dollar cycles. Yet, it is also true that the US currency is affected by third-party effects, so as Global Liquidity grows so the demand for US dollar safe assets is satisfied by other units, and hence the US unit can weaken independent of movements in the amount of liquidity supplied by the US Federal Reserve.

A second key feature of this US dollar-led, global financial system is the frequent large-sized capital shifts between the US dollar 'core' and economies on the periphery. Admittedly, the economies that define this periphery have changed almost completely since the end of Bretton Woods: In the 1970s and 1980s, this fringe was dominated by the other advanced G7 economies, such as the UK, Germany and Japan, but from the early 1990s onwards, the periphery has been increasingly populated by Emerging Market economies, and, to the extent that it is still viewed as outside the core, most notably by China. China adopted the US currency as a benchmark in 1994, making the Yuan convertible in current account transactions from 1996. Although she is lately viewed as a competitive threat to the US, ironically, China's demand helps to sustain the US dollar system. China not only invoices most of her trade in the US unit, but she has lately been a large investor in US government debt securities and a sizeable borrower of the US currency, as well as delivering her own timely fiscal and monetary policy boosts to support the dollar-oriented World trading system.

The US authorities have long seen international monetary tensions and imbalances as being caused by foreigners' inappropriate exchange rate policies. Consequently, US policy-makers often seek to put pressure on creditor economies, such as Germany, Japan and (now) China, to revalue their currencies upwards, rather than tackle America's own domestic savings imbalance directly. The counterparts to a US current account deficit should be correctly seen as a domestic savings shortage and a capital account surplus, rather than a lack of trade competitiveness per se. Contrary to some views, the US is not required to run a permanent current account deficit in order to supply the World with more US currency, because she only need accumulate long-term international assets against these short-term dollar claims, or, in practice, to act much as she does now. Notwithstanding, US ire focuses on trade relations and 'Japan-bashing' and, more recently, 'China-bashing', to force these competitors to allow their currency units to appreciate in value and to open up their markets to American business, e.g. the Super

301 trade initiative aimed at Japan in the late 1980s and the latest rounds of US-China trade talks. Through the 1970s and 1980s, Germany and Japan were the main creditor economies. The initial break-up of Bretton Woods saw the Deutschmark revalued. Arguably, this also spurred the creation of the Euro, which by spreading the burden of currency appreciation over other European economies, cushioned the negative shock to German competitiveness. Later in the decade, US officials used so-called 'open mouth operations' to talk-down the US dollar against the Japanese Yen, while the forceful 1985 Plaza Accord proved successful in getting the Yen to be revalued higher.

Gross Capital Flows

The US dollar's importance in the pricing of both World trade and World capital means that US dollar shocks are quickly propagated internationally. Many Emerging Market economies, most notably China, either fix to or at least shadow the US dollar exchange rate, so that US monetary expansions and contractions are often amplified by these economies. Dollar-based carry trades—buying currencies with high-interest rates and selling low-interest-rate currencies—can further reinforce the procyclical effects of Global Liquidity through cross-border capital flows. These cross-border flows are themselves a key component of our estimates of Global Liquidity, and, for many economies, they have outsized effects on the domestic liquidity totals. Through deliberate exchange rate targeting policies or simply because their domestic financial markets are too thinly traded, many Emerging Market economies are forced to passively respond to the rapid ebb and flow of global capital, so leading to exaggerated swings in domestic liquidity and to frequent financial crises. But the larger, developed economies are not immune. A major symptom, suffered particularly by European banks during the 2000s, has been the divergence between their sluggish domestic deposit growth and their more rapid credit growth. This financing gap forced banks to raise funds through short-term borrowings on international interbank and money markets and by issuing bonds. These shifts in bank funding patterns across Europe and the associated growth in cross-border bank-related financial flows highlight a systematic relationship between international capital flows and domestic credit growth.

We earlier evidenced how broader cross-border activities and capital flows are tied together by a 'global factor' operating through liquidity conditions and risk appetite. When major Central Banks, such as the US

Federal Reserve and the Chinese People's Bank (PBoC), tighten monetary policy, not only do their domestic output, capital spending, consumer confidence, real estate markets and inflation all shrink, but there are significant second-round effects on global financial markets. For example, sensitive international asset prices plunge, risk spreads widen, cross-border capital flows skid lower and leverage shrinks in both offshore wholesale lending markets and eventually across global banks. These effects can be spread further by global banks borrowing from offshore wholesale markets, in, say, London and New York, and lending on to local and regional banks in the Emerging Markets. Their loans are likely to be secured against, probably, local currency-denominated collateral. Plainly, when borrowings are denominated in US dollars, the potential currency mismatch can heighten risks. On the other hand, it can also mean that the US dollar weakness may boost the credit-worthiness of local borrowers and so encourage further leverage. Rey (2015) terms this a *Global Financial Cycle* that drives coordinated fluctuations in the pace of international financial activity. *"[The] Global Financial Cycle can be associated with surges and dry outs in capital flows, booms and busts in asset prices and crises … The empirical results on capital flows, leverage and credit growth are suggestive of an international credit channel or risk-taking channel and point towards financial stability issues"*.[7]

Ironically, the growing World monetary tensions ahead of the GFC were missed by the policy-makers, possibly because international economic analysis focusses too much on the size of current account imbalances and by implication on the size of their counterparts, net capital flows, rather than drilling deeper into the richer data that comprise the overall foreign balance sheet. We draw up a notional foreign balance sheet in Fig. 8.4. Capital flows are conventionally split between private sector and official flows, with private sector flows further broken down into (1) foreign direct investments (FDI), (2) portfolio investments involving the buying and selling of stocks and bonds and (3) flows of bank lending and bank deposits. They cover activity by both domestic residents and foreign nationals. Differences between total inflows and total outflows are financed by changes in a country's holdings of foreign exchange reserves, i.e. official flows. It is also important to carefully distinguish what exactly is meant by 'gross' because the items that are included depend crucially on the level of aggregation. For example, a domestic investment fund resident in the US may buy US$100 million of UK equities and sell US$80 million of German equities, thereby adding an incremental US$20 million to US foreign assets. This latter figure is what we take as the gross (asset) flow,[8] but it plainly disguises the US$180 million of international equity transactions that were undertaken. At a

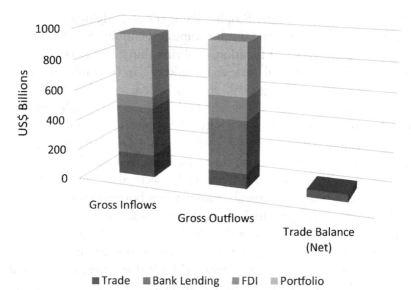

Fig. 8.4   Notional gross foreign sector balance sheet (illustrative)

higher level of aggregation, we may also find that because foreigners simultaneously added US$150 million to their US assets, so raising America's foreign liabilities equivalently, the net US international investment position deteriorated by a net outflow of US$130 million (i.e. $-130 = 20 - 150$).

The chart tries to show that these often-hidden private sector financial flows are both active and frequently dwarf in size, as well as in volatility, parallel movements in trade flows. An increase in foreign assets describes, say, US purchases of European and Asian securities, or international lending by US banks. Similarly, a rise in foreign liabilities represents, for example, German or Japanese purchases of US stocks and bonds, and real investments by non-residents in the US economy. These movements in asset and liability flows may roughly offset one another so that net capital flows become small and insignificant, but gross asset and liability flows could still be large. Moreover, distinguishing gross flows by type identifies risk-seeking, entrepreneurial and more technology-embedded capital flows, compared to the risk-averse capital in search of safety. The former classes are more likely to promote faster economic growth. In other words, simply netting out capital flows, as implicitly happens when discussing trade and current account imbalances, loses a significant amount of information. What's more, these capital flows may actively drive the current account, rather than passively accommodating it. For example, a large expansion in local currency bank lending to foreigners may ultimately result in faster domestic export growth. Similarly, an increase in outward FDI could itself lead to a step-up in export activity, assuming that the capital equipment is domestically manufactured. Another example, could involve a simple carry trade where an increase in foreign portfolio investment in, say, high-yielding Emerging Market debt, is financed through greater US dollar borrowing. A still more convoluted example might involve external US dollar funding of local banks. These banks could take on the currency risk and use these assets to increase their local currency lending, which, in turn, dissipates through outward portfolio flows or faster import growth.

Although all this would seem to show that the financial sector can actively initiate monetary shocks through the capital account, according to the traditional view, financial flows are no more than the accounting counterparts to savings and investment decisions. The current account position supposedly measures the borrowing needs of the national economy, with exchange rates then acting as automatic stabilisers that steer changes in exports and imports sufficient to eliminate external imbalances. When a country experiences an appreciation of its currency, this is predicted to cause a net export contraction. Experience, in fact, shows the opposite, since rising exchange rates often run in parallel with strong capital inflows and accelerating economic activity. For example, in the mid-2000s, the US current account deficit widened to historical highs and, contrary to many expert predictions, the US dollar soared in value. Notwithstanding, several economists still single out large current account imbalances as the key factor contributing to the 2007–2008 GFC. Current account surpluses in several Asian Emerging Market economies are said to have fuelled the credit booms and heightened risk-taking in the Western deficit countries that were at the core of the GFC, both by pushing down World interest rates and by directly financing the booms. Former US Federal Reserve Chairman Ben Bernanke (2005) famously dubbed this phenomenon the *Global Savings Glut*.[9] However, our previous discussion challenges these views, because: (1) any country's cross-border financing activity cannot be inferred from net capital flows, as opposed to gross flows; (2) what defines the 'border' that separates the residence of investors from the beneficial ownership of assets is critical, and (3) market interest rates are determined in broader credit markets and not simply by net savings. Thus, it seems more likely that the GFC and the Asian Crisis that preceded it were casualties of both the excessive elasticity of the international monetary and financial system and the depth offered by Western asset markets (e.g. New York and London), rather than by the high savings rates of Asian households.

In practice, capital inflows and outflows show high correlations and have consequently grown faster in gross than in net terms. Although economics, per se, has little to say about gross flows, the greater globalisation and deeper integration of trade may explain the relative sluggishness of net flows. An alternative reason might come from a drop in the size of relative investment returns between countries, but lower relative returns would also likely mean a negative not positive correlation between inflows and outflows. Consequently, the high correlation in the gross flow data is more likely explained by common risk factors, such as a Global Liquidity shock. This could, for example, involve a widespread jump in bank borrowing in US dollars, as domestic banks tap abundant offshore wholesale markets. Figure 8.5 shows a long-term perspective of gross flows for the overall World Economy starting from 1990. The anomalous surge in cross-border activity to 19.1% of World GDP in 2006, rising to a peak of 22.3% just ahead of the GFC can be seen clearly from the chart. This should have been a stark warning to policy-makers. By 2018 the pace of global flows had slid back to 6.6% of World GDP, or roughly around its late 1990s clip.

In practice, gross capital flows command an even larger fraction of activity between the major advanced economies than for the Emerging Market economies. These developed economies are consequently classified as being more *integrated* into global financial markets. Figure 8.6 shows gross and net capital flows for the aggregate of six major international investors—the US, China, Japan, the UK, Germany and France—measured relative to their overall GDP. The gross flow data parallels the widespread international balance sheet expansion in the years prior to the 2007–2008 GFC, which we

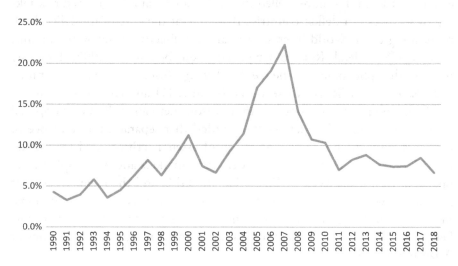

Fig. 8.5 World gross capital flows (% World GDP), 1990–2018 (*Source* IMF)

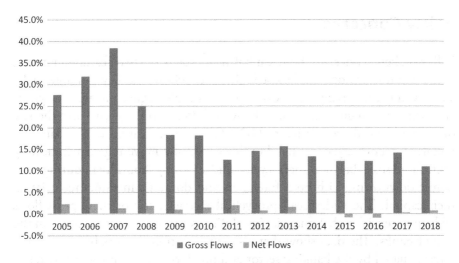

Fig. 8.6 Gross and net flows of international capital—six major economies, 2005–2018 (percent of GDP) (*Source* IMF)

previously reported for the US in Fig. 8.1. Gross flows peaked at nearly 40% of these countries' overall GDP in 2007 just ahead of the crisis, before skidding to barely 10% of GDP in 2018. Throughout these years, net capital flows never rose above low single-digit percentages and consequently failed to flash any early warnings about the magnitude of the approaching GFC. More comprehensive research conducted by the IMF shows that gross capital inflows into the Advanced Economies reached a peak of around 26% of GDP in 2007, while gross outflows hit 25% of GDP (a combined 51% of GDP). At the same time, gross outflows from Emerging Market economies touched 6% of their collective GDP, or well below the near-11% peak reading for gross inflows (a joint total of 17% of GDP).

For completeness, we must also consider foreign remittances, which are strictly classified as transfers of income. More than three-quarters of total cross-border remittances flow from the rich advanced and Middle Eastern economies to the Emerging Market economies. These payments prove more stable than conventional capital flows because they cannot be suddenly withdrawn. The World Bank officially estimates that annual remittance flows to low- and middle-income countries rose to a record high of US$529 billion in 2018, an increase of nearly 10% over the 2017 total, and larger than their inward FDI. Global remittances, which include flows to high-income countries, reached US$689 billion in 2018, up from US$633 billion in 2017. Among countries, the top remittance recipients were India with US$79 billion, followed by China (US$67 billion), Mexico (US$36 billion), the Philippines (US$34 billion) and Egypt (US$29 billion).

Policy Concerns

Policy-makers' concerns about capital flows focus on two features. First, as Fig. 8.7 confirms flows tend to be highly procyclical and they can potentially amplify the underlying business cycle. A simple regression analysis yields an elasticity as high as 2½ times between World GDP growth and the size of gross capital flows relative to GDP. Closer examination of the data also reveals that both asset and liability flows typically move together indicating both large-scale balance sheet cycles and a strong home bias during economic downturns, with both foreigners and domestic investors repatriating their capital. The widespread procyclical characteristic of these gross flows adds to potential global financial instability. A second concern centres on the role of banks. The data show that a sizeable portion of cross-border flows is intermediated by the banking sector and much of this comprises short-term, wholesale funding, which is therefore liable to reverse quickly when financial conditions deteriorate. In other words, there are high risks of 'sudden stops'. Analysis of the past volatility of these gross flows confirms these fears: gross banking inflows and outflows into and out of both the Advanced and Emerging Market economies are consistently more volatile than either the equivalent FDI and portfolio flows. According to the ECB (2016), banking flows typically suffer more than twice the volatility of other broad flow types and in financial crises this has jumped to, at least, 4–5 times larger.

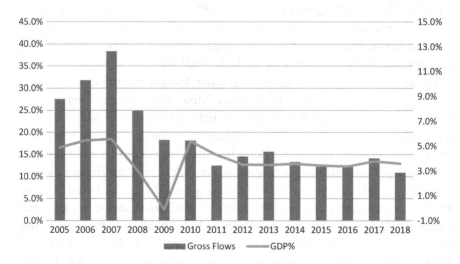

Fig. 8.7 Gross flows of international capital—six major economies and World real GDP growth, 2005–2018 (percent of GDP and annual % change) (*Source* IMF)

The economic cost and the threat to domestic banks of too rapid international financial integration are issues raised by Lane and Milesi-Ferretti (2008). For example, there is a strong positive relationship between the development of local financial systems and the scale of cross-border flows, which can adversely feedback on domestic credit growth. In traditional interpretations, current account imbalances influence real economy macro-variables which, in turn, disturb credit markets. Yet, as we have already noted, the current account when taken by itself is a misleading indicator, because a financial channel can still operate and affect credit markets even when the current account stands in balance. Shin (2012) emphasises the role of gross capital flows between Europe and the US in fuelling America's mid-2000s credit boom. Large gross cross-border financial flows changed the funding environment and the balance sheet structure of US domestic credit providers. This occurred even though the capital flows netted out to zero because European banks raised funding in the US to buy their US-based assets. Greater financial integration allows domestic banks to fund from foreign depositors, foreign interbank participants and offshore money markets, as well as through international bond issues. Inter-office funding provides a further channel, via domestically owned banks with overseas affiliates. Not surprisingly, Lane and McQuade (2013) find that, in practice, the data strongly suggest that domestic credit growth is very closely linked with net inflows of debt. The 2008–2011 Icelandic banking crisis provides a classic example of this.

As Fig. 8.6 suggests, the volume of gross flows serves as a valuable barometer of underlying lending standards. This means it can also be a useful cross-check on Global Liquidity. Looked at in this way, the huge US current account deficit, sustained over two decades, which persuaded many experts ahead of the GFC that the US dollar would slump, actually hid a massive build-up of short-term offshore gross US dollar borrowings by foreigners that required all too frequent refinancing. These were offset by foreign holdings of longer term US 'safe' assets, such as US Treasuries. Not surprisingly, the unfolding of the GFC was accompanied by a sharp US dollar appreciation, as those foreign financial institutions that had also used short-term dollar funding to invest in riskier long-term dollar assets were forced to hurriedly deleverage. European banks who were large players in the US MBS (mortgage-backed securities) market proved prominent casualties. Once the crisis broke, these financial institutions found themselves short of dollars and over-leveraged. A staggering US$8.0 trillion of the US$10.1 trillion cash offered by the US Fed through the swap lines, noted earlier, was taken up by the European Central Bank (ECB) alone. Thus, by attempting to reduce their US dollar liabilities, European investors further bid up the value of the dollar.

Global Financial Centres

Money centres, such as Venice, Amsterdam and Genoa, have long featured in World history as concentrations of footloose savings, often willing to finance speculative ventures. In the nineteenth century, London dominated. According to Walter Bagehot, editor of the *Economist* newspaper:

> Lombard Street ... is by far the greatest combination of economical power and economical delicacy that the world has even seen. Of the greatness of the power there will be no doubt. Money is economical power. Everyone is aware that England is the greatest moneyed country in the world; everyone admits that it has much more immediately disposable and ready cash than any other country. But very few persons are aware how much greater the ready balance — the floating loan-fund which can be lent to anyone or for any purpose — is in England than it is anywhere else in the world. A very few figures will show how large the London loan-fund is, and how much greater it is than any other. The known deposits—the deposits of banks which publish their accounts—are, in:
>
> London (31st December, 1872) £120,000,000
> Paris (27th February, 1873) £13,000,000
> New York (February, 1873) £40,000,000
> German Empire (31st January, 1873) £8,000,000
>
> And the unknown deposits—the deposits in banks which do not publish their accounts—are in London much greater than those many other of these cities. (Walter Bagehot, *Lombard Street*, 1873)

There is constant debate about whether cross-border flows are the result of 'pull' factors that draw capital into attractive foreign investments, or from 'push' factors that drive surplus capital out from the major financial centres. In truth, both apply, but from experience we find that push factors dominate both in terms of their magnitude and macro-finance policy implications. Changes in both underlying monetary policies and in the risk-seeking activities of investors trading from these centres can lead to large outflows of cross-border capital. Tax avoidance and lower reporting requirements admittedly help to explain the rise of some of the smaller offshore centres. According to Zucman[10] (2013), 8% of the global financial wealth of households is held offshore, of which at least 6%, or around US$4–5 trillion, is officially unrecorded, but domiciled in these centres.

There has always been a tradition of foreign investments seeking out these concentrated savings pools. For example, in the nineteenth century many foreign companies, such as American railroads and imperial plantations, listed their securities on the London Stock Exchange to be closer to this surplus capital. Table 8.1 shows the latest GFCI rankings of the World's major financial centres. Although this survey does not directly measure the size of these savings pools, it lists the key players. Few would dispute the dominant positions of New York and London; Frankfurt appears lower in the table than it probably deserves given the capital it controls; Boston with her insurers and investment managers and Chicago with her futures pits both still rank highly. The final column of Table 8.1 shows the change from ten years ago. There have been only minor changes at the top of the table, but the standout fact is the huge jumps seen in the ranking of the Chinese money centres, notably Shanghai and Beijing, which together with Shenzhen, as well as Hong Kong, highlight the growing sway of Chinese money. Pacific Asia's importance is underlined by the growing status once again of Tokyo, and the rise of Dubai, Sydney, Melbourne, San Francisco, Los Angeles and Vancouver, all at the expense of East Coast and Mid-West American and European money centres.

Table 8.1 GFCI ranking of global financial centres, 2019 data (and change from 2009 survey)

	Ranking 2019	Ranking 2009	Change
New York	1	2	1
London	2	1	−1
Hong Kong	3	4	1
Singapore	4	3	−1
Shanghai	5	35	30
Tokyo	6	15	9
Toronto	7	11	4
Zurich	8	5	−3
Beijing	9	51	42
Frankfurt	10	8	−2
Sydney	11	16	5
Dubai	12	23	11
Boston	13	9	−4
Shenzhen	14	NA	NA
Melbourne	15	28	13
San Francisco	16	17	1
Los Angeles	17	NA	NA
Montreal	18	26	8
Vancouver	19	25	6
Chicago	20	7	−13

Source GFCI

The Offshore Swap and Eurodollar Markets

This dominant role played by the US unit in cross-border markets makes the value of the US dollar a useful gauge of global credit conditions. We noted that when an international currency depreciates, there is a tendency for foreigners to borrow more in that unit. This often motivates so-called, 'carry trades'. A substantial part of international banking flows is made up of carry trades, where borrowings in low-cost jurisdictions simultaneously fund investments in prospectively higher return markets. For example, investors may borrow in Yen and invest in US dollars, or equivalently borrow in US dollars and invest in higher yielding Emerging Market bonds. Cross-border borrowing often entails a currency mismatch, which can make flows sensitive to exchange rate movements and particularly to the US dollar, which is the main borrowed currency. When increased supplies of US dollars lead to a depreciation in its value, this can spur additional demand from international borrowers who are incentivised to bias their capital issuance towards dollar-denominated instruments. In addition, global banks are able to provide hedging services more cheaply because cross-border US dollar credit is abundant, but as the US dollar strengthens, they find it harder to rollover these credits. Not surprisingly, periods of heightened currency volatility are typically associated with sharp contractions in cross-border activity. In fact, over the 2002–2008 period ahead of the GFC, the US dollar fell by around one-third in value and cross-border banking flows correspondingly soared in size: in 2002, flows from the US to Europe (i.e. banks resident in the US with claims on borrowers in Europe) totalled US$462 billion. This figure jumped to US$1.54 trillion in 2007, while, according to the BIS, the return leg from Europe to the US leapt from US$856 billion in 2002 to over US$2 trillion in 2007.

A large pool of 'offshore' Eurodollars traditionally provides an important source of short-term funding for many US-based banks. See Fig. 8.8 Eurodollars are a generic term for unsecured foreign currency deposits, not exclusively US dollars, that are held at banks outside of the currencies' legal jurisdiction, and probably housed in the global financial centres named in the preceding section. The US Federal Reserve has chosen since 1990 to impose a zero-reserve requirement on Eurodollar deposits, so effectively treating them as close substitutes for Fed Funds. In fact, the daily volume of Eurodollar funding is around 3–4 times larger than Fed Funds at around US$150 billion. Although these offshore deposits are now transacted in all major global financial centres, the Eurodollar market originally developed in post-WW2 Europe. It started in the 1960s following contemporary concerns among the

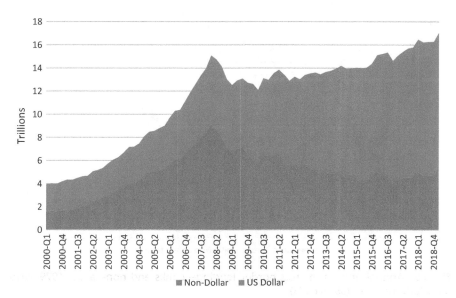

Fig. 8.8 Cross-border and foreign currency borrowing—banks and non-banks, 2000–2019 (quarterly, US$ in trillions) (*Source* BIS)

former Soviet Bloc countries about the potential safety of their US dollars held in the US. Since then, competition has attracted Middle-Eastern oil money to London, while more recently many US multinationals hold large offshore dollar deposits in these markets. Figure 8.9 highlights the annual growth in cross-border lending between banks. The underlying pace of this volatile series has plainly slowed since the GFC, mainly through a reduction in the balance sheet commitment of European banks,[11] following tighter regulation and reduced profitability, but also in the wake of US President Trump's recent tax amnesty and moves to separately regulate banks' subsidiaries.

Money market funds, other institutional investors, corporations and foreign central banks are all active lenders in the Eurodollar market. BIS data show that the stock of US dollar-denominated debt of non-banks operating outside the US currently stands at some US$17 trillion, so easily exceeding the volume of domestic US dollar lending by US banks, with interbank liabilities at a similar US$16.9 trillion. Admittedly, this overall pool of debt has flatlined since the GFC, although bonds have become more important within the total, rising from around 45% of total international credit to non-banks in 2000 to over 56% by 2018. The banking data includes both US banks and, for example, Chinese banks collecting US dollar deposits in London. These pools are large, counted in several trillions of dollars, and

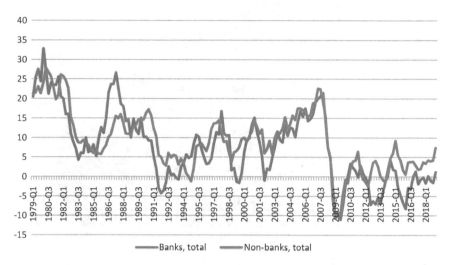

Fig. 8.9 Annual growth in cross-border lending—banks and non-banks, 1979–2019 (quarterly, percent) (*Source* BIS)

tend to be ready sources of wholesale funding. Consequently, they have provided an extra means of leveraging and, hence, amplifying the cycle of Global Liquidity. Although history shows substantial co-movement in international lending to banks and non-banks, the stock of cross-border and foreign currency borrowing by non-banks has lately grown faster according to Fig. 8.10. It now exceeds its previous 2008 peak of US$15 trillion, with US dollar-denominated debts touching nearly 70% of the total.

Cross-border liquidity can also be created through certain derivative transactions when they involve new credits, such as currency swaps. These transactions, which are growing in popularity, even among the Central Banks, occur when two parties exchange funds denominated in different currencies, agreeing to later reverse the trade, possibly as long as some years later. In contrast to carry trades, which involve forex risk, currency swaps entail interest rate risk. With local interest rates across many economies currently low or negative, domestic investors have been keen to purchase higher yielding foreign securities. However, the costs of buying, say, 10-year US Treasuries, fully hedged against currency movements, can substantially erode the already meagre returns on local currency bonds. In a swap deal, each asset earns a period return from money-market interest rates in the currency the investors hold and the sellers pay interest on the currency position they have sold. A swap's so-called *basis* is a shorthand measure for the degree of deviation from covered interest rate parity (CIP[12]). The basis is defined as the difference between the cost of borrowing directly in, say, US dollars and

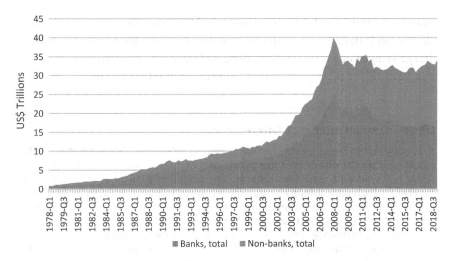

Fig. 8.10 Non-bank cross-border and foreign currency borrowing by currency denomination, 1978–2019 (quarterly, US$ in trillions) (*Source* BIS)

the 'synthetic' cost from borrowing in a foreign currency and then swapping the foreign currency back into US dollars. The US dollar is frequently the borrowed currency and the basis swap spread effectively measures how much more a bank has to pay to borrow US dollars by this roundabout route, rather than taking a straightforward US dollar loan priced at LIBOR.[13] In other words, the US Treasury basis measures the yield on an actual US Treasury note minus the yield on this equivalent synthetic US Treasury security constructed from a foreign bond of similar maturity.

The spread is a direct measure of the global scarcity of dollar safe assets. A positive (negative) basis means that the US dollar interest rate is higher (lower) than the foreign interest rate adjusted for the cost of the swap. A positive basis is often wrongly taken to indicate a US dollar 'shortage', but there is no shortage in reality. Rather, a positive basis signals an excess demand for dollars, and the 'price' i.e. the basis, adjusts to square the market. An average of the spread on the major G-10 currencies is an indicator of the scarcity cost of being without the US currency. CIP theory says that these various positions are entirely fungible and, hence, there should be no basis, but several times since the 2008 crisis we have seen strong counter-evidence of a positive basis. Although the persistence of a positive basis has raised doubts about market efficiency, the CIP assumption of risk-less arbitrage needs to be challenged because there is never complete fungibility. The tendency of textbooks to focus only on traditional banks needs to be corrected and broadened, while the motivations behind these cross-border transactions could be better understood. We have shown that traditional banks are no longer the only market participants and for many investors the arbitrage is neither risk-free, nor costless. Not every investor is able to borrow at LIBOR, or is prepared to take on the implied credit risk.

LIBOR—London Interbank Offered Rate

It is planned to cease quoting LIBOR (London Interbank Offered Rates), USD LIBOR, and similar interbank rates by the end of 2021. These rates are expected to be replaced with new benchmarks. The ubiquitous LIBOR is a widely-used family of benchmark interest rates that has been used for more than 30 years. Millions of contracts and financial instruments, estimated as of mid-2018 by the Bank for International Settlements to be about US$400 trillion, use some form of LIBOR as a reference rate. This includes both wholesale rates, such as floating rate notes (FRNs) and interest rate swaps, and even some residential mortgages. LIBOR's problems stem from the revelations that, at certain key times in the past, it was manipulated by certain market participants for their own gain, so tarnishing its reputation for fairness. On top, regulatory changes and banking reforms have also combined to reduce the size of the interbank lending market in recent years.

Working groups in several jurisdictions have already identified their preferred risk-free reference rate alternatives to LIBOR. Unlike LIBOR, these choices are based on actual transactions and cover institutions beyond banks. They are, however, backwards-looking and they may reference both secured or unsecured lending. In the UK the chosen rate is Sterling Overnight Index Average (SONIA), an unsecured overnight rate. In the US dollar markets, the new reference will be the Secured Overnight Financing Rate (SOFR). These are published, respectively, by the Bank of England and US Federal Reserve. The European Central Bank (ECB) recently announced ESTR as the successor to its LIBOR-like Euro overnight index average (EONIA). ESTR is a transactions-based unsecured overnight rate that reflects wholesale overnight funding costs of the Eurozone banks.

Dollar Risks—A New Triffin Dilemma?

The *Triffin Dilemma* essentially concerns whether the US can meet its foreign liabilities with net assets, be these existing investments or potential future cash flows. It was originally associated with: (1) the final days of the Bretton Woods fixed exchange rate regime in the late-1960s; (2) America's then rapidly deteriorating current account position and (3) her progressive loss of gold reserves. Yet, when looked at in broader terms, it has little to do with US current account deficits per se. The Triffin Dilemma is also neither specifically about a lack of gold-backing for the US dollar, nor about the dangers of excessive US monetary expansion. Rather, it highlights the threat of a potential loss of confidence in the value of dollars held internationally by foreign investors. The problem, consequently, remains relevant today even in an international monetary system that lacks a gold anchor. Gourinchas and Rey (2007) put this argument well:

> Triffin saw that in a world where the fluctuations in gold supply were dictated by the vagaries of discoveries in South Africa or the destabilizing schemes of Soviet Russia, but in any case unable to grow with world demand for liquidity, the demand for the dollar was bound to eventually exceed the gold reserves of the Federal Reserve. This left the door open for a run on the dollar. Interestingly, the current situation can be seen in a similar light: in a world where the US can supply the international currency at will, and invests it in illiquid assets, it still faces a confidence risk. There could be a run on the dollar not because investors would fear an abandonment of the gold parity, as in the seventies, but because they would fear a plunge in the dollar exchange rate. In other words, Triffin's analysis does not have to rely on the gold-dollar parity to be relevant.

Assuming that the demand for US dollar liquidity keeps growing, but the relative size of the US economy continues to shrink relative to the Rest of the World, a new run on the dollar into one or several alternative reserve currencies, such as the Euro, gold and ultimately the Chinese Yuan, remains possible. This could parallel the tumultuous and domino-like falls seen during Interwar years, when international capital first fled sterling in 1931, and, despite a lack of alternatives, then tried to flee from the US dollar in 1933. Notwithstanding, a break in confidence equivalent in scale to the end of Bretton Woods would probably require the US to renege on a large part of her foreign obligations. These are predominantly US dollar denominated and such a move would seem, for now, unlikely. In fact, more likely, is the opposite risk that a lack of sufficient international dollar liquidity and dollar-denominated securities could at the same time derail global financial markets. This means that the overall ability of the US to be both a global insurer and to act as a global liquidity provider crucially depends on the capacity of the economy to issue credible 'safe' assets. During recent times of global crisis, US Treasuries, and sometimes also German Bunds, have proved to be the only large-scale international assets able to provide an effective insurance. We know that the demand for 'safe' assets lowers domestic bond term premia. Gourinchas et al. (2019) estimate the resulting inflation-adjusted excess returns from America's FDI and foreign portfolio investments averages around 2% annually above the yield on US 'safe' assets. This premium potentially allows the US to run larger trade deficits. This so-called[14] 'exorbitant privilege' represents real economic power for America through *seigniorage*, namely the difference between the face value of its currency and the production (or printing) costs. International envy over American seigniorage still runs deep. It motivated Europe to create the Euro currency unit as a rival international monetary standard, and arguably now exercises China, whose officials are on record as wanting to displace the US dollar in Asia.[15] Yet, the US dollar may not be easily replaced. Take the British pound as a historical benchmark: the US economy overtook Britain in economic size in 1870, but it was not until 1955, nearly nine decades later, that the US dollar finally surpassed the pound sterling as the main international currency.

Warning Signs of Future Crises

In summary, the private sector is often responsible for cross-border spillovers of liquidity, because financial institutions frequently span different countries and operate across multiple currencies. Even though this globalisation of finance should, in theory, promote efficiency and faster growth, it comes at the cost of sometimes violent cycles of leveraging and de-leveraging. Rapidly moving cross-border flows are themselves affected by the availability and cost of US dollars, the main international funding currency. These liquidity shocks tend to be closely correlated and procyclical, and they are growing in size as World financial markets become both more innovative and more deeply integrated. What's more, they can travel across national borders even when net capital flows are themselves small because gross flows will still affect the overall balance sheet size of the financial sector. Consequently, we need to look beyond economists' traditional obsession with national current account (or net) imbalances by focusing in more detail on these gross flows, and by distinguishing between the national and residential decision-making better understand currency exposures and risks.

The data reported in Tables 8.2 8.3, 8.4, 8.5, 8.6, and 8.7 evidence these challenges in the detailed international accounts and foreign balance sheets of the US, China, Japan, Germany, the UK and France. Taken overall, 76.4% of America's foreign asset stock is covered by liabilities of US debt and short-term credits, whereas equivalent holdings of foreign debt and credits by US residents only comprise 44.6% of foreign assets. This confirms the implicit leverage in the US international balance sheet and its

Table 8.2 United States—international investment position, 2005–18 (US$ in millions)

	2005	2006	2007	2008	2009	2010	2011	2012	2013	2014	2015	2016	2017	2018	Average	Percent (%)	Stdev (%)
Assets	13,357.0	16,409.9	20,704.5	19,423.4	19,426.5	21,767.8	22,208.9	22,562.2	24,144.8	24,882.9	23,430.6	24,060.6	27,799.1	25,398.6	21,826.9	100.0	17.3
FDI	4047.2	4929.9	5857.9	3707.2	4945.3	5486.4	5214.8	5969.5	7120.7	7242.1	7057.1	7421.9	8910.0	7528.4	6102.7	28.0	24.4
Portfolio	4629.0	6017.1	7262.0	4320.8	6058.6	7160.4	6871.7	7984.0	9206.1	9704.2	9570.2	10,011.4	12,543.8	11,281.1	8044.3	36.9	30.3
Equity	3317.7	4329.0	5248.0	2748.4	3995.3	4900.2	4501.4	5321.9	6472.9	6770.6	6756.2	7146.3	9129.5	7826.2	5604.5	25.7	32.3
Debt	1311.3	1688.1	2014.1	1572.4	2063.3	2260.1	2370.3	2662.1	2733.2	2933.6	2814.0	2865.0	3414.4	3454.9	2439.8	11.2	27.0
Other	4492.8	5243.0	7307.3	11,101.7	8018.8	8632.4	9585.3	8036.3	7369.6	7502.3	6419.7	6220.1	5895.5	6140.0	7283.2	33.4	24.1
Gold & forex. reserves	188.0	219.9	277.2	293.7	403.8	488.7	537.0	572.4	448.3	434.3	383.6	407.2	449.7	449.1	396.6	1.8	28.7
Liabilities	15,214.9	18,218.3	21,984.0	23,418.7	22,054.1	24,279.6	26,664.3	27,080.2	29,513.4	31,828.3	30,892.2	32,242.2	35,524.1	35,115.7	26,716.4	122.4	23.1
FDI	3227.1	3752.6	4134.2	3091.2	3618.6	4099.1	4199.2	4662.4	5814.9	6378.9	6729.2	7596.1	8925.5	8518.4	5339.1	24.5	37.1
Portfolio	7337.8	8843.5	10,327.0	9475.9	10,463.2	11,869.3	12,647.2	13,978.4	15,541.3	16,921.8	16,645.8	17,360.0	19,482.2	18,738.1	13,545.1	62.1	29.1
Equity	2304.0	2791.9	3231.7	2132.4	2917.7	3545.8	3841.9	4545.4	5864.6	6642.5	6209.1	6570.2	7951.9	7453.7	4714.5	21.6	42.6
Debt	5033.8	6051.6	7095.3	7343.4	7545.6	8323.5	8805.3	9433.5	9676.7	10,279.3	10,436.8	10,789.8	11,530.3	11,284.4	8830.7	40.5	22.7
Other	4649.9	5622.2	7522.8	10,851.6	7972.2	8311.3	9817.8	8438.9	8157.2	8527.6	7517.2	7286.1	7116.4	7859.3	7832.2	35.9	19.5
Net assets	−1857.9	−1808.5	−1279.5	−3995.3	−2627.6	−2511.8	−4455.4	−4518.0	−5368.6	−6945.4	−7461.6	−8181.6	−7725.0	−9717.1	−4889.5	−22.4	−55.8
FDI	820.0	1177.3	1723.7	616.0	1326.7	1387.3	1015.6	1307.1	1305.8	863.2	327.9	−174.3	−15.5	−990.0	763.6	3.5	97.7
Portfolio	−2708.9	−2826.4	−3064.9	−5155.1	−4404.7	−4708.9	−5775.5	−5994.9	−6335.1	−7217.5	−7075.7	−7348.6	−6938.4	−7457.0	−5500.8	−25.2	−31.3
Equity	1013.7	1537.1	2016.3	616.0	1077.6	1354.5	659.5	776.5	608.3	128.1	547.1	576.1	1177.6	372.5	890.1	4.1	56.8
Debt	−3722.5	−4363.5	−5081.3	−5771.0	−5482.3	−6063.4	−6435.0	−6771.4	−6943.4	−7345.7	−7622.7	−7924.7	−8116.0	−7829.5	−6390.9	−29.3	−21.5

Source IMF

Table 8.3 China—international investment position, 2005–18 (US$ in millions)

	2005	2006	2007	2008	2009	2010	2011	2012	2013	2014	2015	2016	2017	2018	Average	Percent (%)	Stdev (%)
Assets	1223.3	1690.4	2416.2	2956.7	3436.9	4118.9	4734.5	5213.2	5986.1	6438.3	6155.8	6507.0	7148.8	7324.2	4667.9	100.0	43.9
FDI	64.5	90.6	116.0	185.7	245.8	317.2	424.8	531.9	660.5	882.6	1095.9	1357.4	1809.0	1899.0	691.5	14.8	90.8
Portfolio	116.7	265.2	284.6	252.5	242.8	257.1	204.4	240.6	258.5	262.5	261.3	367.0	492.5	498.0	286.0	6.1	36.0
Equity	0.0	1.5	19.6	21.4	54.6	63.0	86.4	129.8	153.0	161.3	162.0	215.2	297.7	270.0	116.8	2.5	83.8
Debt	116.7	263.7	265.0	231.1	188.2	194.1	118.0	110.8	105.5	101.2	99.3	151.8	194.8	227.9	169.2	3.6	36.5
Other	216.4	253.9	468.3	552.3	495.2	630.4	849.5	1052.7	1186.7	1393.8	1392.5	1684.8	1611.4	1759.2	967.7	20.7	56.0
Gold & forex reserves	825.7	1080.8	1547.3	1966.2	2453.2	2914.2	3255.8	3387.9	3880.4	3899.3	3406.1	3097.8	3235.9	3168.0	2722.8	58.3	36.6
Liabilities	872.0	1174.5	1474.5	1567.0	2149.0	2640.6	3208.9	3538.3	4177.0	4835.6	4483.0	4556.7	5048.1	5194.1	3208.5	68.7	48.3
FDI	471.5	614.4	703.7	915.5	1314.8	1569.6	1906.9	2068.0	2331.2	2599.1	2696.3	2755.1	2725.7	2762.3	1816.7	38.9	48.1
Portfolio	132.6	244.6	392.7	271.5	381.7	433.6	411.3	527.6	573.4	796.2	817.0	811.1	1099.4	1096.4	570.7	12.2	53.8
Equity	119.6	230.4	375.1	254.3	366.4	415.9	374.3	453.4	484.5	651.3	597.1	579.5	762.3	684.2	453.4	9.7	40.9
Debt	13.0	14.2	17.6	17.2	15.2	17.8	37.1	74.2	88.9	144.9	220.0	231.6	337.0	412.2	117.2	2.5	113.6
Other	267.8	315.5	378.1	380.0	452.6	637.3	890.7	942.6	1272.4	1440.2	969.6	990.5	1223.1	1335.4	821.1	17.6	50.2
Net assets	351.3	515.9	941.7	1389.7	1287.9	1478.3	1525.6	1674.9	1809.1	1602.7	1672.8	1950.4	2100.7	2130.1	1459.4	31.3	36.9
FDI	−407.1	−523.8	−587.7	−729.8	−1069.0	−1252.4	−1482.1	−1536.1	−1670.8	−1716.5	−1600.4	−1397.8	−916.6	−863.3	−1125.2	−24.1	−40.5
Portfolio	−15.9	20.6	−108.1	−19.0	−138.9	−176.5	−206.9	−287.0	−314.9	−533.7	−555.7	−444.1	−606.9	−598.4	−284.7	−6.1	−79.8
Equity	−119.6	−228.9	−355.4	−232.9	−311.9	−352.9	−287.8	−323.6	−331.5	−490.0	−435.1	−364.3	−464.7	−414.1	−336.6	−7.2	−29.7
Debt	103.8	249.5	247.3	213.9	173.0	176.4	80.9	36.5	16.6	−43.7	−120.6	−79.8	−142.2	−184.3	51.9	1.1	286.7

Source IMF

Table 8.4   Japan—international investment position, 2005–18 (US$ in millions)

	2005	2006	2007	2008	2009	2010	2011	2012	2013	2014	2015	2016	2017	2018	Average	Percent (%)	Stdev (%)
Assets	4294.9	4697.2	5360.1	5731.5	6041.7	6893.1	7502.6	7613.5	7575.3	7811.7	7883.1	8444.1	8967.4	9222.9	7002.8	100.0	22.1
FDI	390.6	454.8	547.5	690.8	753.2	846.2	972.3	1054.1	1133.0	1177.2	1260.2	1360.2	1547.4	1667.2	989.6	14.1	40.1
Portfolio	2114.9	2343.5	2523.6	2376.7	2845.9	3305.2	3379.3	3559.8	3430.7	3398.0	3513.0	3779.3	4104.7	4082.7	3196.9	45.7	20.3
Equity	408.6	510.4	573.5	394.7	594.0	678.5	665.8	687.2	1198.7	1190.1	1274.8	1405.9	1676.8	1655.3	922.5	13.2	49.7
Debt	1706.3	1833.1	1950.1	1982.0	2251.8	2626.7	2713.4	2872.6	2232.0	2207.9	2238.2	2373.4	2427.8	2427.3	2274.5	32.5	14.7
Other	946.4	1004.1	1321.7	1639.4	1388.8	1645.0	1857.7	1734.6	1743.6	1984.0	1877.2	2084.1	2054.1	2207.7	1677.7	24.0	23.2
Gold & forex reserves	843.0	894.8	967.4	1024.6	1053.9	1096.7	1293.4	1264.8	1268.0	1252.5	1232.8	1220.4	1261.3	1265.3	1138.5	16.3	13.7
Liabilities	2763.1	2889.0	3165.2	3242.1	3125.2	3751.3	4083.4	4155.2	4482.0	4799.3	5068.1	5564.9	6058.4	6120.8	4233.4	60.5	27.3
FDI	104.9	112.9	137.7	213.9	212.4	230.0	242.2	222.2	185.7	196.9	205.6	241.7	252.9	282.2	202.9	2.9	25.7
Portfolio	1542.4	1762.9	1942.9	1541.7	1537.0	1866.8	2026.3	2085.3	2393.2	2363.1	2660.1	2784.4	3345.3	3170.8	2215.9	31.6	26.8
Equity	1126.1	1255.0	1245.9	756.2	829.6	988.8	847.2	965.4	1446.6	1402.1	1551.2	1554.2	1947.2	1616.0	1252.2	17.9	28.1
Debt	416.4	507.9	697.0	785.5	707.4	878.0	1179.1	1120.1	946.7	961.0	1108.9	1230.2	1398.1	1554.7	963.6	13.8	33.9
Other	1115.8	1013.2	1084.6	1486.6	1375.8	1654.4	1814.9	1847.5	1903.1	2239.4	2202.4	2538.8	2460.1	2667.8	1814.6	25.9	30.6
Net assets	1531.8	1808.2	2194.9	2489.4	2916.5	3141.9	3419.2	3458.1	3093.3	3012.4	2815.0	2879.2	2909.1	3102.1	2769.4	39.5	20.6
FDI	285.7	341.9	409.8	477.0	540.8	616.2	730.1	831.9	947.3	980.3	1054.6	1118.6	1294.5	1385.0	786.7	11.2	45.2
Portfolio	572.5	580.6	580.7	835.0	1308.9	1438.4	1353.0	1474.2	1037.5	1035.0	852.9	994.9	759.3	911.9	981.0	14.0	32.0
Equity	-717.5	-744.5	-672.4	-361.5	-235.6	-310.3	-181.3	-278.2	-247.9	-211.9	-276.4	-148.3	-270.4	39.3	-329.8	-4.7	-68.9
Debt	1290.0	1325.1	1253.1	1196.5	1544.4	1748.7	1534.3	1752.5	1285.3	1246.9	1129.3	1143.2	1029.7	872.6	1310.8	18.7	19.5

Source IMF

Table 8.5 Germany—international investment position, 2005–18 (US$ in millions)

	2005	2006	2007	2008	2009	2010	2011	2012	2013	2014	2015	2016	2017	2018	Average	Percent (%)	Stdev (%)
Assets	5015.5	6245.7	7676.3	7096.3	7554.1	8739.3	8862.4	9633.5	9581.7	9303.1	8593.4	8709.0	10,035.3	9804.9	8346.5	100.0	17.5
FDI	996.7	1236.0	1545.3	1459.6	1605.3	1634.9	1696.2	1928.8	2092.6	1995.9	1958.4	1973.8	2328.5	2385.6	1774.1	21.3	22.3
Portfolio	1817.9	2266.4	2624.8	2149.2	2507.9	2555.7	2380.4	2760.1	3083.6	3075.7	2905.6	2976.8	3519.0	3298.6	2708.7	32.5	17.4
Equity	771.4	884.2	954.0	589.5	707.1	739.7	647.2	747.4	919.6	939.8	952.0	1009.0	1287.3	1145.7	878.1	10.5	22.0
Debt	1046.5	1382.1	1670.8	1559.6	1800.8	1816.0	1733.2	2012.7	2164.0	2136.0	1953.6	1967.7	2231.6	2152.9	1830.5	21.9	18.3
Other	2099.2	2631.8	3370.0	3349.5	3260.1	4332.2	4547.1	4695.6	4207.3	4038.6	3555.8	3573.2	3987.7	3922.5	3683.6	44.1	19.6
Gold & forex reserves	101.7	111.6	136.2	138.0	180.8	216.5	238.9	248.9	198.2	192.8	173.7	185.3	200.1	198.2	180.1	2.2	24.5
Liabilities	4654.8	5624.5	6983.1	6449.5	6669.1	7855.2	8051.0	8594.8	8237.5	7853.7	7054.6	7016.7	7896.8	7456.5	7171.3	85.9	15.0
FDI	813.2	1029.9	1246.9	1137.2	1212.4	1210.5	1252.0	1448.0	1599.4	1469.3	1391.4	1404.6	1665.0	1691.1	1326.5	15.9	18.6
Portfolio	2114.0	2508.0	3259.0	2839.7	3042.7	3015.5	3044.9	3359.4	3398.5	3210.3	2867.0	2751.1	3058.6	2682.8	2939.4	35.2	11.9
Equity	445.2	622.9	908.9	472.3	647.3	667.6	565.8	701.6	862.3	761.3	732.0	720.9	889.3	694.2	692.3	8.3	20.2
Debt	1668.9	1885.1	2350.0	2367.5	2395.4	2347.9	2479.1	2657.8	2536.2	2449.0	2134.9	2030.2	2169.3	1988.6	2247.1	26.9	12.4
Other	1727.6	2086.6	2477.2	2472.5	2414.1	3629.1	3754.1	3787.5	3239.6	3174.1	2796.2	2861.0	3173.2	3082.6	2905.4	34.8	21.3
Net assets	360.7	621.3	693.2	646.8	885.0	884.2	811.4	1038.7	1344.3	1449.3	1538.9	1692.3	2138.5	2348.4	1175.2	14.1	50.7
FDI	183.6	206.1	298.3	322.4	392.9	424.4	444.2	480.9	493.3	526.6	566.9	569.2	663.6	694.6	447.6	5.4	34.8
Portfolio	−296.1	−241.6	−634.2	−690.6	−534.8	−459.9	−664.6	−599.2	−314.8	−134.6	38.7	225.6	460.3	615.8	−230.7	−2.8	−183.9
Equity	326.2	261.4	45.1	117.2	59.8	72.1	81.4	45.9	57.4	178.5	220.0	288.1	398.0	451.4	185.9	2.2	75.0
Debt	−622.3	−503.0	−679.3	−807.8	−594.6	−531.9	−745.9	−645.1	−372.2	−313.0	−181.3	−62.5	62.3	164.4	−416.6	−5.0	−74.1

Source IMF

Table 8.6 United Kingdom—international investment position, 2005–18 (US$ in millions)

	2005	2006	2007	2008	2009	2010	2011	2012	2013	2014	2015	2016	2017	2018	Average	Percent (%)	Stdev (%)
Assets	10,341.9	12,892.6	16,521.0	16,790.1	14,393.7	15,954.7	17,097.1	16,477.4	15,875.2	15,941.5	14,256.4	13,490.3	14,499.7	14,218.4	14,910.7	100.0	12.4
FDI	1642.7	1947.8	2301.1	2097.2	2043.7	2102.4	2108.1	2227.4	2367.2	2165.8	2080.2	1925.4	2127.6	2128.5	2090.4	14.0	8.4
Portfolio	2434.6	3318.8	3803.3	2463.8	2943.4	3025.0	2801.9	3173.9	3389.9	3469.5	3312.3	3026.0	3653.8	3411.8	3159.2	21.2	12.8
Equity	1247.2	1653.4	1871.6	1041.3	1380.3	1499.0	1344.5	1628.1	1899.4	1949.4	1878.9	1805.0	2341.2	2109.3	1689.2	11.3	21.2
Debt	1187.4	1665.5	1931.7	1422.6	1563.2	1526.0	1457.4	1545.9	1490.5	1520.1	1433.5	1221.0	1312.6	1302.5	1470.0	9.9	12.9
Other	6221.4	7581.0	10,363.2	12,176.2	9341.6	10,749.7	12,099.3	10,978.1	10,016.9	10,200.5	8734.4	8404.4	8567.4	8523.3	9568.4	64.2	17.7
Gold & forex reserves	43.2	45.0	53.5	52.9	65.0	77.6	87.8	98.0	101.2	105.6	129.5	134.6	150.8	154.8	92.8	0.6	41.7
Liabilities	10,397.5	13,118.9	16,762.9	16,566.5	14,785.3	16,144.6	17,385.4	17,237.8	16,398.0	16,577.0	14,821.2	13,549.3	14,736.2	14,543.7	15,216.0	102.0	12.7
FDI	1191.6	1520.1	1578.9	1376.7	1427.1	1484.4	1537.0	1973.9	2083.7	2066.1	2005.4	1908.9	2112.7	2220.5	1749.1	11.7	19.1
Portfolio	2568.5	3410.1	4030.1	2953.7	3912.8	3987.4	4034.1	4352.7	4513.0	4495.2	4374.0	3818.0	4533.0	4475.6	3961.3	26.6	15.3
Equity	1107.8	1495.3	1634.3	841.8	1305.8	1413.6	1376.3	1666.8	1969.9	1909.2	1844.9	1548.5	1990.0	1968.6	1576.6	10.6	22.1
Debt	1460.6	1914.8	2395.8	2111.9	2607.1	2573.9	2657.8	2685.9	2543.1	2586.0	2529.0	2269.5	2543.0	2506.9	2384.7	16.0	14.4
Other	6637.4	8188.7	11,153.8	12,236.2	9445.4	10,672.8	11,814.3	10,911.2	9801.3	10,015.8	8441.9	7822.5	8090.4	7847.6	9505.7	63.8	18.0
Net assets	−55.6	−226.3	−241.8	223.6	−391.6	−189.9	−288.3	−760.4	−522.8	−635.5	−564.8	−59.0	−236.5	−325.3	−305.3	−2.0	−84.7
FDI	451.1	427.7	722.1	720.5	616.6	618.1	571.1	253.4	283.5	99.8	74.8	16.5	14.9	−92.0	341.3	2.3	83.4
Portfolio	−133.8	−91.2	−226.8	−489.8	−969.4	−962.4	−1232.2	−1178.8	−1123.1	−1025.7	−1061.6	−792.0	−879.2	−1063.8	−802.1	−5.4	−49.6
Equity	139.4	158.1	237.3	199.5	74.5	85.5	−31.8	−38.8	−70.5	40.2	33.9	256.5	351.2	140.7	112.5	0.8	108.9
Debt	−273.2	−249.3	−464.1	−689.3	−1043.9	−1047.9	−1200.4	−1140.0	−1052.6	−1065.9	−1095.6	−1048.5	−1230.4	−1204.4	−914.7	−6.1	−37.8

Source IMF

Table 8.7 France—international investment position, 2005–18 (US$ in millions)

	2005	2006	2007	2008	2009	2010	2011	2012	2013	2014	2015	2016	2017	2018	Average	Percent (%)	Stdev (%)
Assets	4640.1	5969.1	7347.8	7351.9	7848.1	7692.5	7719.9	8070.0	8078.4	7933.8	7089.8	7081.8	7929.6	7809.4	7325.9	100.0	13.0
FDI	911.9	1143.2	1382.7	1320.4	1504.8	1557.0	1608.5	1709.0	1771.0	1691.7	1632.1	1643.3	1855.2	1887.0	1544.1	21.1	17.7
Portfolio	1873.3	2437.7	2965.0	2605.3	2983.2	2806.2	2413.9	2626.8	2872.9	2752.8	2549.5	2530.4	2928.3	2710.4	2646.8	36.1	11.0
Equity	524.9	716.8	826.9	474.8	646.0	665.8	519.3	652.6	812.3	770.7	748.0	754.6	962.3	796.5	705.1	9.6	19.2
Debt	1348.4	1720.9	2138.1	2130.6	2337.1	2140.4	1894.6	1974.2	2060.6	1982.1	1801.5	1775.8	1966.0	1913.9	1941.7	26.5	12.3
Other	1780.6	2289.9	2884.4	3323.3	3227.1	3163.1	3525.6	3549.7	3289.5	3345.9	2770.0	2761.3	2989.7	3045.4	2996.1	40.9	16.2
Gold & forex reserves	74.4	98.2	115.7	102.9	133.1	166.2	171.9	184.5	144.9	143.4	138.2	146.8	156.4	166.6	138.8	1.9	22.6
Liabilities	4674.2	6076.6	7587.0	7720.1	8242.8	7919.1	7920.7	8423.3	8561.7	8341.4	7399.2	7431.9	8483.1	8116.1	7635.5	104.2	14.0
FDI	644.7	813.4	996.3	949.2	1032.3	1014.8	1055.0	1116.9	1206.9	1097.5	1051.3	1068.6	1278.1	1279.7	1043.2	14.2	16.2
Portfolio	2081.9	2585.3	2926.4	2592.3	3299.0	3234.8	3121.1	3482.3	3862.2	3706.3	3359.2	3329.9	3817.1	3318.0	3194.0	43.6	15.8
Equity	690.4	990.3	1060.4	624.8	825.8	774.0	647.7	811.0	1009.2	902.2	853.5	878.6	1077.8	682.7	844.9	11.5	17.9
Debt	1391.4	1594.9	1866.0	1967.5	2473.2	2460.8	2473.4	2671.3	2853.0	2804.1	2505.7	2451.3	2739.3	2635.3	2349.1	32.1	19.6
Other	1947.6	2677.9	3664.3	4178.6	3911.5	3669.5	3744.6	3824.1	3492.6	3537.6	2988.7	3033.5	3387.9	3518.4	3398.4	46.4	16.9
Net assets	-34.1	-107.5	-239.2	-368.2	-394.7	-226.5	-200.9	-353.3	-483.4	-407.6	-309.4	-350.2	-553.5	-306.7	-309.6	-4.2	-45.1
FDI	267.2	329.8	386.4	371.2	472.5	542.3	553.5	592.1	564.1	594.2	580.8	574.8	577.1	607.3	500.9	6.8	22.8
Portfolio	-208.6	-147.5	38.6	13.0	-315.8	-428.6	-707.2	-855.4	-989.3	-953.5	-809.7	-799.4	-888.8	-607.6	-547.1	-7.5	-66.7
Equity	-165.6	-273.5	-233.5	-150.1	-179.7	-108.3	-128.4	-158.3	-196.9	-131.5	-105.4	-124.0	-115.5	113.8	-139.8	-1.9	-62.8
Debt	-43.1	126.0	272.2	163.1	-136.1	-320.4	-578.8	-697.1	-792.4	-822.0	-704.3	-675.5	-773.3	-721.4	-407.4	-5.6	-98.9

Source IMF

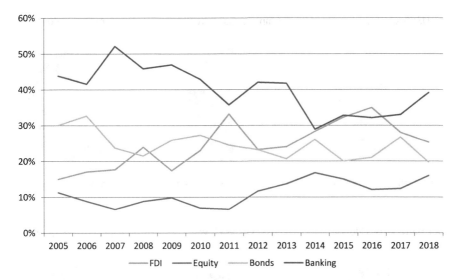

Fig. 8.11 Trends in gross World cross-border flows (major advanced economies), 2005–2018 (percent of total) (*Source* IMF)

hedge fund-like structure, because it essentially leverages purchases of risk assets (e.g. circa 5-times) with short-term 'safe' asset liabilities (21.8%). The US is the main exporter of risk-seeking capital, while Emerging Markets are the main exporter of risk-averse capital. US gross capital flows peaked at US$3.76 trillion in 2007, or almost double their 2005 total. We noted earlier that this rapid balance sheet growth was ignored at the time, while the more closely watched net capital flow figure stayed remarkably stable, averaging around US$730 billion over the 2005–2008 period, so inadvertently allaying fears of future trouble ahead of the GFC. Although US gross equity flows have since surpassed their 2007 peak in 2014, both gross FDI and gross debt flows remain reassuringly well-below this high-water mark. Figures 8.11 and 8.12 summarise the broader capital flow evidence across the six major economies over the 2005–2018 period. The data in Fig. 8.11 reports gross capital flows by category: FDI increased from 15% of aggregate activity to more than 25%, whereas gross banking flows have dropped from their 2007 peak of 52% to under 40%. Within the mix of gross portfolio flows, bonds have suffered a similar slide to banking flows, falling from 30% in 2005 to under 20% in 2018, while equity flows have climbed in importance from barely 7% in 2007 to nearly 16% of all gross capital activity in 2018. Measured by gross flows, FDI represented 28.2% of US capital movements over the 2005–2018 years, according to Fig. 8.12, with debt securities

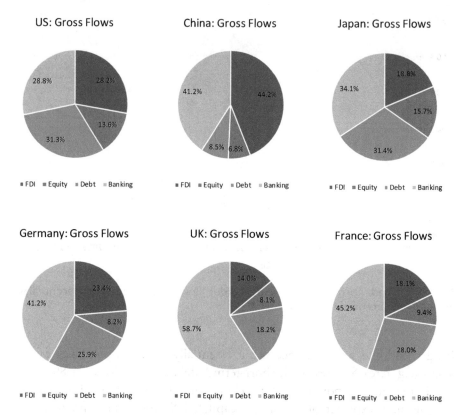

Fig. 8.12 Structure of capital flows—major economies, percentage share by gross flow type, average 2005–2018 (*Source* IMF)

making up a further 31.3% and banking flows 28.8%. The most volatile categories are banking flows, with a standard deviation of 56.1% of their mean value, followed by debt flows at 46.2%. The decline in the aggregate share taken by the traditionally more volatile banking and debt flows may improve the stability of the international financial system.

The dominance of banking and debt flows is plain to see across other major economies. These flows directly, or indirectly through collateral, drive changes in domestic credit and, hence, in global liquidity. Banking flows alone accounted for 58.7% of average UK capital movements over the 2005–2018 period; 45.2% of French flows; 41.2% of German flows; 41.2% of Chinese flows and 34.1% of Japanese flows. The importance of banking to the UK is underscored by their 64.2% average share of UK foreign assets over the period and the near-equivalent 63.8% of UK foreign liabilities. Bonds played a larger role in Germany, accounting for 25.9% of gross flows and 26.9% of Germany's foreign liabilities. FDI made up a sizeable 44.2% of Chinese gross capital flows over this period and 38.9% of China's foreign liabilities. Official gold and forex reserves at 58.3% dominate China's stock of foreign assets, which emphasises the Chinese government's active role in recycling dollars. The private financial sector plays a small part in recycling, which explains the still minor international role played by the Yuan. We note in Chapter 9, the anomaly in the Chinese international data. For example, Chinese gross banking activity is dominated by Chinese residents borrowing US dollars: lending in Yuan to foreigners and foreign purchases of Chinese domestic bonds is to date minimal. China is re-exporting US dollars, when she should be exporting Yuan. This has to change.

Notes

1. From the movie *All the President's Men* about the Watergate break-in.
2. See: Gopinath, G, *The International Price System*, Jackson Hole Economic Symposium, 2016.
3. See also: https://libertystreeteconomics.newyorkfed.org/2019/02/the-us-dollars-global-roles-where-do-things-stand.html.
4. 'Pull, Push, Pipes' Speech by Governor Mark Carney, Tokyo, 6 June 2019.
5. The 2010 Dodd–Frank Act took some powers away from the Federal Reserve Board. Certain emerging market economies, such as Mexico and Brazil, have previously accessed temporary US dollar swap lines, but these have now lapsed.
6. Also known as global value chains (GVC).
7. Helene Rey, IMF Mundell Fleming Lecture, 2015.
8. Gross capital inflows are formally defined as the net acquisition of domestic assets by non-residents; gross capital outflows as the net acquisition of foreign assets by residents, excluding official reserves; and net capital flows as the difference between gross capital inflows and outflows.
9. It is sometimes called the *Asian Savings Glut* and the *Excess Savings* view.
10. Gabriel Zucman, The Missing Wealth of Nations, *QJE* 128(3), August.
11. Foreign assets comprise around two-thirds of overall European bank assets, compared to around one-third for US banks.
12. Under CIP, interest rate differentials between currency pairs are fully reflected by their forward exchange rate parity.
13. London Interbank Offered Rate.
14. By French Finance Minister Valery Giscard d'Estaing, 16 February 1965.
15. See the speech by Chinese Major-General Qiao Liang, April, 2015 quoted in Chapter 1.

References

Bank for International Settlements. 2019. Triennial Central Bank Survey of Foreign Exchange and Over-The-Counter (OTC) Derivatives Markets in 2019. https://www.bis.org/statistics/rpfx19.htm.

Bernanke, Ben S. 2005. The Global Saving Glut and the U.S. Current Account Deficit. Federal Reserve Board, Remarks made at the Sandridge Lecture, Virginia Association of Economists, Richmond, Virginia, March.

Bruno, Valentina, and Hyun Song Shin. 2015. Capital Flows and the Risk-Taking Channel of Monetary Policy. *Journal of Monetary Economics* 71 (April): 119–132.

European Central Bank. 2016. Dealing with Large and Volatile Capital Flows and the Role of the IMF. Occasional Paper No. 180, September.

Goldberg, Linda S., and Robert Lerman. 2019. The U.S. Dollar's Global Roles: Where Do Things Stand? Liberty Street Economics, February.

Gourinchas, Pierre-Olivier, and Helene Rey. 2007. International Financial Adjustment. *Journal of Political Economy* 115 (4) (August): 665–703.

Gourinchas, Pierre-Olivier, Helene Rey, and Maxime Sauzet. 2019. The International Monetary and Financial System. LBS Working Paper, April (Forthcoming, *Annual Review of Economics*).

Lane, Philip R., and Peter McQuade. 2013. Domestic Credit Growth and International Capital Flows. ECB Working Paper No. 1566, July.

Lane, Philip R., and Gian Maria Milesi-Ferretti. 2008. The Drivers of Financial Globalization. *American Economic Review* 98 (2): 327–332.

Rey, Hélène. 2013. Dilemma Not Trilemma: The Global Financial Cycle and Monetary Policy Independence. Jackson Hole Conference, August 2013.

Rey, Hélène. 2015. IMF Mundell Fleming Lecture.

Shin, Hyun Song. 2012. Global Banking Glut and Loan Risk Premium. *IMF Economic Review* 60: 155–192.

Tooze, Adam. 2018. *Crashed.* London: Penguin.

Zucman, Gabriel. 2013. The Missing Wealth of Nations. *Quarterly Journal of Economics* 128 (3) (August): 1321–1364.

9

China and the Emerging Markets

The Chinese Monetary and Financial System

Overall Chinese Liquidity, excluding the People's Bank, stands close to RMB200 trillion (US$28 trillion), with State-owned banks (SOBs) the dominant lenders. Sitting alongside, according to Figs. 9.1 and 9.2, the shadow banks also play a significant role in the Chinese monetary system, where they account for upwards of one-third of total liquidity, or only a slightly smaller share than their US equivalents. Although we do not consider capital issues to be a source of new liquidity (technically they simply recycle existing savings within the private sector), they average around 11% of money raised and are included in the official estimates of *total social financing*. The main Chinese shadow banking activity consists of lending by trust banks and by non-bank financial institutions, often against financial collateral. Foreign currency loans, which are subsequently converted into Yuan, used to be a more significant source of funds, but their use has been lately discouraged by the Central Bank, the People's Bank of China (PBoC).

Figure 9.3 highlights the remarkable stability seen in commercial bank lending (mainly the SOBs). Around this trend, fluctuations in overall Chinese Liquidity are driven by larger swings in shadow banking activity. The shadow banks experience a more pronounced credit cycle. These are frequently anti-cyclical which may indicate that shadow banks thrive on evading mainstream monetary controls? They tend to be funded through wholesale money and capital markets; they are dependent on buoyant collateral values, and many turn out to be subsidiaries of the major banks.

© The Author(s) 2020
M. J. Howell, *Capital Wars*,
https://doi.org/10.1007/978-3-030-39288-8_9

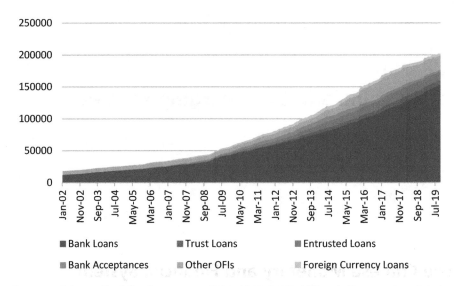

Fig. 9.1 Chinese liquidity by source, 2002–2019 (RMB billions) (Source *CrossBorder Capital*, People's Bank)

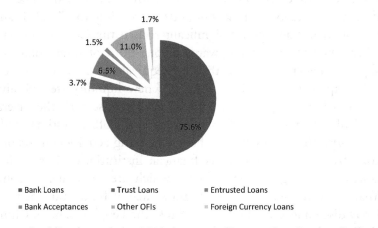

Fig. 9.2 Chinese liquidity by source, 2019 (percent) (Source *CrossBorder Capital*, People's Bank)

Moreover, some shadow banks have been tainted both by their association with local authorities, and in several cases with dubious real estate deals. Hence, the sometimes sudden halt in their activities is the result of periodic central government censure.

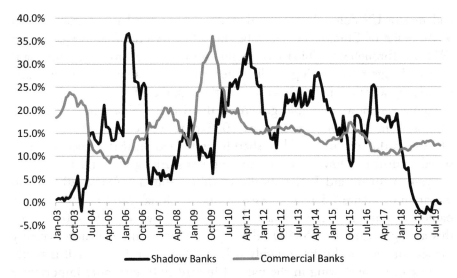

Fig. 9.3 Chinese liquidity growth by source, 2003–2019 (percentage change YoY) (Source *CrossBorder Capital*, People's Bank)

China's Financial Immaturity

Structurally, China enjoys a large domestic savings surplus, which has historically been big enough to more than cover the public sector deficit, and correspondingly it allows her to run a current account surplus. However, despite recently re-imposing restrictions on capital outflows, the recent slide in China's current account and slowdown of inward foreign direct investment (FDI) has drained her still enormous forex reserves. Although this is still largely a cyclical concern, it does raise deeper structural questions. Specifically, China's foreign balance sheet reflects her overall financial immaturity. China's gross foreign asset base is around US$7½ trillion compared to $10 trillion for Germany and over US$25 trillion for the US: a figure that is commensurate with the size of America's GDP. Not only is China's balance sheet far smaller in size, both relatively and absolutely, it is heavily skewed towards official holdings of forex reserves (average 58%, 2005–2018), with gross liabilities dominated by inward FDI (average 39% of gross assets), of which roughly half appears to be financed by RMB-denominated bank loans.

Cross-border capital flows between the core Developed economies and the Emerging Market economies on the periphery strictly need to be split into the large, dominant flows to China and smaller-sized flows to other, sometimes more, financially mature Emerging Markets. China's huge accumulation of US dollar forex reserves is the counterpart to sizeable inward FDI[1] and her large and mostly US dollar-denominated trade surplus that has essentially arisen in the wake of China's 2001 membership of the World Trade Organisation (WTO). Throughout, China has sought to maintain a broadly stable Yuan/US$ exchange rate, refusing to allow her currency to appreciate in the same excoriating way that the Japanese Yen did through the 1970s and 1980s.

Figure 9.4 shows the rapid growth in the size of China's current account surplus from the 2001 lows to its 2007 peak at close to 10% of GDP. Thereafter, the surplus has fallen sharply, and based on IMF projections it is slated to drift still lower over the coming years. Alongside, FDI has proved buoyant, with inward FDI typically totalling around US$150–200 billion per annum. Figure 9.5 reports what we term China's *fundamental balance*, namely the current account plus net FDI flows. Over the 2007–2015 years, this averaged close to US$400 billion per annum, although more recently the size of this surplus has roughly halved. The reason for this fall is partly because of some slowing in the pace of inward FDI, but more importantly because of stronger outward FDI, much of which is associated with *Belt and Road Initiative* projects. Looking ahead, with interest rates low and geopolitical tensions rising, China is more likely to increase her outward FDI, rather than accumulate more US Treasuries. Recent concerns over China–US relations have led many to predict that China could quickly sell off her vast[2]

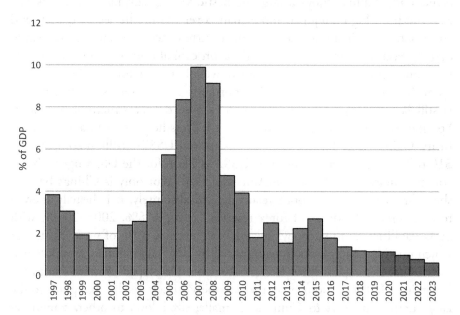

Fig. 9.4 China current account balance, 1997–2023 (percent of GDP) (*Note* IMF Projections for 2020–2023. *Source* IMF)

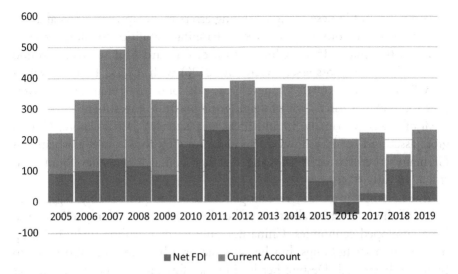

Fig. 9.5 China fundamental balance—current account plus net FDI, 2005–2019 (US$ in billions) (Source *CrossBorder Capital*)

US$1.1 trillion nest egg of US Treasury securities, but more likely is a reluctance by China to buy more US assets and a rechannelling of her surplus into regional investment projects. This, in turn, will help to foster an RMB-economic zone closer to home.

Notwithstanding her favourable overall net foreign asset position that now exceeds US$2 trillion, the mix of China's international balance sheet is strongly biased because of the underlying immaturity of her financial sector and specifically by the latter's minor international presence and relatively small gross foreign flows. In short, China's asset holdings are heavily skewed towards the US dollar, and specifically dominated by official holdings of short-to-medium term US Treasury securities. Much like the US itself, but unlike, say, Germany, China's foreign revenues are mainly denominated in US dollars. China badly needs to get off this dollar hook and China herself has to start using the Yuan abroad. In practice, large-sized inflows of foreign exchange have to be recycled back into foreign assets, either by the private or the public sectors, to prevent them driving the Yuan exchange rate higher. This explains the pro-active role of the Chinese State through its agencies, such as SAFE[3] and the PBoC. As a result, China's gross foreign assets are dominated by more than US$3 trillion[4] of official forex reserves that make up 58% of all foreign asset holdings (average 2005–2018). This huge forex pot compares to only 16.3% for Japan, and a tiny 2% for Germany and 0.6% for the UK, which all have more mature domestic financial sectors.

In comparison, Chinese foreign banking assets make up 21% of total assets (Germany 44%), offset by a stock of banking liabilities totalling 18% of all assets (Germany 35%). China's stock of outward FDI stands at around 15% of her total gross assets (Germany 21%) with inward FDI equivalent to 39% (Germany 16%). Chinese gross portfolio investment abroad averages some 6% of assets, with foreign gross portfolio investment into China 12% of assets (Germany 33 and 35%, respectively). What's more, China's gross asset and liability flows prove to be roughly three times as volatile as Germany's, perhaps again showing that her capital market development is still at an early stage.

These comparisons are revealing. China is unquestionably lagging in terms of the internationalisation of her financial sector. Compared to rival large developed economies, China not only needs to substantially build up her foreign asset holdings, but her international balance sheet also needs to be more diversified. Despite her healthy net foreign asset position, the size of China's foreign balance sheet, as measured by the sum of gross assets and liabilities, rather than their net difference, is seriously sub-par. Put another way, China's foreign liabilities are largely risk assets, such as FDI, whereas her foreign assets are dominated by safe assets. Thus, the US dollar proceeds from selling her real capital stock to foreigners are re-exported as dollars and recycled back into US Treasuries. According to Table 9.1, gross Chinese international banking inflows plus outflows total 39% of all foreign assets, while in Germany they exceed 79%, in the US 69% and in the UK 128%. China's gross cross-border portfolio activity is even weaker standing at 18% of all foreign assets, compared to 99% for the US, 78% for both Germany and Japan, and 48% for the UK. In other words, the Chinese private sector does a poor job of recycling inward capital. This is shown in Fig. 9.6 which compares gross private sector cross-border asset flows for China and the World average, measured as a percentage of GDP. In financially more mature economies, such as Germany, the UK and Japan, the private sector undertakes a greater recycling role through its international investments, at a pace at least twice that of China and even ignoring the short-lived pre-GFC spike in 2007.

Specifically, foreigners' holdings of Chinese bonds are barely one-tenth of comparable German figures and Chinese international bank lending could easily double as a share of gross assets or, when the FDI component of lending is stripped out, possible even quadruple. What these gaps suggest are, respectively, the absence of: (1) a domestic sovereign bond market with reserve currency status that foreigners can freely invest in, and (2) an international market in RMB-denominated trade credit. The necessary condition

Table 9.1 China gross international balance sheet, 2013–2018 (US$ in billions, averages defined 2005–18)

China, PR: Mainland: international investment position

Millions of US dollars

Please click here for country specific metadata	2013	2014	2015	2016	2017	2018	Average	Percent	Stdev
Assets	5986.1	6438.3	6155.8	6507.0	7148.8	7324.2	4667.9	100.0%	43.9%
FDI	660.5	882.6	1095.9	1357.4	1809.0	1899.0	691.5	14.8%	90.8%
Portfolio	258.5	262.5	261.3	367.0	492.5	498.0	286.0	6.1%	36.0%
Equity	153.0	161.3	162.0	215.2	297.7	270.0	116.8	2.5%	83.8%
Debt	105.5	101.2	99.3	151.8	194.8	227.9	169.2	3.6%	36.5%
Other	1186.7	1393.8	1392.5	1684.8	1611.4	1759.2	967.7	20.7%	56.0%
Gold & forex reserves	3880.4	3899.3	3406.1	3097.8	3235.9	3168.0	2722.8	58.3%	36.6%
Liabilities	4177.0	4835.6	4483.0	4556.7	5048.1	5194.1	3208.5	68.7%	48.3%
FDI	2331.2	2599.1	2696.3	2755.1	2725.7	2762.3	1816.7	38.9%	48.1%
Portfolio	573.4	796.2	817.0	811.1	1099.4	1096.4	570.7	12.2%	53.8%
Equity	484.5	651.3	597.1	579.5	762.3	684.2	453.4	9.7%	40.9%
Debt	88.9	144.9	220.0	231.6	337.0	412.2	117.2	2.5%	113.6%
Other	1272.4	1440.2	969.6	990.5	1223.1	1335.4	821.1	17.6%	50.2%
Net assets	1809.1	1602.7	1672.8	1950.4	2100.7	2130.1	1459.4	31.3%	36.9%
FDI	−1670.8	−1716.5	−1600.4	−1397.8	−916.6	−863.3	−1125.2	−24.1%	−40.5%
Portfolio	−314.9	−533.7	−555.7	−444.1	−606.9	−598.4	−284.7	−6.1%	−79.8%
Equity	−331.5	−490.0	−435.1	−364.3	−464.7	−414.1	−336.6	−7.2%	−29.7%
Debt	16.6	−43.7	−120.6	−79.8	−142.2	−184.3	51.9	1.1%	286.7%

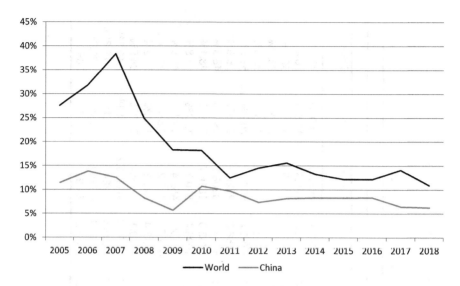

Fig. 9.6 Gross private sector capital flows—China compared to World average, 2005–2018 (% of GDP) (Source *CrossBorder Capital*)

for the internationalisation of Chinese government bonds will likely require some relaxation of existing capital controls, and the development of a transparent financial infrastructure with standard metrics. In turn, a market in RMB trade credit, itself requires more of China's trade to be invoiced in RMB. Both trends are rising, albeit slowly. However, China is unlikely to be hurried, because losing control of the exchange rate through a speculative attack would be an unwelcome blow to her economic prestige. More likely than any significant relaxation of outward capital controls could be the narrower aim of establishing a semi-closed RMB-zone, perhaps including Central Asia, and possibly other Asian peer economies. Already, the People's Bank is establishing a network of regional swap lines for the Yuan across Asia.

Chinese private sector financial corporations have so far been unable to build up substantial Yuan claims against foreigners and, with their predominantly Yuan-denominated liabilities, to date these institutions show neither the expertise nor the desire and ability (given official controls) to take on any currency risk by directly holding dollars themselves. Consequently, the State manages this currency pool through its own foreign exchange reserves (SAFE); the CIC Sovereign Wealth Fund (SWF),[5] and by directing outward FDI into foreign projects, such as the *Belt and Road* initiative. Moreover, as already noted, China is unlikely to want to add significantly to her

US dollar reserves in the future. Given these circumstances, China seems best served by maintaining the exchange rate stability of the Yuan against the US dollar, or even against a basket of regional peer currencies.[6] A much weaker Yuan could encourage capital flight, while a strong Yuan would damage export performance and might so increase China's external funding needs. Indeed, the growing interconnectedness of Asian industry, linked by sprawling regional supply chains, underscores the increasing importance of intra-Asian currency stability. Put another way, if all Asian currency units move higher in step against the US dollar, any potential loss of competitiveness will be shared out among the participants. Consequently, we should expect to see the emergence of a de facto regional currency bloc, like the Euro, characterised by exchange rate stability within the bloc and greater flexibility between blocs. This evolution would allow greater external diversification of Chinese capital, particularly within the Asian sphere.

The Gurley-Shaw-Goldsmith view on financial structure described in Chapter 6 implies that financial systems have a normal tendency towards constantly increasing liquidity as a natural part of their development, particularly in fast-growing economies. Because China's financial development has lagged, in terms of institutional depth, international investors have been forced to rely more on US capital markets. This may have dangerous consequences for international financial stability if it leads to a structural shortage of 'safe' asset collateral and a greater workload for the US Fed. Figure 9.7

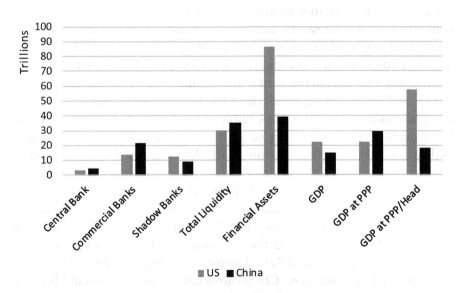

Fig. 9.7 China versus US—comparative size of monetary systems, end-July 2019 (US dollars in trillions, except PPP/head in US$ '000s) (Source *CrossBorder Capital*)

compares the relative sizes of the US and Chinese economies, and their respective pools of money (M2 definition) and liquidity. The data show how China has the larger Central Bank, a bigger pool of traditional bank assets, and a large, albeit slightly smaller shadow banking system. Overall, Chinese liquidity at US$35.6 trillion is around one-fifth bigger than the equivalent US$29.2 trillion pool of US Liquidity. China's GDP measured in current US dollars stands at US$14.2 trillion, but re-expressed in purchasing power parity (PPP) terms it nearly doubles to US$27.3 trillion, or nearly one-third bigger than the US$21.3 trillion US economy.

The deepening of Yuan-based international markets is an essential next step. Although China enjoys an excess of savings over domestic investment, she still needs to attract foreign capital. This is partly because, from a qualitative dimension, FDI often embodies latest technologies and international management skills, and partly because, in quantitative terms, it will enable China to diversify her domestic asset base. Put another way, China is predominantly a re-exporter of dollars through her capital account, but she would prefer to be a bigger exporter of Yuan. This will facilitate the internationalisation of the Yuan and go some way to fulfilling China's stated goal of displacing the widespread use of the US dollar in Asian markets. China could then capture sizeable *seigniorage* gains. For example, China has a large, high yielding domestic bond market that should potentially attract foreign investors. A transparent, liquid Chinese government bond market should attract both more domestic and foreign investors. Not only would Chinese bonds command a sizeable weighting in the benchmark indexes and so attract foreign capital, but an efficient domestic bond market would itself serve as a useful benchmark for the valuation of other Chinese assets, such as equities. Equally, in terms of the banking and credit markets, demanding payment for goods and assets in Yuan and encouraging foreigners to use Yuan is a straightforward way to increase Chinese wealth, achieved at the negligible cost of printing paper money or by encouraging adoption of a digital-Yuan. China's major companies have already established domestic payments platforms, such as Alipay and WeChat, which could likely extend to an e-wallet containing both electronic and State-backed digital monies. Selling foreigners Yuan-denominated assets, such as bonds, will also encourage them to borrow Yuan. Similarly, pricing more exports in Yuan will lead to the development of a much-needed Yuan-based trade credit market. All these initiatives should raise gross cross-border financial activity and increase holdings of Yuan-denominated foreign assets, e.g. Chinese bank loans and trade credit to foreigners, and Yuan-denominated foreign liabilities, e.g. foreign holdings of Chinese securities. China's gross balance sheet size should begin to increase and diversify towards the World average.

It is also possible, indeed likely, that the internationalisation of the Yuan involves the rapid development of offshore trading and deposit markets in Yuan, i.e. Euro-yuan, that parallel the equivalent existing Eurodollar markets. Recall that the initial impetus behind the growth of the Eurodollar markets was contemporary Soviet concerns over the integrity of their US dollar deposits held in banks located in mainland USA, particularly as Cold War tensions grew. Many investors would share similar concerns today about the integrity of any Yuan deposits held in mainland Chinese institutions in the event of an escalation of geopolitical tensions. It is worth noting that the parallel tensions in the Cold War era did not halt the use of the US dollar in international trade, but simply hastened the development of the Eurodollar markets, particularly in London. There seems no reason why a similar offshore Euro-yuan market cannot develop.

The recent September 2019 attempt by the Hong Kong Stock Exchange to bid for the London Stock Exchange, alongside the near-simultaneous announcement of the termination of quotas on foreign investment into Chinese financial assets are examples of this lust for 'intelligent' and risk-seeking foreign capital. Equally, further access to foreign savings could come from the US ADR (American Depository Receipt) programme in Chinese shares and the possible inclusion of more Chinese stocks and bonds in benchmark indexes. The latter would mean more potential investment from passive international investment funds. However, all these inflows represent a worrying drain from the US dollar pool. US politicians have recently pushed back against these threats, and it seems likely that the US Administration will resist such easy access to American savings. Some experts are even suggesting imposing hard limits on US portfolio flows into China. After all, capital is at war.

The Impact of Capital Flows on Emerging Markets

In general, cross-border capital inflows into the Emerging Markets often prove to be powerful drivers of domestic asset markets. However, capital inflows also come with costs. According to research from Barings[7]: "… *every Emerging Market crisis is first-and-foremost a currency crisis*". There is a long tradition across many Emerging Market economies of national policy-makers targeting exchange rate stability against the US dollar, for trade competitiveness reasons, and so allowing their foreign exchange reserves to rise and fall accordingly. These flows affect domestic asset markets in three ways: (1) *volume*: foreign institutional investors and lenders located in the major developed economies are large-sized relative to the often small local asset markets in the developing World; (2) *information*: indigenous funds held offshore by wealthy Emerging Market residents can move quickly into and out of the home markets as they detect changes in local economic conditions, and (3) *policy*: because national Central Banks frequently target exchange rates, they consequently allow capital flows to be monetised through large reserve pools of foreign exchange. The often-underdeveloped local financial markets mean that the effect of these flows on domestic money and credit aggregates cannot be fully sterilised. Hence, net capital inflows into Emerging Market economies frequently lead to domestic credit booms, through these second-round effects, rather than to appreciating currencies. Yet, this effect is not always symmetric, because although capital outflows may initially tighten credit markets, the threat of negative second-round effects on the domestic economy can force policy-makers to sacrifice their currencies by choosing devaluation rather than risk an economic slump.

We showed in Chapter 5 how this monetary transmission occurs in a similar way to the so-called Balassa–Samuelson effect described in the economics literature. Rising real exchange rates follows positive capital flow shocks that are often, but not exclusively, induced by underlying productivity factors. In other words, fast-growing Emerging Market economies are likely to experience upward pressure on their real exchange rates. By definition, the real exchange rate consists of a nominal exchange rate and a relative price level. However, we do not restrict ourselves here to high street prices and instead define this 'price' level broadly to include asset prices, as well as wages and service sector prices. In a supply chain dominated World, we can assume that most goods prices are determined internationally, not domestically, while wages tend to be 'sticky' due to the resistance to pass costs on along the chain. An increase in the real exchange rate therefore implies that either the nominal exchange rate can rise; domestic asset prices can rise, or there is some combined increase of the two. Consequently, when national monetary authorities target their nominal exchange rates at constant levels, upward pressure on the real exchange rate is ultimately expressed through rising asset prices. This likely explains why the high productivity growth Asian economies, such as Singapore, Hong Kong and Korea, often enjoy large asset price gains and they can often feature speculative funds chasing investment in real estate developments.

We can trace the monetary transmission that accompanies Emerging Market exchange rate targeting policies and culminates in an asset price boom. An initial liquidity shock appears either through faster export

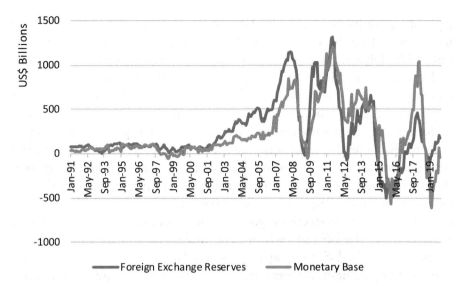

Fig. 9.8 EM foreign exchange reserves and base money, 1991–2019 (US$ in billions, annual change) (Source *CrossBorder Capital*)

growth and/or stronger capital inflows. The resulting forex reserve changes are transmitted through the monetary base and, in turn, on to the broader credit aggregates, such as overall bank lending. Figure 9.8 shows the sizeable swings in Emerging Market forex reserves and the parallel growth in Emerging Market high-powered money (correlation coefficient 0.807), measured in US dollar terms. For example, when capital inflows are translated into local currencies by the Central Bank and accumulated as foreign exchange reserves, the resulting increase in base money can provide the new funding for multiple expansion in bank credit. Equally, domestic private banks can engage in, say, forex swaps to gain extra funding, with greater confidence in the stability of the currency regime. These mechanisms, which can also work in reverse, apply unless local policy-makers can sterilise the effects of the changes in base money by offsetting actions elsewhere, such as through the Central Bank buying and selling of other financial assets.

Typically, because Emerging Markets are at the same time both emergent economies and underdeveloped financial systems, their domestic financial markets are less able to fully sterilise the effects of cross-border capital flows. In fact, even in the case where economies operate fully flexible exchange rates, Rey (2015) shows that they are still vulnerable to these global factors. What this means is that international capital movements have an exaggerated impact on Emerging Market economies, making asset price bubbles far more likely because of procyclical second-round effects. This makes them especially sensitive to changes in US monetary policy and to any resulting movements in the benchmark US dollar exchange rate. Thus, whereas periods of US dollar strength prove unfavourable, dollar weakness is associated with positive Emerging Market financial market performance. A strong US currency not only adversely affects Emerging Markets through the broader impact of tighter US monetary policy, but it will have direct negative effects on foreign borrowers who have to repay in now more expensive US dollars.

By focussing on these exchange rate effects, this framework helps to explain why the prevailing US dollar system incorporates an additional amplification mechanism. As we have already argued, this operates through the real exchange rate and engages when other economies catch-up with and overtake slipping US productivity growth. The resulting reverse productivity gap pressurises the US real exchange rate to devalue, but the importance of finance within the US economy compels the US authorities to try to maintain prevailing domestic collateral values, i.e. asset prices, by pumping in more liquidity into their financial markets. Consequently, the nominal US dollar exchange rate has historically taken the bulk of the adjustment burden by depreciating over the long-term, despite periodic increases in its demand. On top of a knock-on effect as Emerging Market policy-makers follow the US easing, the weaker US dollar exchange rate, in turn, reduces the immediate debt repayment burden and encourages ever more cross-border borrowing by the private sector, including unhedged carry-trades, thereby raising dollar foreign debt levels and increasing cross-currency mismatches. Unwisely, many Emerging Market borrowers have previously succumbed to this temptation. Alongside, the ease of international borrowing allows the US to maintain a low savings rate and a large fiscal deficit, with a growing current account deficit as the arithmetic counterpart. Because changes in trade flows mostly involve manufacturing industry, America's rising trade deficit has become associated with secular de-industrialisation, and because manufacturing is the potential source of most productivity gains, this decline further undermines the long-term level of the US real exchange rate. Complex feedbacks can multiply, as we originally set out in Chapter 3. Cross-border capital inflows back into the US, such as European banks' dollar mortgage lending ahead of the GFC, may also reinforce the initial Federal Reserve monetary policy easing to promote domestic asset bubbles. This, in turn, ultimately compels the Fed to retighten and so can trigger debt crises back in the Emerging Markets themselves. The result is that capital shifts rapidly and sometimes violently between the core and the periphery, and then back again.

Admittedly, these direct US dollar effects may have lately lessened somewhat because China and many other Emerging Markets now undertake relatively more of their borrowing in local currencies. Nonetheless, in absolute terms Emerging Market economies remain major cross-border borrowers. They are still vulnerable to disruption,[8] evidenced by the fact that one-fifth of all surges in cross-border capital flows end in national financial crises, according to the IMF. The data show that Emerging Market economies are at least three times more likely to experience a financial crisis after a surge in cross-border capital flows. Figure 9.9 demonstrates how these crisis periods frequently follow a spike in capital inflows. Although cross-border capital inflows appear, at first sight, to boost GDP growth, those Emerging Market economies suffering above-average capital flow volatility, in fact, grow substantially slower. Not surprisingly, many Emerging Market economies have chosen to self-insure against capital flow volatility, notably in the wake of the 1997/1998 Asian Crisis, by accumulating huge reserves of 'safe' assets through both the establishment of SWF and through the accumulation of large foreign exchange reserve cushions. Figure 9.10 shows that the Emerging Market economies collectively hold around US$7 trillion in foreign exchange reserves, with evidence of strong accumulation during the early to mid-2000s.

Figure 9.11 reports the recent unusually weak pattern of net private sector capital flows into the Emerging Market economies. Capital outflows have lately exceeded capital inflows. Admittedly, this becomes less true when

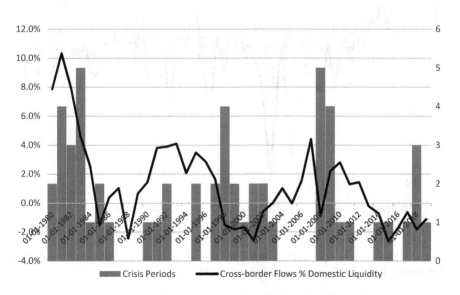

Fig. 9.9 Cross-border capital flows to Emerging Markets (percent of domestic liquidity) and number of crisis periods, 1980–2019 (*Source* IMF, *CrossBorder Capital*)

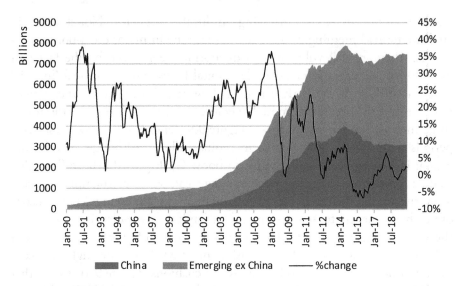

Fig. 9.10 Foreign exchange reserves of Emerging Markets, 1990–2019 (monthly, US dollars in billions and YoY%) (Source *CrossBorder Capital*)

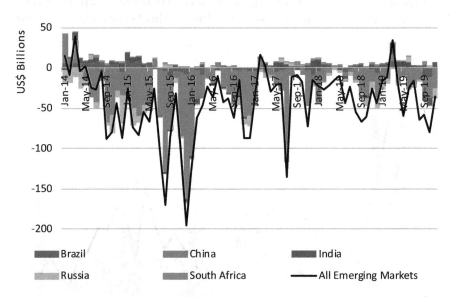

Fig. 9.11 Net cross-border capital flows to Emerging Markets, 2014–2019 (monthly, US dollars in billions) (Source *CrossBorder Capital*)

China is excluded from the sample, because of the large-scale 'capital flight' from China that took place over the 2014–2017 period. Here and coincident with Premier Xi Jinping's anti-corruption drive, China temporarily lowered her external capital controls to comply with conditions laid down by the IMF for the Yuan to join the SDR reserve currency unit from 2016. Notwithstanding, this general phenomenon of capital 'flowing uphill' from high to low return markets, namely from the Emerging to the Developed Market economies, has been eponymously dubbed the *Lucas Paradox*, after the well-known US economist. Yet, the picture looks more plausible when the entire foreign balance sheet and movements in gross flows are once again considered, because this evidences how capital flows broadly into various Emerging Market investments. In other words, these inflows of risk capital have lately been more than offset by the demand of Emerging Market residents for 'safe' assets, such as government bonds and hard currencies issued by the rich, advanced economies, as well as by foreign debt repayments by Emerging Market borrowers.

Separating out these inflows of risk capital, the data reported in Fig. 9.12 confirm that Emerging Market capital inflows are dominated by purchases of debt securities and they are also highly cyclical. We have added the *CrossBorder Capital* index of World cross-border flow activity alongside to

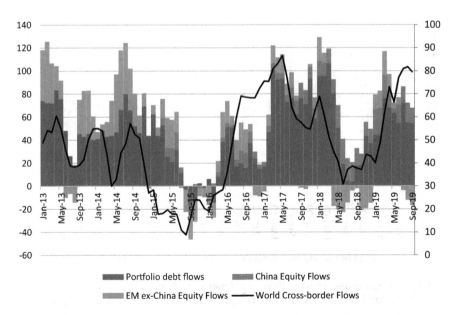

Fig. 9.12 Cross-border portfolio inflows to Emerging Markets and CBC index of cross-border flows, 2013–2019 (US$ billions and index, 0–100) (*Source* IMF, *CrossBorder Capital*)

emphasise that these swings are likely driven by some global factor. A deeper question concerns whether these capital inflows to Emerging Markets are driven more by so-called 'pull' factors, related to positive domestic economic features, e.g. faster national growth, than by 'push' factors, related to looser monetary conditions in the Developed Economies, e.g. a US Federal Reserve policy easing? The evidence is admittedly two-way, but from our experience, and supported by the data in Fig. 9.12, the 'push' factors tend to dominate. These can be better understood by once again looking at the overall foreign balance sheet, because in a liquidity boom not only do cash-rich foreign investors buy up local securities, but local banks can also obtain easier funding terms by borrowing in foreign markets. Both are recorded as capital inflows and represent increases in gross foreign liabilities. Consequently, as the Global Liquidity cycle expands, so gross flows and the overall size of the foreign balance sheet increase significantly.

On the other hand, the data in Fig. 9.13 seem, at first sight, to support the 'pull' case by highlighting the strong co-movement between the *CrossBorder Capital* sub-indexes of capital flows to Emerging Markets and Chinese domestic liquidity flows. The correlation between the two data series is high (correlation coefficient 0.505). It is underscored by the latest

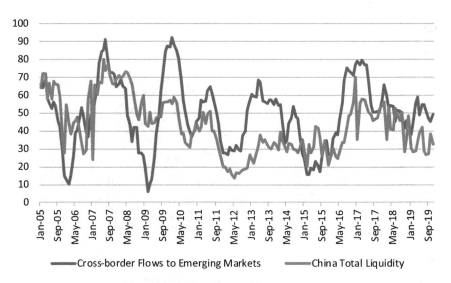

Fig. 9.13 Cross-border capital flows to Emerging Markets and Chinese liquidity, 2005–2019 (monthly, indexes 'normal' range 0–100) (Source *CrossBorder Capital*)

research from the Kiel Institute[9] in Germany, which confirms the critical role played by the Chinese business cycle. Their analysis finds that each percentage point rise in Chinese GDP growth leads to a 1.7% increase in Chinese capital outflows as a per cent of GDP, with a similar-sized and significant positive 'push' effect from looser domestic Chinese monetary policy. In other words, capital inflows into the non-Chinese Emerging Markets could be attracted by expectations of better regional prospects following an expansion of the increasingly dominate Chinese economy. On the other hand, a third, 'push' factor, namely US monetary policy, may explain both features. A looser US monetary stance could 'push' US capital into Emerging Markets and simultaneously force the Chinese People's Bank to match America's new looser monetary policy in order to maintain the prevailing Yuan/US dollar exchange rate parity. However, the Kiel researchers find that these US 'push' factors tend to be statistically weaker.

In conclusion, looking at gross flows and analysing the entire foreign balance sheet are important tools that help us to properly understand Emerging Market flows. The act of benchmarking national currencies against the US dollar leads to a procyclical and essentially volatile Emerging Market investment cycle. This is not helped by the fact that many Emerging Market economies are sandwiched between the capital 'push' from the US-led Global Liquidity cycle and the 'pull' from the attractions of being associated with the fast-growing Chinese economy. The archetypal Emerging Market Crisis follows a Global Liquidity boom and usually involves heavy foreign borrowing by local banks. The rich detail behind these gross flows is hidden by the 'net' capital flow numbers. These also unquestionably obscures the financial immaturity of China and specifically the underuse of Yuan instruments in global markets. Consequently, China fails to fully-benefit from *seigniorage* and is instead forced to use and export the US dollar, rather than the Yuan.

Notes

1. FDI: foreign direct investment.
2. This total refers to officially disclosed holdings. In practice, other Chinese State entities likely hold another US$1 trillion of US securities.
3. SAFE: State Administration of Foreign Exchange.
4. Chinese forex reserves touched US$4 trillion in 2014.
5. CIC: China Investment Corporation established in 2007.

6. De facto this is already happening. The correlation between the CNY and other Asian units has risen steadily from 0.27 in 2015, to 0.36 through 2016–2018 and to 0.52 in 2019.
7. Baring Securities, *Emerging Markets* research report, 1994.
8. AR Ghosh, JD Ostry, and M. Qureshi, When do capital inflows surges end in tears? *American Economic Review*, 2016.
9. China's Overseas Lending, Sebastian Horn, Carmen Reinhart and Christoph Trebesch, Kiel WP #2312, June 2019.

Reference

Rey, Hélène. 2015. IMF Mundell Fleming Lecture.

10

The Liquidity Transmission Mechanism: Understanding Future Macro-valuation Shifts

The Financial Economy Versus the Real Economy

The concept of a *financial cycle* (see Borio 2012) describes the often febrile interactions between investors' and credit providers' risk appetites, collateral values and the availability of funding. The resulting upswing in credit and liquidity provision typically drives up stock markets, real estate values and other risk asset prices. By further increasing the value of collateral this, in turn, allows the private sector to borrow ever more credit until, at some point, the cycle tops-out and reverses. Financial cycles can be of different lengths and amplitudes to standard economic cycles, nonetheless, they have a tendency to amplify prevailing macroeconomic dislocations. Historically, the financial cycle demonstrates a unique ability to predict future economic trends, while the downswing frequently coincides with major banking crises and recessions.

Yet, traditional economics textbooks see it differently. They treat financial flows as little more than the accounting counterparts of savings and investment decisions. Consequently, financial markets are supposed to respond passively, rather than drive the real economy. In practice, financial markets are moved by these inflows and outflows of liquidity and by changes in the risk-taking behaviour of investors. Both affect risk premia. For example, when there is insufficient liquidity, risk premia on investment assets are higher. Put another way, by thinking of financial intermediaries as undertaking 'risk-sharing', then the greater the size of their balance sheets the more

© The Author(s) 2020
M. J. Howell, *Capital Wars*,
https://doi.org/10.1007/978-3-030-39288-8_10

risk they can take on. Hence, more liquidity means bigger intermediary balance sheets, more risk-sharing and, in turn, less system-wide risk. Many Central Banks now accept that liquidity plays a key role in financial markets. In the words of the European Central Bank[1] (ECB):

> …obtaining a higher valuation of assets can be seen to be the implicit, if not explicit, rationale for large-scale asset purchases/quantitative easing by some major central banks … [These] measures providing liquidity to the financial system via collateralised lending as in the case of the ECB might also indirectly support asset valuation by helping to avoid disorderly deleveraging and fire sales by banks … The focus on the size and composition of central bank balance sheets obviously contrasts with the irrelevance proposition on non-standard policy measures put forward in the neo-Wicksellian tradition. Such measures would be seen as irrelevant even when the zero lower bound has been reached, to the extent that they do not change the future expected path of interest rates (Eggertson and Woodford, 2003). However, interest rates and associated risk premia, while disregarding quantity variables, would not appear sufficient to capture the way monetary policy operates when the efficiency of financial markets and financial intermediation are impaired amidst deleveraging pressures and heightened uncertainty and risk aversion. In such circumstances the role of the central bank as the issuer of the ultimate safe and liquid asset – money – and its capacity as intermediary and risk absorber of last resort come to the fore. This has been the case for the Euro-system and the US Federal Reserve alike.

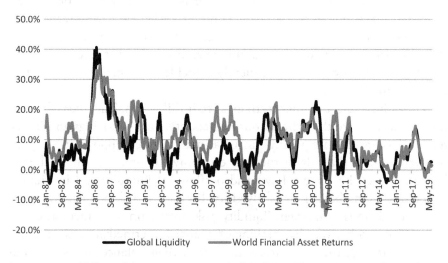

Fig. 10.1 World financial asset returns and Global Liquidity, 1981–2019 (annual percentage changes) (Source *CrossBorder Capital*)

Figure 10.1 confirms that Global Liquidity is often the determining factor behind World asset price movements. Yet, this close co-movement hides the complex feedbacks that operate between liquidity flows and investors' desired asset allocation. Our flow of funds-based model, detailed earlier in Chapter 4 and summarised in Fig. 10.2 below, argues that financial liquidity explicitly drives investors' risk appetite, and, hence, asset allocation. Rising collateral values then positively feedback to underpin new liquidity creation. While financial liquidity is usually necessary for an asset boom, it is not always enough by itself, because bull markets typically need a fundamental theme to stimulate and sustain investor interest. In other words, trends in asset allocation and swings in the behaviour of the investment crowd will affect and often amplify the transmission of liquidity to asset prices and, ultimately, its pass-through into the real economy. To better understand these trends in asset allocation, Fig. 10.3 plots the cross-sectional data on per capita incomes and the value of financial assets per head for several economies. Both sets of data are expressed in logarithmic terms, so that the fitted non-linear relationship describes what is known mathematically as a power function. The loading on financial assets is 1.48, which tells us that roughly speaking every 10% growth in the size of per capita incomes is associated with a near-15% increase in the value of financial assets per head. Economists would correspondingly describe financial assets as *luxury goods*, because of this high income elasticity of demand. It follows that as economies develop and mature, the financial sector should outpace the real economy. This cross-country evidence accords with historical experience and confirms the early observations made several decades ago by Yale economist Raymond Goldsmith, who first introduced the *financial interrelations ratio*. This concept is defined as the aggregate value of intangible assets divided by the value of tangible assets, as calculated from national balance sheet data. It is used to measure the density of an economy's financial structure and the relative rates of growth between its financial assets and its tangible wealth. Goldsmith argued that each country's financial development goes through a similar sequence of well-defined stages, each characterised by a rising financial interrelations ratio. Typically, the ratio reaches a limit slightly above one, when its increments become progressively smaller thereafter. According to Goldsmith, the share of the assets of financial institutions in total national assets should still show an increasing trend which continues well after the rise in the financial interrelations ratio has slowed down or ceased.

To see this intuitively, consider the development over time of pension and life insurance funds. By using mortality tables, actuaries can estimate the

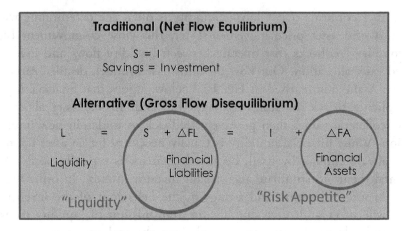

Fig. 10.2 The flow of funds model (summary)

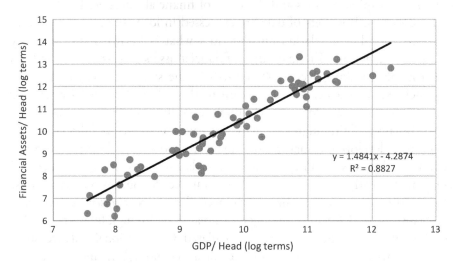

Fig. 10.3 Financial assets and GDP per head, 2018 (US$ in 000s, log terms) (Source *CrossBorder Capital*)

future pattern of required pay-outs. Assuming workers subscribe for pensions at, say, age twenty years and retire at age sixty-five, assets with a maturity (or strictly a duration[2]) of forty-five years are needed to match these liabilities. Therefore, as industrial labour forces grow, and as pension entitlement and the popularity of life insurance expand, so the demand for longer-dated assets will increase. On top of these secular forces that are connected to long-term liabilities, we must add cyclical ones linked to investors' sentiment and investors' attitudes towards risk-taking. Economics teaches that the more roundabout production techniques, those that tie up capital for longer, also tend to be among the most profitable. Consequently, as investors' mood changes from pessimism to optimism they lengthen their investment horizons and they are prepared to discount prospects for profitability further out into the future. Similarly, vice versa. This means that we should not expect the asset composition of an economy to stand still, but rather to both increase towards a longer duration structure over time and to cycle around this trend as investors' mood changes. In other words, the demand for appropriate asset duration to match expected liabilities is a dominant driver of asset allocations.

In practice, we can measure an economy's overall asset mix in several ways. For example, from the average duration of its assets; from the ratio between holdings of long-term and short-term assets; from the split between equities and bond holdings, and from the division between holdings of, so-called, safe assets and risky assets. Given that cash and government bonds tend to be safer and often shorter duration investments, whereas equities and real estate are often longer duration and riskier, these various proposed measures will often give similar results. To express our ideas more succinctly, we will use a simple framework with just two assets, namely a safe, liquid asset, such as cash or bank deposits, and a risk asset, such as equities. Since cash and bank deposits are uniquely legal tender (i.e. ultimate means of settlement) they provide a robust valuation benchmark. The central measure of asset allocation then becomes the P/M or price-to-money ratio, where the 'P' represents the market value of risk asset holdings, here equities, and the 'M' denotes the pool of liquidity or money holdings. A high P/M ratio tells us that investors are allocating more to risk assets, e.g. equities, than they are to safe assets, e.g. cash.

The General Transmission of Liquidity Shocks

Financial assets are usually valued relative to the future incomes they provide, such as the conventional P/E and E *earnings power* model and the less popular, but equivalent, P/GDP and GDP model that is allegedly favoured by veteran US investor Warren Buffett. See, for example, the classical statement in *Security Analysis* by Graham and Dodd (1934). Yet, Beryl Sprinkel (1964) identified the frequent inconsistencies between the business cycle and equity markets:

> It is true that economic activity and stock prices go in the same direction about two-thirds of the time, but it is the other third that is most interesting and potentially most profitable ... Usually, stock price changes move well ahead of subsequent business cycle changes so that economic activity and share prices are moving in separate directions at the turning points in the market.

Occasionally, stock prices forge a pattern all their own, apparently unrelated to the underlying business and profit trends. *Money and Stock Prices* (1964)

In a similar vein, the legendary investor Stan Druckenmiller, told Barron's magazine in a 1988 interview: *"Earnings don't move the overall market; it's the Federal Reserve Board.... Focus on the central banks and focus on the movement of liquidity.... Most people in the market are looking for earnings and conventional measures. It's liquidity that moves markets ... the best environment for stocks is a very dull, slow economy that the Federal Reserve is trying to get going ...".*

Using our liquidity-based framework, financial assets can alternatively be valued as part of a portfolio that balances different risks against, say, cash, for a given profile of liabilities. Expressed by using the previously defined symbols:

$$P_t = \frac{P_t}{M_t} \times M_t \tag{10.1}$$

This expression tells us that asset price movements derive from two components: (1) changes in the P/M ratio between equities and liquid assets, i.e. the portfolio allocation decision, and (2) changes in the flow of new money, M. From our experience, the P/M ratio, in turn, largely depends on four factors, the first three of which are long-term: (a) the structure of taxation, (b) the demographic profile of the economy, (c) the expected inflation rate and (d) investors' risk appetite. In the shorter term, say though the business cycle, when tax rates, demographics and core inflation are roughly unchanged, the main driver of the P/M ratio is investors' mood. Given that this is a psychologically based factor and likely to gyrate between the extremes delineated by investors' degree of greed and fear, it follows that the P/M should itself show an overall tendency to mean- or, at least, trend-revert.

In fact, this simplified expression derives from the more general statement:

$$MC_t = \frac{MC_t}{M_t} \times M_t \tag{10.2}$$

where,

$$MC_t = P_t \times A_t \tag{10.3}$$

and where MC_t denotes market capitalisation; M_t is money or liquidity circulating in the financial sector; P_t represents asset prices and A_t is the number of securities or assets in existence.

Changes in the desired asset mix (MC/M) can occur through changes in the average prices of risk assets (P) and/or through changes in the volume of outstanding financial instruments whether through new issuance or retirements (A). Assuming that these latter changes typically add up to only a small net percentage of overall holdings, then fluctuations in the P/M ratio and in M will combine and drive asset prices. When A_t is fixed, it follows that:

$$\%\Delta P_t = \%\Delta(P_t/M_t) + \%\Delta M_t \qquad (10.4)$$

where $\%\Delta$ represents the period percentage change.

Although the P/M and P/E valuation frameworks are conceptually different, they are connected. This can be seen from the following expression:

$$\frac{P_t}{E_t} = \frac{P_t}{M_t} \times \frac{M_t}{GDP_t} \times \frac{GDP_t}{E_t} \qquad (10.5)$$

This decomposition suggests that the P/E is itself a hybrid statistic that is composed of three factors: (1) a measure of relative asset ownership or asset allocation (P/M); (2) excess liquidity compared to the size of the economy (M/GDP) and (3) aggregate profit margins (E/GDP). In other words, the traditional P/E valuation benchmark is, in practice, driven by three factors: (a) investor sentiment, (b) liquidity and (c) industrial profitability. The influence of each factor is broken out in Table 10.1 for World equity markets. The final column reports the market value to GDP ratio for comparison.

According to this data, the World P/M ratio peaked at 1.36 times in 1999, a huge near five-fold rise from its 1980 level, and it touched a more recent low of 0.65 in 2008. The P/M ratio currently stands just below the mid-way point at 0.96 times. In a two-asset World, an equity-to-cash ratio of 0.96 is equivalent to a portfolio split virtually evenly between equity holdings and liquid assets. Although the World P/M ratio fell sharply in 2008, the main driver of the GFC was less a market valuation extreme, as occurred in year 2000, and was more about skidding liquidity (M) following the collapse of the US shadow banking sector. This then led to a subsequent fall in the P/M ratio as investors grew more risk-averse. Similarly, the 1997/1998 Asian Crisis was triggered by a sudden reversal of cross-border capital flows, which, in turn, destroyed domestic liquidity. Since the GFC, the rebound in World equity prices owes much to the huge volumes of

Table 10.1   Inside the World P/E multiple, 1980–2018 (times)

	P/E	P/M	M/GDP	E/GDP (%)	P/GDP
1980	9.2	0.31	0.55	1.9	0.17
1981	9.7	0.29	0.51	1.5	0.15
1982	9.8	0.31	0.50	1.6	0.15
1983	12.0	0.36	0.50	1.5	0.18
1984	13.1	0.36	0.47	1.3	0.17
1985	12.6	0.41	0.54	1.8	0.22
1986	16.0	0.49	0.63	1.9	0.31
1987	21.4	0.49	0.76	1.7	0.37
1988	20.3	0.59	0.74	2.1	0.44
1989	21.1	0.67	0.73	2.3	0.49
1990	20.6	0.49	0.78	1.8	0.38
1991	16.6	0.55	0.80	2.6	0.44
1992	21.3	0.52	0.77	1.9	0.40
1993	20.9	0.63	0.79	2.4	0.50
1994	25.5	0.62	0.83	2.0	0.52
1995	19.5	0.69	0.85	3.0	0.59
1996	20.2	0.80	0.81	3.2	0.65
1997	20.2	0.98	0.74	3.6	0.72
1998	21.4	1.10	0.82	4.2	0.90
1999	25.6	1.36	0.84	4.5	1.14
2000	28.8	1.25	0.76	3.3	0.95
2001	24.1	1.09	0.73	3.3	0.79
2002	21.9	0.84	0.75	2.9	0.63
2003	17.1	1.03	0.81	4.9	0.83
2004	19.9	1.10	0.84	4.6	0.92
2005	17.4	1.23	0.79	5.6	0.98
2006	18.2	1.33	0.85	6.2	1.12
2007	17.2	1.29	0.96	7.2	1.24
2008	14.7	0.65	1.02	4.5	0.66
2009	9.6	0.87	1.10	10.0	0.96
2010	18.7	0.92	1.13	5.5	1.04
2011	15.9	0.77	1.15	5.6	0.89
2012	12.8	0.84	1.16	7.7	0.98
2013	15.0	0.97	1.14	7.4	1.11
2014	15.7	1.00	1.11	7.1	1.11
2015	17.1	0.97	1.07	6.1	1.04
2016	16.2	0.99	1.06	6.4	1.04
2017	19.0	1.12	1.10	6.5	1.23
2018	20.1	0.96	1.08	5.2	1.04

Source *CrossBorder Capital*

liquidity injected by Central Banks through quantitative easing (QE) policies, which have helped to spur a recovery in investors' risk appetite.

The charts in Figs. 10.4 and 10.5 show the co-movements between the
P/E, and the P/M (correlation coefficient 0.47) and P/GDP (correlation

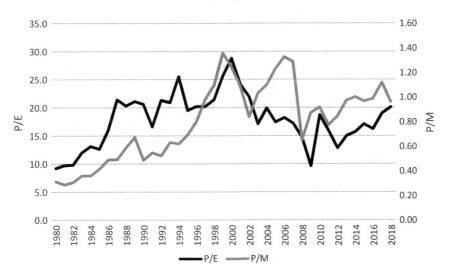

Fig. 10.4 World P/E and P/M ratios, 1980–2018 (times) (Source *CrossBorder Capital*)

coefficient 0.30) ratios, respectively. The data also reveal a strong positive correlation between the P/M and the excess liquidity term (correlation coefficient 0.57). This tells us that increases in liquidity tend to be associated with asset allocation shifts towards risk assets. In other words, when liquidity is plentiful, then risk-taking should be widespread. On the other hand, periods of scarce liquidity are associated with market panics when investors rush for 'safety'. This seems plausible, because as the pool of available liquidity increases, defaults and other systemic risks should diminish, thereby reducing the need to hold precautionary safe assets and so allowing investors to expand their investment horizons towards holding more risk assets. Alternatively, when tight liquidity raises systemic risks, investors will shift their holdings towards safer assets, such as cash deposits.

There is no right or wrong in preferring one valuation benchmark, such as the P/E, rather than another, say the P/M. Ultimately, the choice of valuation method is subjective and it comes down to analysing future opportunities from either the perspective of the investment security (i.e. using the P/E) or from the standpoint of the investor (i.e. via the P/M). The traditional P/E is a well-established statistic and plainly the more practical when assessing the merits of individual securities. However, it is compromised when there are no earnings and when earnings are particularly volatile. Moreover, it is less clear what it really means at the aggregate market level, as the P/E decomposition hinted earlier. The attraction of the P/M alternative is that it relates to investors rather than to investments, i.e. securities,

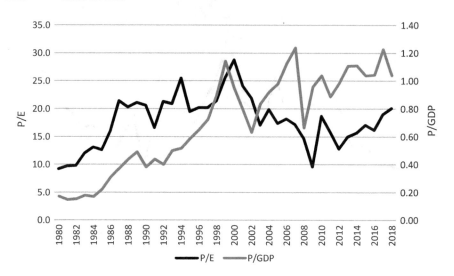

Fig. 10.5 World P/E and P/GDP ratios, 1980–2018 (times) (Source *CrossBorder Capital*)

and it works particularly well when trying to analyse the changing mood of the investment crowd. As such, it lends itself directly to behavioural interpretations and it allows us to better understand the influence of liquidity on asset allocation. To summarise, we tend to favour the P/M or *investor power* model for three reasons: (1) it is a more intuitive way of understanding investor behaviour because it has a direct association with asset allocation; (2) liquidity, a key determinant of investor and market action is easily incorporated into the framework, and (3) we find the P/M ratio is, in practice, more stable and mean- or trend-reverting than the conventional P/E multiple, which in, say, profit recessions can surge higher, because the 'E' collapses, and so distort any future valuation opportunities (Fig. 10.4).

The Transmission of Liquidity Shocks to Bonds and Forex Markets

Whereas the previous section has focussed more generally on investor positioning and takes equities as its main example, this section is a more granular study of how liquidity affects the fixed income and currency markets. Liquidity shocks are primarily transmitted through domestic financial markets, along two channels, by changing the implicit risk and term premia that are notionally embedded in asset prices. These term and risk premia reflect balance sheet mismatches, such as currency exposure (i.e. forex risk); the interest rate term structure of government bond holdings (i.e. maturity risk), corporate credit quality (i.e. default risk), or some combination of the three (i.e. duration risk).[3] We identify two key liquidity transmission channels in modern financial systems:

1. *Quantity*: changes in the absolute volume of liquidity directly affects investors' appetite for risk-taking. When liquidity is plentiful, risk-taking is widespread, but periods of scarce liquidity are frequently associated with market panics as investors rush to 'safety'. This behaviour is captured by movements in various interest rate spreads and risk premia, such as the maturity spread or yield curve slope.
2. *Quality*: money and liquidity are hierarchical, and so the quality mix of liquidity will affect the 'price' of money, i.e. the exchange rate. A vibrant private sector that throws off cash is likely to attract investment. However, since domestic money is less useful in international markets, the quality mix is poor (good) when Central Banks are aggressively supplying more (less) than the private sector needs. This results in a weaker (stronger) exchange rate. By a similar reasoning, a better quality of liquidity mix should also favour private sector corporate bonds over government securities.

To better understand these transmission channels, we need to frame liquidity in terms of the supply and demand for safe assets. We define a 'safe' asset more formally in Chapter 11, but essentially it derives from the asset's ability to cover expected liabilities. The canonical 'safe' asset is the 10-year US Treasury note. Treasuries are considered 'safe' assets by the majority of investors, whereas corporate bonds are usually deemed to be riskier assets, because of their greater risk of default, which is, in turn, implicitly assessed from the credit quality grades assigned to issuers by the credit-rating agencies, such as Moody's and the Standard & Poors company. More liquidity has potentially large effects on systemic risk by reducing frictions and lowering the odds of default. Economic agents typically default because they are illiquid and not necessarily because they are insolvent. Modern finance theory contends that this should be impossible because a solvent entity can in theory always borrow, yet defaults still happen. The reduced threat of default implied by a greater availability of liquidity persuades risk-averse investors to cut back on their holdings of safe assets and switch instead towards riskier assets, like equities. Generally, when liquidity is plentiful the demand for risk assets tends to exceed the demand for safe assets, and similarly vice versa.

It follows that changes in Central Bank Liquidity provision, e.g. QE policies, operate through this risk-taking channel by affecting the supply and demand for safe assets and, hence, bond term premia. This, in turn, as we show below, affects the level and shape of the interest rate term structure. However, the attention of most bond market investors typically focusses on the policy rate announcement, with commentators frequently rivalling one another to guess whether, say, the Fed is going to announce a cut in its target Fed Funds rates by 25 bp or even 50 bp. However, this is only one factor behind asset returns and by no means the most powerful. What, in our view, matters more than the short-term rate is the entire term structure of interest rates stretching out across future tenors, say, 5 years, 10 years and even 30 years ahead.

The term structure is conventionally expressed through so-called spot yields,[4] or the average yield on a notional zero-coupon bond, over that time horizon. Thus, a 2-year bond paying 2% in year 1 and 3% in year 2, has a spot yield of 2.5%. The term structure of interest rates at any yield tenor can be thought of as consisting of: (1) a policy rate expectations component, measuring the average policy rate over that horizon, and (2) a term premia that compensates the investor for tying funds up for a longer period rather than continuously rolling-over a shorter-term instrument. Thus, each spot yield (y_t^m) along the term structure comprises an expected short-term interest rate (r_t) over a holding period (m) plus a nominal term (or bond maturity[5] risk) premium (tp_t^m):

$$y_t^m = \frac{1}{m} \sum_{i=0}^{m-1} E_t r_{t+i} + tp_t^m \tag{10.6}$$

where y_t^m is the spot yield of a bond of maturity m, at time t; E_t denotes the expectations operator; r_t is the interest rate; tp_t^m represents the nominal bond term premium over a holding period m.

These term premia cover future inflation and market volatility risks, and they include the effects from the excess supply or excess demand for bonds arising from, say, government austerity policies that limit new issuance and/or from tighter regulations that require more 'safe' assets. As systemic risks grow, investors will demand more-and-more safe assets, thereby, forcing down term premia.

The conventional narrative is that Central Banks control the path of policy rates, which they have lately signalled through 'forward guidance' policies, and they themselves can drive down term premia and, hence, long-term yields through the buying-in of government bonds through LSAP (large-scale asset purchases), or QE (quantitative easing) policies. Event studies that use average responses calibrated across different markets purport to show that, as a broad rule of thumb, asset purchases worth 10% of GDP reduce

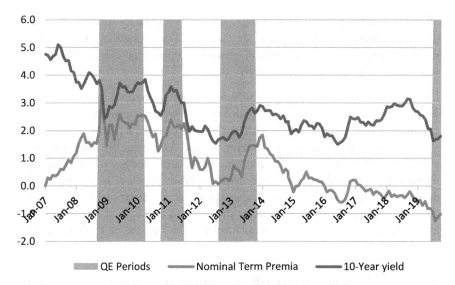

Fig. 10.6 US QE periods, US Treasury 10-year yields and term premia, 2007–2019 (percent) (Source *CrossBorder Capital*)

10-year yields by around 50-100 bp. In other words, according to this view, a monetary expansion involving simultaneous rate cuts and QE should therefore mean lower yields across the term structure and probably even lower longer term yields, i.e. a yield curve flattening. Yet, the evidence shows precisely the reverse. The chart in Fig. 10.6 highlights the clear positive correlation between Federal Reserve QE periods and US Treasury 10-year term premia: term premia rise (not fall) by an average 135 bp under QE programmes (shaded) and they have fallen as the QE programmes expire or turn into QT (quantitative tightening).

The error is that the standard narrative ignores the fact that the demand for safe assets can itself change as Central Banks signal their actions. Private sector demand for safe assets depends upon what investors' anticipate policy-makers will do. Safe asset demands depend upon systemic risks and specifically on the access to sufficient liquidity for refinancing purposes. If, as a corollary to QE, the volume of cash in financial markets is boosted sufficiently to significantly reduce systemic threats, the demand of investors for safe assets should correspondingly drop:

....many recent LSAP studies (see Krishnamurthy and Vissing-Jorgensen, 2011 and Gagnon, 2016, for a summary) have flaws: for example, they ignore the substitution and dynamic effects that cause changes in the overall demand for safe assets, such as Treasury securities. Consequently, these event studies often reach perverse conclusions about asset prices and rarely acknowledge that the effectiveness of LSAP is typically conditional on the state of the economy, since consistent policy transmission crucially depends of the persistence of extant informational and market frictions. …

LSAP policies effectively force the private sector to substitute cash for bonds. The reduction in the supply of bonds to the private sector decreases the amount of outstanding duration risk and, given preferred habitats, also creates scarcity effects that together lower term premia. However, the impact of the announcement of policy action, combined with the injection of more liquidity into markets, reduces perceived systemic risks, increases investors' confidence and so encourages the private sector to cut its demand for safe assets, including Treasury bonds. This causes the demand curve for maturity to shift leftwards and so drive up term premia as investors become more risk-seeking. (Howell 2017)

In other words, term premia reflect imbalances between the supply and demand for Treasuries. They specifically derive from safety and duration characteristics: in fact, these two are often connected. Central Bank QE policy, enacted through LSAP programmes unambiguously decrease the effective supply of asset duration to the private sector (D), and potentially below their targeted levels (say, D*). This boosts risk-taking and the hunt for longer duration assets, such as equities. Equally, as we acknowledged earlier, the canonical safe asset for most investors is the 10-year US Treasury. A reduction in the supply of Treasuries to the private sector, caused by (1) government austerity policies; (2) tighter regulations and (3) LSAP (large-scale asset purchases) by Central Banks as part of a QE policy, will cause a scarcity and drive term premia lower. However, as noted above, the demand for safe assets is governed by the threat of systemic risk. Low levels of liquidity raise systemic risks because they are associated with higher default rates. Individuals and corporations tend to default because they are denied access to funds, i.e. they are illiquid, rather than because they are necessarily insolvent. Hence, an increase in liquidity by reducing systemic risks leads to a rise in targeted asset duration (D*) and to a fall in the demand for safe assets. This results in higher bond term premia. In turn, this explains the close connection between liquidity, term premia and the slope of the yield curve. However, Central Bank interventions through their open market operations can muddy the waters when they simultaneously buy government bonds as part of their attempts to boost liquidity. This is because private sector credit providers themselves use Treasuries as collateral for their repo funding. Consequently, while the supply of liquidity to the private sector expands,

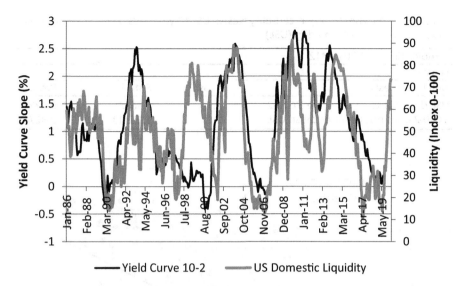

Fig. 10.7 US liquidity (advanced 9 months) and 10-2 year US Treasury yield curve slope, 1986–2020 (percent and index, 0–100) (Source *CrossBorder Capital*)

the availability of long-dated collateral could contract, thereby leaving the net supply of liquidity uncertain.

Thus, despite a potential reduction in the effective supply of 'safe' asset Treasuries for the private sector, the net effect, and the effect arguably shown in the data in Fig. 10.6, is a deeper cut in the excess demand for safety (e.g. D*-D, in duration terms). In other words, LSAP, or QE policies, are associated with lower net demands for safe assets and hence higher bond yields. Reverse QE, or QT, policies, in turn, are linked to falling bond yields. And, given that term premia, by definition, make up a progressively larger-and-larger component of yields as bond maturity extends,[6] QE policies necessarily cause yield curves to steepen. We noted a similar result in Chapter 7. Since long-term interest rates matter when assessing the viability of long-term projects and because bank profitability often rests on the slope of the yield curve, these term structure movements will have an important impact on the real economy. Figures 10.7 and 10.8 use the *CrossBorder Capital* Global Liquidity Indexes[7] (GLI) to evidence the close link between liquidity and the slope of the yield curve. These charts demonstrate the high correlation between a simple index measure of the US liquidity sub-component (advanced by 9 months) and movements in the 10-year less 2-year US Treasury yield spread. Liquidity is strongly one-way Granger causal ($p = 0.0335, 0.3278$). See Table 10.2. This framework appears to confirm that more liquidity, such as via QE, increases term premia and steepens the yield curve, whereas less

Table 10.2 Pairwise Granger causality tests: US 10-year less 2-year treasury yield curve (YC10-2) and US liquidity (USL)

Sample: 1985M01 2019M12			
Lags: 6			
Null hypothesis	Obs	F-statistic	Prob.
USL does not Granger cause YC10-2	419	2.30685	0.0335
YC10-2 does not Granger cause USL		1.15843	0.3278

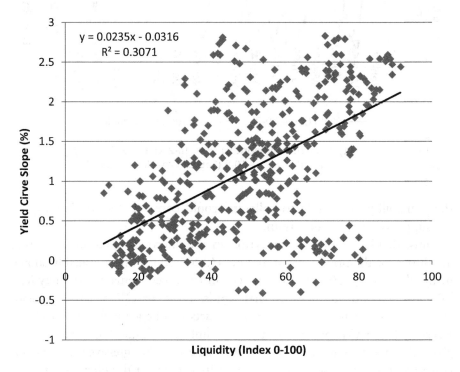

Fig. 10.8 Scatter diagram US liquidity (advanced 9 months) and 10-2 year US Treasury yield curve slope, 1985–2019 (percent and index, 0–100)

liquidity, say a QT, flattens the term structure. The yield curve steepens and flattens procyclically because, as noted, the contribution of term premia to yields increases with maturity. So, any change in term premia affects longer maturity bonds more than the shorter dated tenors.

There may also be another feedback because low term premia, reflecting greater systemic risks and the excess demand for safe assets, can themselves cause prudent policy-makers to further ease monetary conditions. Narrowing term premia express themselves through falling bond yields, and this could, consequently, explain why long-term interest rates often precede similar directional changes in short-term interest rates. Central Bank interventions

Table 10.3 Pairwise Granger causality tests: 10-year US Treasuries (R10) and federal funds (FF)

Sample: 1985M01 2019M12			
Lags: 3			
Null hypothesis	Obs	F-statistic	Prob.
R10 does not Granger cause FF	419	7.42625	0.0000
FF does not Granger cause R10		0.51041	0.6753

will themselves lead on to higher future term premia, which, in turn, can help to explain the seemingly regular cyclical shifts in the yield curve.

Paradoxically, the prevailing consensus believes that Central Banks alone set interest rates, but one implication of liquidity analysis is that the markets play the leading role and Central Banks react to their movements by changing their policy rates to keep up. Put another way, long-term interest rates determine short-term interest rates and not, vice versa, as the textbooks claim. This can be demonstrated statistically using Granger causality tests. The relationship reported in Table 10.3 tells us that there is a near-zero probability that long-term yields fail to Granger cause Fed Funds rates, with odds of more than two-to-one against Fed Funds rates Granger causing long-term yields. The result is true both for levels and for first differences.

Of course, these are not widely held views. According to the Federal Reserve[8]: "*A primary channel through which [Quantitative Easing] takes place is by narrowing the risk premiums on the assets being purchased. By purchasing a particular asset, the Fed reduces the amount of the security that the private sector holds, displacing some investors and reducing the holdings of others. In order for investors to be willing to make those adjustments, the expected return on the security has to fall. Put differently, the purchasers bid up the price of the asset and hence lower its yield. These effects would be expected to spill over into other assets that are similar in nature, to the extent that investors are willing to substitute between the assets. These patterns describe what researchers often refer to the portfolio balance channel*". The former US FOMC member Jeremy Stein (2012) is similarly unequivocal: "*... One thing that seems clear from the data is that if you buy a lot of long-term Treasury securities, this exerts significant downward pressure on their yields and term premiums ...*". Not to be outdone, Andrew Hauser from the Bank of England[9] warns: "*But QT, when it comes, may imply a steeper yield curve than we see today*". And, his colleague, MPC member Gertjan Vlieghe[10] is even more forthright: "*To explain why long-term interest rates declined throughout the post-crisis period, we have to resort to interest rate expectations, we cannot plausibly invoke the mechanical impact of asset purchases.... the data show, most of the fall in long-term interest rates was not due to risk premia, but due to expectations of the future path of policy rates*".

In fact, the yield curve slope itself is a flaky predictor of the future business cycle (Howell 2018). What also seems to matter is the curvature of the term structure, which is often determined by the pattern of term premia (Howell 2019). These term premia frequently detract from the pure efficacy of yield curve predictions, which implies that they may contain more information about the financial economy than about the real economy. This may explain why the Bank of England sets out five broader channels through which QE and liquidity can affect the overall economy:

- Policy signalling effects: QE acts as a signal to market participants of the central bank's commitment to meet inflation targets, which lead market participants to expect policy rates to remain low for longer than otherwise. By anchoring expectations, asset purchases can support increased spending.
- Portfolio rebalancing effects: central bank asset purchases raise the price of assets bought and other assets, leading to investors rebalancing their portfolios to include higher yielding assets. The increase in asset prices helps to depress yields, which lowers borrowing costs for firms. This helps to support increased investment and spending.
- Liquidity premia effects: Asset purchases can improve market liquidity by actively encouraging trading. The effects of this channel only persist while asset purchases are ongoing.
- Confidence effects: Asset purchases may help to boost confidence, leading to an increase in investment and consumer spending.
- Bank lending effects: The higher level of reserves held by banks and liquid assets encourages banks to increase lending to corporates and consumers.

Although we still favour the 'safe' asset or risk channel, like the US Federal Reserve, the Bank of England considers the portfolio balance channel to be the most important element of its approach, which is why purchases have been targeted towards long-term assets held by non-bank financial institutions such as insurers and pension funds. This is to encourage a shift towards riskier investments such as corporate bonds and equities. The impact of the bank lending channel may be dampened by the pressures on banks to reduce the size of their balance sheets and to rebuild their capital reserves.

Yet, the common denominator of each of these official and semi-official views is that more liquidity will drive down government bond yields. If this is at all correct, it is only true fleetingly. Gagnon[11] neatly summarises the numerous academic studies of the effects of Central Bank quantitative easing policies. See Table 10.4. Standardising his various results, Gagnon found that a QE

Table 10.4 Estimated effects of quantitative easing (LSAP) on 10-year bond yields

Study	Sample	Method	Yield reduction (basis points)
United States			
Greenwood and Vayanos (2008)[a]	1952–2005	Time series	82
Gagnon, Raskin, Remache, and Sack (2011)	2008–2009	Event study	78
Gagnon, Raskin, Remache, and Sack (2011)	1985–2007	Time series TP only	44
Krishnamurthy and Vissing-Jorgensen (2011)	2008–2009	Event study	91
Krishnamurthy and Vissing-Jorgensen (2011)	2010–2011	Event study	47
Hamilton and Wu (2012)	1990–2007	Affine model	47
Swanson (2011)	1961	Event study	88
D'Amico and King (2013)	2009–2010	Micro event study	240
D'Amico, English, Lopez-Salido, and Nelson (2012)	2002–2008	Weekly time series	165
Li and Wei (2012)	1994–2007	Affine model of TP	57
Rosa (2012)	2008–2010	Event study	42
Neely (2012)	2008–2009	Event study	84
Bauer and Neely (2012)	2008–2009	Event study	80
Bauer and Rudebusch (2011)[b]	2008–2009	Event study TP only	44
Christensen and Rudebusch (2012)[b]	2008–2009	Event study TP only	26
Chadha, Turner, and Zampolli (2013)	1990–2008	Time series TP only	56
Swanson (2015)[b]	2009–2015	Yield curve TP only	40
Christensen and Rudebusch (2012)[b]	2008–2009	Event study TP only	15
United Kingdom			
Joyce, Lasaosa, Stevens, and Tong (2011)	2009	Event study	78
Joyce, Lasaosa, Stevens, and Tong (2011)	1991–2007	Time series	51
Christensen and Rudebusch (2012)[b]	2009–2011	Event study TP only	34
Churm, Joyce, Kapetanios, and Theodoris (2015)	2011–2012	Intl. comparison	42
Japan			
Fukunaga, Kato, and Koeda (2015)	1992–2014	Time series TP only	24
Fukunaga, Kato, and Koeda (2015)	2013–2014	Event study	17

(continued)

Table 10.4 (continued)

Study	Sample	Method	Yield reduction (basis points)
Eurozone			
Middeldorp (2015)[c]	2013–2015	Event study	45–132
Altavilla, Carboni, and Motto (2015)[d]	2014–2015	Event study	44
Middeldorp and Wood (2016)[c]	2015	Event study	41–104
Sweden			
De Rezende, Kjellberg, and Tysklind (2015)	2015	Event study	68

Notes [a]Greenwood and Vayanos scaled the effect relative to the size of the Treasury market. The estimate here is based on the ratio of Treasury debt to GDP in 2015

[b]These studies further differentiate between signalling effects and portfolio effects. The reported estimate is for the portfolio effect only

[c]The smaller estimate is for German bonds and the larger one is for Italian bonds

[d]The estimate is for an average of Eurozone bonds

Purchases normalised to 10% of GDP. 100 bp equals 1% point. Most studies present a range of estimates. The Table displays the preferred estimate if one exists. If not, it presents the midpoint of the range. For event studies, the purchases are normalised by all long-term bonds, not just government bonds. Some of the non-event studies include non-government bond purchases and others do not. "TP only" denotes studies that attempt to estimate the term premium component of movements in bond yields. For event studies, the normalisation is based on GDP in the final year of the event

Source Gagnon (2016)

programme totalling a benchmark 10% of GDP led to an average reduction of 67 bp in bond yields: slightly more in the case of the Eurozone, and slightly less for Japan. *Pace* academia, what works in practice seemingly does not work in theory! We (and the markets) profoundly disagree, because more liquidity drives down the price of safe assets and drives up the price of risky assets, often in both absolute and relative terms. Thus, periods of abundant liquidity see government yield curves steepen; credit spreads narrow, and equities outperform bonds, led by strong gains in value stocks relative to growth stocks.

Exchange Rates

We have already discussed exchange rates in some detail. Readers are referred back to Chapter 5. However, in outline, we argued earlier that exchange rates depend on the quality mix of liquidity between private sector (or 'good') liquidity and Central Bank (or 'bad') liquidity. Central Bank liquidity represents an additional supply of a currency. While this may favour domestic risk assets, extra supply acts to weaken the exchange rate. In contrast, private sector liquidity is a measure of an economy's cash flow generation. This is likely to move procyclically with the real economy and may even slightly precede the business cycle. Stronger economic activity should encourage investment and incentivise capital inflows. As these are attracted to the currency, the exchange rate should appreciate. Consequently, the difference between private sector liquidity and Central Bank liquidity is likely to predict future exchange rate movements. This view is different from that outlined in the previous section about domestic asset markets, which argued that the sum (not difference) of private sector and Central Bank liquidity determines bond term premia, and it also contrasts with the standard monetarist view of exchange rate determination. Monetarists typically do not differentiate between these different types of liquidity, taking their aggregate sum as a measure of supply. Instead, we favour this *quality theory of money*.

Risk Assets

We have shown how more liquidity reduces the average level of asset duration (D) available to the private sector and by cutting default rates, cuts the odds of systemic risk. This, in turn, increases duration targets (D*), raises the term premia on safe assets, such as government bonds, and, correspondingly, lowers the risk premia demanded on risk assets. In other words, more liquidity

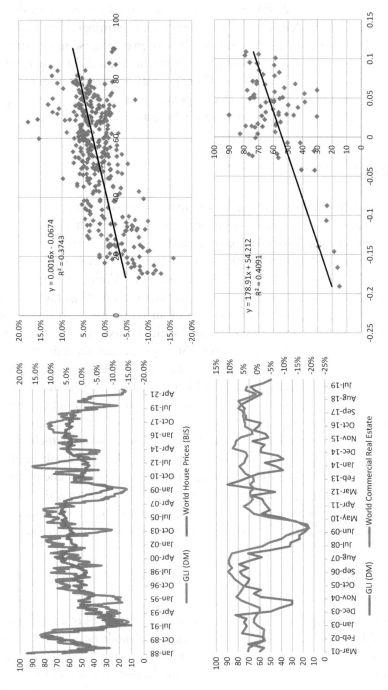

Fig. 10.9 Real estate prices and Global Liquidity, 1988–2019 (indexes and annual percentage change) (*Source* BIS and *CrossBorder Capital*)

should drive a hunt for more duration and so push risk asset prices higher. We examine the two main classes: (1) real estate and (2) equity markets.

Risk Assets 1: Real Estate

The relationship between real estate and liquidity can be separated into the markets for private housing and for commercial buildings, which includes both retail and industrial properties. The lead-times between a liquidity impulse and the reaction of the real estate markets are relative long at around three years in all three cases, but they are strongly positive and statistically significant. The time-series data and regression results are shown in Fig. 10.9. The charts report results for the Developed Economies. The real estate prices are taken from the BIS database and the derived aggregates are constructed as simple rather than weighted averages across economies. House prices consist of monthly observations starting from year 2000, whereas commercial real estate is quarterly data beginning in 1991. The liquidity variable is the *CrossBorder Capital* GLI Index for Developed Markets. According to the regression results detailed in the charts, each 10% point increase in the GLI index ('normal' range 0–100) leads to an approximate 2% annual rise in real estate values, slightly more for commercial buildings and slightly less for housing.

Risk Assets 2: Equities

We have already suggested that: (1) the quantitative flow of liquidity drives the bond and real estate markets and (2) the quality mix of liquidity determines exchange rates. We next intend to show that it is: (3) the positioning of liquidity (and safe assets in general) within investment portfolios that proves to be a major factor behind equity market returns. This implies that there exists some asset allocation 'norm', possibly measured by duration, which investors target, and it, therefore, follows that changes in their risk appetites, relative to this norm, cause them to shift funds into and out of risk assets. Equities (typically a long duration asset) maybe, in fact, the marginal or swing asset class that they can use to quickly adjust their portfolio mix. In other words, imbalances and tensions in the fixed income and foreign exchange markets are often expressed through equities. This is an empirical question. Put yet another way, this may explain why it often pays to be a contrarian investor in equity markets by doing the opposite of the crowd, when it is at its most greedy and most fearful extremes.

The asset mixes implied by the holdings of equities, bonds and liquid assets are reported in Fig. 10.10. The data covers all investors and they are shown as percentages of the three main primary financial asset classes— bonds, stocks and liquid assets. Tangible assets, such as land and real estate, are excluded, and we have looked-through secondary instruments, such as investment funds, to their underlying primary asset constituents. While these asset mixes vary significantly between economies, they appear remarkably stable over time with clear visual evidence of mean-reversion or trend-reversion. For example, the latest data show that US investors hold the highest percentages in equities (36%) and Japanese investors hold the least (20%). British (35%) and mainland European investors (34%) stand close to American levels of equity exposure, whereas Emerging Market investors (24%) are nearer to Japanese levels. Bond exposure shows a similar variation. Eurozone investors (48%) currently have the highest exposure to fixed income, paced by the US (46%) and Japanese investors (45%). Liquid asset holdings are substantially higher in Emerging Markets (45%) than elsewhere. Bringing this together, the aggregated World asset mix is currently invested 31% in equities, or very close to its long-run trend since 1990 of 28%; 40% in bonds and 29% in liquid assets. World equity allocation peaked at 36.4% in October 2007 ahead of the GFC, or more than two standard deviations (i.e. 2 × 4%) above average, and it peaked at a similar extreme deviation in August 2000 at 38.1% during the Y2K bubble. Following the GFC, the equity proportion of portfolios troughed at under 19%, or some two-and-one half standard deviations below average.

What explains the cross-country variation in asset allocation? Why do US investors favour equities, Japanese investors prefer bonds and Emerging Market investors like to hold substantial amounts of cash? Cultural, institutional and demographic reasons feature, together with economic factors, such as expected inflation, the domestic tax structure and per capita incomes. Together these factors define the size and duration of future liabilities. National investors will then choose the asset mix that will appropriately match the pattern and timing of these future liabilities, subject to their risk preferences. For example, investors resident in relatively low per capita income economies, with underdeveloped financial institutions are more likely to hold large amounts of liquid assets. Equally, investors in developed economies with young workforces are more likely to favour equities. However, the representative asset mix will adjust to increasingly favour bonds as workforces age, on average, and when deflationary pressures build. For the most part, these factors are relatively slow-moving, with the exception being changes in investors' risk appetite.

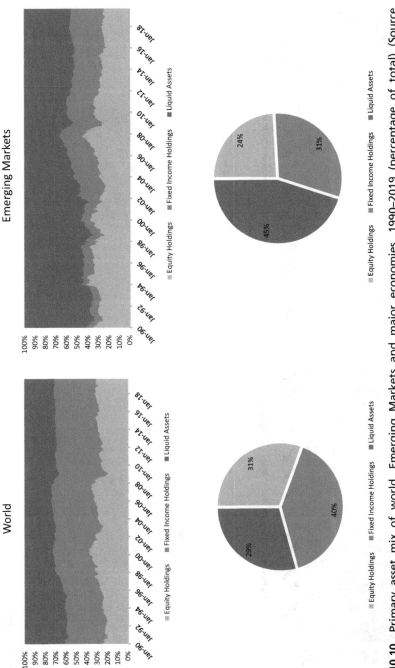

Fig. 10.10 Primary asset mix of world, Emerging Markets and major economies, 1990–2019 (percentage of total) (Source *CrossBorder Capital*)

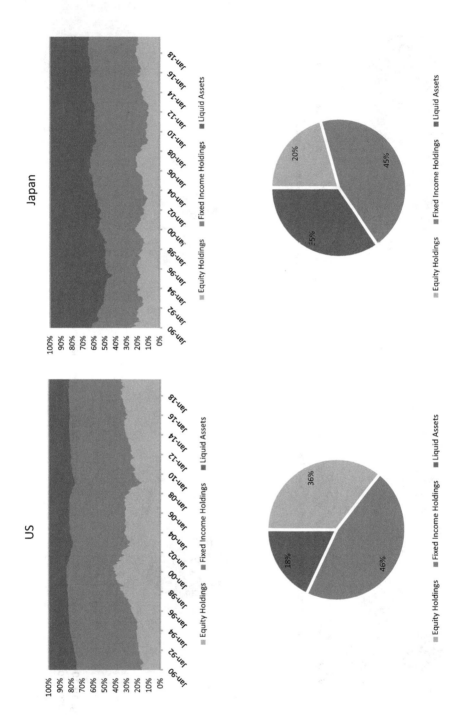

Fig. 10.10 (continued)

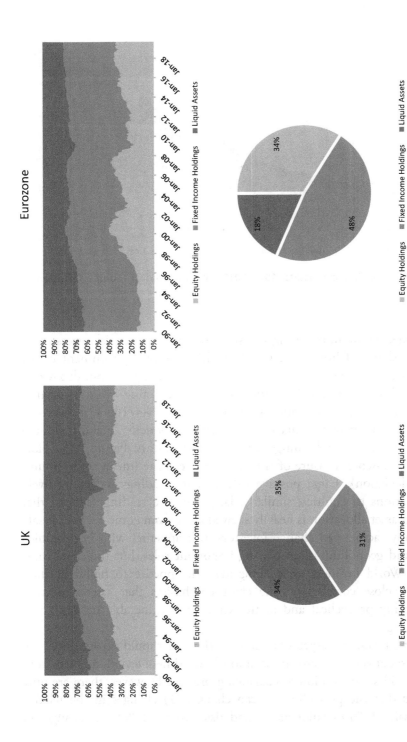

Fig. 10.10 (continued)

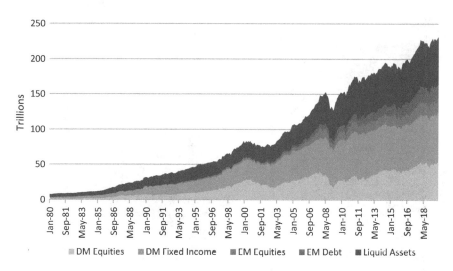

Fig. 10.11 Global financial assets, 1980–2019 (US$ in trillions) (Source *CrossBorder Capital*)

Consequently, by normalising the share of equities (i.e. risk assets) relative to the shares of liquid assets and, in this example, government bonds (i.e. safe assets) as reported in Fig. 10.11, using a rolling 41-month z-score, we can think of the residual variation as largely reflecting investors' changing risk appetite. The mountain-scape diagram in Fig. 10.11 reports our estimates of the major primary asset class components making up the US$230 trillion of asset holdings across World investors. Figure 10.12 plots the resulting z-score measure of risk appetite over time (mean zero, 20-unit standard deviation). Large positive risk appetite readings reflect relatively high allocations to equities, similarly, large negative readings suggest that the current asset allocation is heavily skewed away from equities towards safe assets. Many factors can change investors' risk appetite, with both liquidity flows and geopolitics often playing important roles, but the chart compares the World business cycle alongside risk appetite to highlight their particularly close correlation. The chart emphasises that asset allocation is both highly procyclical and at the same time vulnerable to significant over-shooting.

Assuming investors' target an asset allocation, we should expect the actual asset mix to converge towards these 'norms' over time. Deviations away from the target will set in motion a rebalancing process. However, there are only three ways that the portfolio mix can change: (1) changes in the relative prices of safe (19% of adjustment) and risky assets (21%); (2) changes in

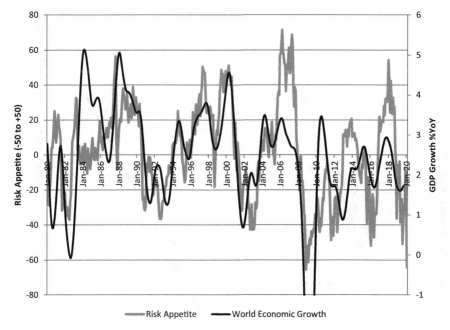

Fig. 10.12 World Risk appetite index ('normal' range -50 to +50) and GDP growth (percent), 1980–2019 (Source *CrossBorder Capital*)

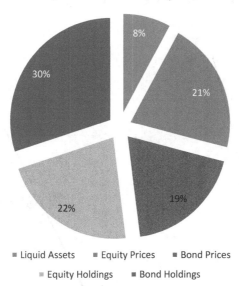

- Liquid Assets - Equity Prices - Bond Prices
- Equity Holdings - Bond Holdings

Fig. 10.13 Contribution to variations in world investors' portfolio mix, 2000–2019 (monthly, percent) (Source *CrossBorder Capital*)

the supply of safe assets (27%) and (3) changes in the supply of risky assets (22%). See Fig. 10.13. In practice, some combination of all of these channels usually takes place.

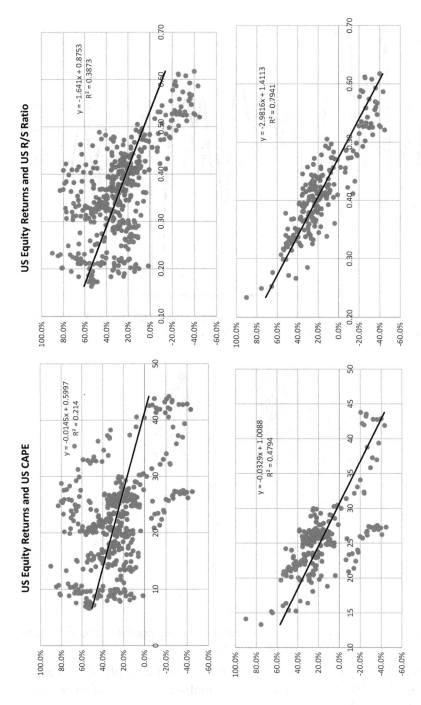

Fig. 10.14 Efficacy of US CAPE and US risk/safe asset ratios as predictors of future 2-year equity returns, 1980–2019 and 2000–2019 (percent) (Source *CrossBorder Capital*)

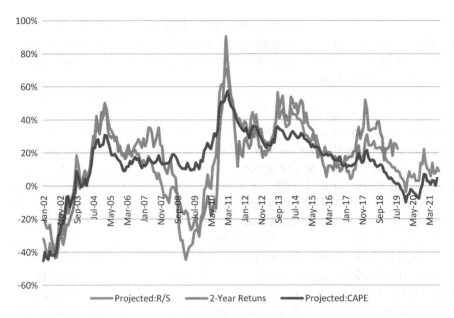

Fig. 10.15 Prediction of future 2-year equity returns using US CAPE and US risk/safe asset ratios, 2002–2021 (percent) (Source *CrossBorder Capital*)

A large move upward in the value of equities could tip the balance of the portfolio too far towards risky assets. This may lead to a reversal of relative asset prices as equities are switched into bonds. In practice, risk asset prices typically take on most of the adjustment burden because the prices of safe assets, i.e. cash and dated government bonds are more limited in how much they can move. On the other hand, changes in the supply of safe assets can be significant. Prior to the 2007–2008 GFC, it was not unusual for the supply of 'safe' assets to grow at 10–15% annual rates. Again, this may lead to investors selling existing bonds and investing new cash into equities. Since the GFC, the supply of safe assets has been deliberately constrained by austerity policies and by Central Banks varying quantitative policies. On top, many US corporations have aggressively bought back their shares with cash. This means, that the behaviour of investors is often more variable than the earnings and dividends that characterise the underlying securities. Therefore, knowing when asset allocations are skewed significantly towards risky assets is likely to anticipate future selling by the mass of investors and hence lower equity returns. The charts reported in Fig. 10.14 show how the ratio (R/S) between risky (equities) and safe (government bonds and cash) affects future stock returns 2-years ahead. We consider two periods (1980–2019 and 2000–2019) and compare the results of the US equity to safe asset ratio (R/S) to the US Shiller CAPE (cyclically adjusted price to earnings) multiple. Future returns can be better explained by the US R/S ratio (R^2 59 and 80%) than by the CAPE (R^2 21 and 50%) over both periods.

The 1980s and 1990s were both decades of significant equity market returns (S&P Composite rose by 1225%), but it was also a twenty-year period of moderate earnings growth (+218.4%). The most significant driver of equities during the period was the sizeable drop in allocations to liquid assets and the increase in the appetite for risk assets, with US equity exposure rising from around 14% to a whopping 42% of national financial wealth by end-1999. Today, equity exposure is around 36% of US financial wealth and noticeably above the post-1990 average allocation of 29%.

Looking ahead, the latest relatively high readings for both the US CAPE and the US R/S ratios point to future lacklustre returns. This is indicated by Fig. 10.15 which reports results using the regression models described in Fig. 10.14. The track record of both valuation metrics can be compared to the outcome from the rolling 2-year returns on the S&P500 index. Both valuation measures appear to serve investors well, but the US R/S ratio performed far better than the US CAPE over the period of the 2007–2008 GFC. In other words, this suggests that asset valuation is a relative rather than an absolute criterion, which necessarily involves an implied arbitrage between risk and safe assets.

Asset Allocation

Asset prices change because of buying and selling actions, fuelled by changes in liquidity and investors' risk appetites, that cause imbalances between demand and supply. Rather than focus on the theoretical valuation of individual securities, we use liquidity and flow of funds to analyse the asset allocation behaviour of the aggregate investor community between various risky and safe assets. Consequently, when their desired asset allocation changes from holding safe assets, such as government bonds, to holding more risky assets, such as equities, so these investors will purchase more equities and their prices should tend to rise. Similarly, vice versa. Therefore, assuming asset allocation mean-reverts to some 'norm' over time, knowing when asset allocations are skewed significantly towards risky assets anticipates future selling and hence lower prospective equity returns.

Arguably the most famous reference work on value investing, Graham and Dodd's Security Analysis, succinctly summarises the art of investment:

The Global **Liquidity** Cycle

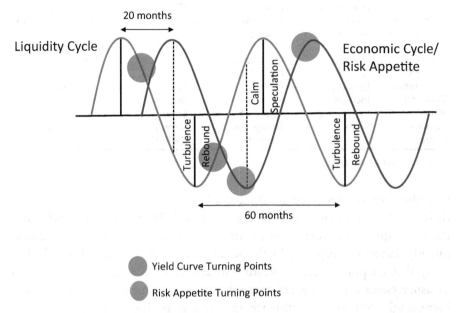

Fig. 10.16 Asset allocation using the Global Liquidity cycle (schematic) (Source *CrossBorder Capital*)

"*...the market is not a weighting machine, on which the value of each issue is recorded by an exact and impersonal mechanism, in accordance with its specific qualities. Rather should we say that the market is a voting machine, whereon countless individuals register choices, which are the product partly of reason and partly of emotion*". Graham and Dodd, *Security Analysis* (1934). We simply add to this that the votes are MONEY.

Hence, knowing these aggregate shifts in the money cycle, or more correctly the liquidity cycle, allows us to better understand asset allocation. The schematic diagram in Fig. 10.16 brings together the main signals and inflections points. We show two cycles: (1) the Liquidity Cycle and the subsequent (2) Business Cycle or Risk Cycle. Investors' risk appetite often coincides closely with the movements in the overall business cycle, and often to slightly precede it, as we demonstrated earlier in Fig. 10.12. Overlaid on the diagram, we have marked the turning points in the slope of the government bond yield curve (red dots) and investors' risk appetite (brown dots). The business cycle tends to follow the liquidity cycle by around 15–20 months, in our experience. Around 6–9 months after the respective peaks and troughs in the liquidity cycle, the yield curve will

Table 10.5 Taxonomy of liquidity and investment regimes

	Rebound	Calm	Speculation	Turbulence
Liquidity	Low/rising	High/rising	High/falling	Low/falling
Yield curve	Trough	Bullish steepening	Peak	Bearish flattening
Investors' risk appetite	Falling	Trough	Rising	Peak
Economy	Slowing	Contraction	Expansion	Boom
Long yields	Small rise	Large fall	Small rise	Rise
Short rates	Large fall	Fall	Rise	Large rise
Duration	Increase	Highest	Decrease	Lowest
Volatility	Large jump	Flat	Large fall	Increase
Equities	Weak	Trough and rising	Strong	Peak and falling
(sector)	*Defensive value*	*Cyclical value*	*Cyclical growth*	*Defensive growth*

Source *CrossBorder Capital*

typically flatten and steepen. Periods of scarce (abundant) liquidity initially see Treasury bond term premia narrow (widen) and the yield curve, the yield spread between long-maturity and short-maturity bonds, consequently, flattens (steepens). In the wake of a negative liquidity shock, it is likely that corporate credit spreads will also start to widen, partly because Treasury yields themselves collapse. This prediction assumes that it becomes increasingly difficult to refinance investment positions, with the further result that the risk appetite of equity investors may collapse and systemic risks begin to escalate. Falls in risk appetite can cause the cancellation and postponement of long-horizon capital projects in the real economy. Paradoxically, the longest duration investment is a part-finished capital project. As these and other projects are stopped and shelved, industrial activity slows. Hence, roughly coincident with business cycle peaks and troughs, investors risk appetite similarly peaks and troughs, but as noted in Fig. 10.12, these moves tend to be more violent, frequently self-reinforcing and they often touch the extremes of fear and greed. This means that around a year following the yield curve inflections, the business cycle itself typically peaks and troughs. This latter feature is separately confirmed by studies of the yield curve and the business cycle (see Howell 2018). Table 10.5 characterises the four phases of the liquidity cycle as *Rebound, Calm, Speculation* and *Turbulence* and summarises these likely features of asset allocation that we have just described. These labels reflect the tempo of the liquidity cycle and do not necessarily describe the contemporary features of asset and economic markets. Typically, the liquidity cycle is around one or two phases ahead. Thus, stock markets peak in the *Turbulence* liquidity regime and bottom in the *Calm* liquidity regime. This tends to coincide, respectively, with the peak of the economic boom and the low point of the economic recession.

Notes

1. Working Paper Series #1528, April 2013.
2. Duration also takes into account the present value of the future stream of coupon and dividend payments as well as the final redemption value. For a zero-coupon bond, maturity and duration are the same.
3. The 'liquidity' of an individual asset measures the holder's ability to obtain legal tender money. As such is has two dimensions: (1) time taken to convert into legal tender, i.e. maturity transformation, and (2) the certainty of the realised price, i.e. credit risk [A third is forex risk]. Duration summarises these dimensions, but they are interconnected because a speedier transformation may mean a lower realised price.
4. Forward rates, equivalent to the incremental spot rates, can also be used. Sometimes for coupon paying bonds the par curve is drawn using their yields-to-maturity. The spot curve shows the yield on a bond at any point in time and does not assume it is held to maturity.
5. For a zero-coupon bond, maturity and duration are the same. For a conventional, non-zero coupon, bond duration is bounded from above by maturity.
6. For example, over the 2000–2019 period term premia movements account for 77% of the variation in US Treasury yields at the 10-year tenor; 50% at the 5-year tenor and only 14% at the 1-year tenor.
7. We devote the later Chapter 13 to an explanation of these Global Liquidity Indexes.
8. US Federal Reserve, December 2009.
9. Andrew Hauser, BoE, July 2019.
10. *Monetary Policy Expectations and Long Term Interest Rates*, speech at London Business School, May 2016.
11. J. Gagnon, Quantitative Easing: An Underappreciated Success, PIIE Policy Brief No. 16-4, Washington, DC, 2016.

References

Borio, Claudio. 2012. The Financial Cycle and Macroeconomics: What Have We Learnt? BIS Working Papers No. 395, December.
Gagnon, J. 2016. Quantitative Easing: An Underappreciated Success. PIIE Policy Brief No. 16-4. Washington, DC.

Graham, Benjamin, and David Dodd. 1934. *Security Analysis*. New York: McGraw-Hill.

Howell, Michael J. 2017. *Further Investigations into the Term Structure of Interest Rates*. London: University of London.

Howell, Michael J. 2018. What Does the Yield Curve Slope Really Tell Us? *The Journal of Fixed Income* 27 (4): 22–33.

Howell, Michael J. 2019. Measuring Bond Investors' Risk Appetite Using theInterest Rate Term Structure. *The Journal of Investing* 28 (6) (October): 115–127.

Sprinkel, Beryl W. 1964. *Money and Stock Prices*. Homewood: Irwin.

Stein, Jeremy C. 2012. Monetary Policy as Financial-Stability Regulation. *Quarterly Journal of Economics* 127 (1): 57–95.

11

Financial Crises and Safe Assets

The Financial Cycle

Finance may have evolved through the eighteenth and nineteenth centuries from national pools of surplus funds, but today we have a global banking and financial system, made up of private firms acting largely independently of their domestic economy's needs. We argue in Chapter 8 that capital imports do not accurately measure another country's net savings, rather they often represent a credit flow from one financial institution outside the country to another one inside. For example, although both the UK and the US run large and persistent current account deficits, their financial sectors are major sources of international credit. Consequently, the 2007–2008 GFC was not about unsustainable current account deficits, but largely hinged on unsustainable bank balance sheets, which resulted in a Global Liquidity collapse.

The standard economics and finance paradigms ignore money and liquidity. Markets are assumed to exist everywhere and at all times, and frictionless trade is supposed to occur. Yet paradoxically, illiquidity is the ultimate friction and without sufficient liquidity there would be a widespread market failure and no trade. Illiquidity can occur both when the supply of money and credit breaks down, and when heightened uncertainty (again assumed away in the standard framework) causes investors to hoard 'safe' assets, such as cash, for precautionary reasons. In practice, 'no trade' rather than 'trade' is more likely to be the normal state. Hence, fluctuations in the quantity of liquidity matter greatly. Put another way, in the real-world imperfect markets and market failures are commonplace, and the efficient market hypothesis (EMH), the bedrock of finance theory, simply does not apply. Financial crises happen.

© The Author(s) 2020
M. J. Howell, *Capital Wars*,
https://doi.org/10.1007/978-3-030-39288-8_11

Our earlier definition of Global Liquidity is built around the two concepts of: (1) *Funding Liquidity*—a monetary liquidity measure, defined as the ability to convert monetary assets into goods, financial instruments and services, domestically and internationally, and (2) *Market Liquidity*—a measure of financial market depth, defined as the ease of trading in assets relative to trading in money, and reflecting the cost of converting a financial asset into money. Although we mainly focus on funding liquidity, it is closely connected with market liquidity and the two frequency interact through collateral effects. We argued earlier that neither should not be seen in isolation or as independent. We also show how these Global Liquidity flows are highly procyclical and how they can quickly evaporate, setting in motion self-sustaining and adverse dynamic effects, such as those often seen during financial crises.

The dominant players behind Global Liquidity are the US Federal Reserve, China's PBoC and the cross-border funding markets, e.g. Eurodollars. China controls her huge retail deposit base largely through the management of bank reserves. Alongside, she accumulates US dollars since her exports and FDI are largely invoiced in the US unit, but, given the private sector's dominant domestic Yuan liabilities, the Chinese State undertakes to manage economy-wide forex risk. The asymmetry, as we argued in Chapter 9, sees China essentially re-export large quantities of US dollars, rather than exporting Yuan. At the same time, US liquidity increasingly depends on the wholesale money markets, which receive these Chinese and similar US dollar inflows from corporate and institutional cash pools (CICPs). However, the wholesale markets are leveraged and collateral-based, and they suffer from a structural shortage of high-quality safe asset instruments, which forces demand to spillover into riskier longer maturities and flakier credit substitutes. A further amplification mechanism kicks in when, encouraged by interest rate and regulatory arbitrage, US dollar wholesale deposits head into the offshore Eurodollar markets, where they are typically lent back to US and Emerging Market borrowers. In turn, the resulting cross-border capital inflows into the Emerging Market economies both serve as additional bank collateral and also get multiplied up when local Central Banks intervene in their forex markets.

These swings in the liquidity cycle drive risk appetite, which, in turn, feedsback positively on to funding liquidity via market liquidity, thereby amplifying the cycle. Together market liquidity, funding liquidity and risk appetite make up what has been termed by academics the *financial cycle*. This is shown in Fig. 11.1, with these three key components charted

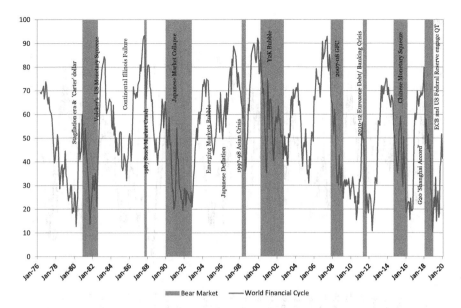

Fig. 11.1 The World financial cycle—hybrid of funding liquidity, market liquidity and investors' risk appetite, 1976–2019 (Index 0–100) (Source *CrossBorder Capital*)

separately in Fig. 11.2. In the words of Rey[1] (2015): *"[The] Global Financial Cycle can be associated with surges and dry outs in capital flows, booms and busts in asset prices and crises … The empirical results on capital flows, leverage and credit growth are suggestive of an international credit channel or risk-taking channel and point towards financial stability issues"*.

Is Stability Destabilising?

Yet, on paper at least, the World financial system should be more stable, following the changes enacted since the 2007–2008 GFC. For example, there is more and, arguably, better official regulation. Banks have greater capital buffers since the Basel III regulations, and their funding has become less reliant on wholesale markets. Central Banks are more active and the latest mix of cross-border capital flows embraces fewer volatile components. Liquidity Coverage Ratios (LCRs) now require 100% of liquidity to be matched, for 30 days ahead, for each foreign legal subsidiary. It is now harder to access deposits across borders, and even if foreign assets are not explicitly penalised, they are far more closely scrutinised. In addition, although regulation is still predominantly national, international oversight is more important, such

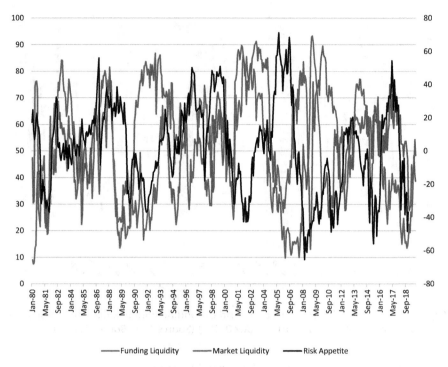

Fig. 11.2 Components of World financial cycle—funding liquidity, market liquidity and investors' risk appetite, 1980–2019 (Index 0–100) (Source *CrossBorder Capital*)

as the greater involvement of the IMF and BIS, and the recognition of the dangers of regulatory arbitrage between incongruent regimes. This occurred ahead of the GFC, when tight regulation of US banks through leverage ratios forced them to sell their loans, largely to European banks, who were more constrained by their capital ratios. This led to an amplifying feedback mechanism, or what was later dubbed a 'liquidity pump'.

At the same time, it is worth recalling Churchill's justly famous dictum that in the beginning we create our institutions and, in the end, they create us. His wisdom frequently applies to finance. For example, many policy-makers have unquestioningly adopted Wicksell's view that monetary systems are inherently stable and are only destabilised by errant Central Bank actions: "*To combat depression by a forced credit expansion is to attempt to cure the evil by the very means which brought it about; because we are suffering from a misdirection of production, we want to create further misdirection – a procedure which can only lead to a much more severe crisis as soon as the credit expansion comes to an end*".[2] On the other hand, according to Kaufman[3] (2017), the US Federal Reserve still does not fully understand the connections between its monetary policy and the financial markets. Similarly, our concerns focus on policy-makers, in general, in: (1) not understanding the need for balance sheet capacity to facilitate debt rollovers, and their associated (2) failure to supply sufficient safe assets. Put another way, many regulators and policy-makers have never properly adapted to the evolving financial structure. On top, these same authorities promoted the further concentration of the financial system, but alongside they have demonstrated slow and often erratic responses to the growing financial tensions. Examples include the rapid accumulation of debt Worldwide, as well as its progressive slide in quality, as illustrated in the US by the dramatic loss in AAA grade borrowing status.[4] At the same time, there have been the widespread and uncontrolled use of derivatives, maturity and foreign exchange mismatches, growing securitisation and off-balance sheet financing. In short, a rapacious pace of innovation, while, the GFC itself highlighted the crucial delay in tackling the BNP Paribas fund suspension in 2007 and the short-sighted error made by sanctioning the Lehman bankruptcy.

These were not the only errors. Former Fed Chairman Alan Greenspan, Treasury Secretary Robert Rubin and his deputy Larry Summers, together promoted the Gramm-Leach-Bliley Act of 1999 that ultimately removed the 1933 Glass-Stegall Act that, among the other safeguards brought in after the 1929 Crash and subsequent Depression, had for decades separated US commercial and investment banking. This new legislation accelerated the concentration among US financial firms and further weakened Federal Reserve control. This may help to explain how more than three-quarters of America's financial assets are now controlled by the ten largest financial conglomerates. Yet, as recently as 1990, the then ten largest firms controlled barely 10%. This fact voices the popular *crie-de-coeur* of 'too big to fail' and forces the US authorities to be still more interventionist, so reaching well-beyond their traditional mandates.

Rather than 'too big to fail', what should be of more concern is 'too interconnected to fail'. The brilliantly prescient cartoonist David Low sketched a hilariously accurate lampoon for the London Evening Standard at the depth of the Depression (May 24, 1932). His cartoon, showing the World economy adrift on the high seas with the caption: *"Phew, that's a nasty leak. Thank goodness it's not at our end of the boat"*, parodied the foolishness of policy-makers' response to the early 1930s Central European banking crisis. Brought up to date, it could easily apply to the recent 2010–2012 Eurozone banking crisis. Europe's banks were subsequently saved by ECB President Draghi's famous three words[5]—*"...whatever it takes"*—that ushered in the massive quantitative easing programme. His words echoed the earlier forceful determination of *"Making sure 'It' doesn't happen here..."* the famous anti-deflation speech made by former Fed Chairman Ben Bernanke in

November 2002. Yet, in its latest iteration, the data shows that global debt is now growing fastest among non-financial companies, with government debt also expanding, and household debt levels strained and seemingly near to a saturation point. A 2019 report by the *Robert Triffin International Institute*[6] focusses on these cross-border risks and warns about the fragile state of funding. The report notes that the US dollar debt of non-banks outside of the US stands at record levels, and by drilling deeper it exposes substantial currency mismatches and worryingly high private sector leverage, with the newly rising reliance on international bond markets creating additional latent risks. Overall, there is a growing unease among practitioners about the dominance of the US dollar, and concern over the inadequacy of an international financial safety net.

All this surely questions the abilities of the international financial system to generate further meaningful increases in credit, and of the Central Banks to be able to tighten policy sufficiently when a future need arises, say, from higher inflation? We emphasised in earlier chapters how modern finance has inevitably geared itself towards refinancing existing debts, rather than continuing to provide new credit. Thus, while the shadow banks are typically involved in two-thirds of funding, e.g. 're-packaging' of existing loans, they supply only 15% of new credit, according to IMF estimates. What shadow banks essentially do is to transform traditional bank assets and liabilities by refinancing them in longer and more complex intermediation chains, e.g. A lends to B who lends to C, etc. The fragility of the financial system, evidenced so disastrously in the 2007–2008 GFC, is highlighted by this intermediation process because when A lends to B, and B lends to C, etc. through to Z, any break in this wholesale lending chain can notionally bankrupt an alphabet of 'twenty-six' firms and not just one. On top, the widespread use of market-based collateral introduces a hierarchy into liabilities, making the system both more procyclical and more than ever dependent on the interventions of Central Banks. This latter dependence can surely only deepen in a future World of electronic and digital monies? The ongoing dominance of refinancing activity over new financing makes access to credit lines more important than interest rates and emphasises that QE (quantitative easing) and QT (quantitative tightening) are critical policy levers. In the real economy, money matters, but in financial markets it is credit and liquidity that really count. According to the textbook model, credit is normally created via banks, with new liquidity provided by Central Banks and funding backstopped by State deposit guarantees. Ahead of the 2007–2008 GFC, securitisation was widespread, new liquidity came from interbank markets and funding was backstopped by credit default swaps (CDS). The pre-GFC model clearly failed, but in its latest precarious incarnation, featuring dominant wholesale markets, new liquidity is provided by CICPs (corporate and institutional cash pools) and funding is backstopped by sometimes flaky collateral.

The drive for greater financial elasticity, in turn, has fuelled a jump in cross-border flows outside of the realm of US Federal Reserve interest rate and regulatory control, so providing an additional source of leverage. International integration has consequently jumped. In fact, by so much that the velocity of cross-border flows and the scale of the associated financial spillovers seriously questions the continuing validity of economist Robert Mundell's famous trilemma, which describes the ability of open economies to operate independent monetary policies. In practice, it seems that domestic economies can never be fully insulated from these international monetary shocks. This should raise concerns over potential financial instability and go a long way to explain the well-known concentration and bunching together of recent international financial crises, as noted by Reinhart and Rogoff (2009), Schularick and Taylor (2012), and Jordà et al. (2018). Indeed, in practice, international financial crises tend to be preceded by build-ups in leverage, with the scale of instability almost certainly amplified by government austerity policies and by the rise of shadow banks and CICPs. This experience appears to confirm Hyman Minsky's well-documented *financial instability hypothesis* (FIH), which argues that liabilities experience three different financing regimes: (1) hedged, (2) speculative and (3) Ponzi. Whereas the hedged regime is stable for both markets and economies, speculative and Ponzi are unstable. Speculative schemes need liquidity to allow their debts to be rolled over: Ponzi schemes demand both liquidity and rising asset prices. Neither can be guaranteed and, according to Minsky "...*stability leads to instability*", meaning that ultimately the hedged regimes regress through time towards the speculative and Ponzi regimes.

With its vast and visible stock-piles of past capital accumulation, modern capitalism has to operate a huge refinancing system. This, in turn, demands a stable credit instrument that is able to support these debt rollovers. Gold is not sufficiently elastic and the supplies of State money and debt are often compromised by policy-makers' concerns over their low inflation mandates and a desire to honour the prevailing free market/laissez faire ideology. The resulting safe asset supply shortfall encourages private sector initiatives to create substitutes, but these by definition frequently lie beyond the realm of State regulation and consequently miss out on State support. What's more, these private sector instruments can be highly procyclical, so in downturns when liquidity is most needed, it is simply not there. Such nagging ill-discipline makes them poorly suited to serve as 'safe' assets.

Bagehot famously noted[7] that *money does not manage itself*. Indeed, the story of financial crises is often a story of the failure of these safe assets, which may explain why crises can be so wrenching and traumatic. Investors are prepared to take losses on their risky investments, but they do not expect to take losses on supposedly safe ones. Policy-makers are always trying to make the financial system safer by encouraging investors to invest more in safe assets. However, by not supplying enough safe assets and then having to hastily react and bailout the system, they end-up creating moral hazard by making many risky investments safe, while some of the most dangerous investments turn out to be those that were once believed to be completely safe. Indeed, the ferocity of this long monetary debate over the elasticity and safety of means of settlement looks set to escalate, given the rapid evolution and deployment of electronic and digital monies, and the likely growing emphasis on collateral, as we briefly outlined in Chapter 7.

A Worldwide Shortage of 'Safe' Assets?

Every financial crisis, it seems, involves some form of failure of safe assets. Keynes put it slightly differently by pointing out that there can be no such thing as liquidity for the investment community as a whole: someone has to take on risk. We know that, in times of financial stress, the wholesale funding markets demand higher quality collateral. This usually takes the form of long-term US Treasury debt or its international equivalent. However, this is currently in scarce supply, which must surely mean that the financial system is more vulnerable? Large-scale asset purchases (LSAP) by the Federal Reserve and other Central Banks have squeezed the wholesale markets by stripping them of the best collateral. Some academic experts have argued that because interest is paid on reserves and near-zero yields exist nearly everywhere, Central Bank money has become indistinguishable from all other financial assets. This is a contentious viewpoint. We have noted how 'liquidity' has two dimensions: low duration and limited credit risk, which means that it can be instantly turned into legal tender without discount. We can think of a 'safe' asset in similar terms, but with the difference that the time horizon is adjusted to take into account the timing of the asset owners' future liabilities. A 'safe' asset can, therefore, be defined by its ability to cover expected liabilities, whereas a non-safe asset may not match expected liabilities, either in their size (a solvency problem) or in the pattern of cash needs over time (a liquidity problem). This timing mismatch can be expressed through the finance concept of *duration*, or what can be thought of as the effective time horizon of the investment. Like maturity, duration is usually measured in years. The yield premium on an asset may partly compensate for this timing mismatch (or illiquidity). It is also likely that the longer that capital is tied-up, the greater its potential future return. Therefore 'risky' assets, as defined by their deviation away from some desired duration, should earn higher returns. In other words, a 'safe' asset has low credit risk and will match the duration of the asset owners' expected future liabilities. An excess demand for safe assets, say, government bonds is usually expressed through higher bond prices, or, put more accurately, via narrower bond term premia. We noted earlier, in Chapters 7 and 10, that the period since the 2007–2008 GFC, which has been characterised by both quantitative easing and the so-called 'austerity' policies, has been associated with large swings in term premia. In particular, whenever liquidity and/or safe assets are in scare (abundant) supply term premia narrow (widen).

Two observations follow: First, the most important price in the global financial system is always the price of the dominant economy's (or economies') sovereign debt, which today is made-up of the yield on US Treasuries plus the value of the US dollar. Second, the canonical 'safe' asset for many US domestic and international institutional investors is consequently the 10-year US Treasury note, because it more closely matches the duration of liabilities, such as future pension pay-outs, than, say, cash.[8] However, the textbooks tend to think in terms of cash, or even sometimes gold bullion, as the main safe assets, while the fast-growing corporate and institutional cash pools (CICPs) arguably favour a US dollar-denominated instrument of somewhat shorter maturity. Asset allocators actively decide the portfolio mix between holdings of risky and safe assets. Safe assets are more likely to match desired duration, but they will likely offer smaller returns. Although risky assets can deliver greater rewards, this may come at the cost of mismatched duration. A balance is required. Taking government bonds and cash as 'safe' assets and equities and corporate debt as risky, the risk/safe asset mix is likely to change through the economic cycle, but ultimately it should mean-revert back to a level determined by expected future liabilities, as demonstrated in Chapter 10. In turn, these liabilities will depend on long-term factors such as demographics, taxation, underlying inflation and risk aversion. Figure 11.3 reports the ratio between the value of holdings of all equity securities, i.e. risk assets, by US and World investors and their respective holdings of safe assets. According to the chart, the value of risk assets holdings compared to 'safe' assets currently looks somewhat extended for both World (circa 45%) and US (circa 55%) investors, compared to history. This

Fig. 11.3 US and World investors' market value of equity holdings to safe asset ratio (all investors), 1980–2019 (Source *CrossBorder Capital*)

warns of higher risk levels, but admittedly not to the same degree as in either year 2000, following the Y2K bubble, or ahead of the 2007–2008 GFC.

Safe Assets

A 'safe' asset can be defined from its ability to cover expected liabilities. Unlike a legally defined 'reserve asset', a 'safe' asset is assessed subjectively. A non-safe asset may not match expected liabilities, either in their size (a *solvency* problem) or timing (a *liquidity* problem). The yield premium on an asset may partly compensate for these mismatches. Typically, when there is an inadequate supply of safe assets, either portfolios are constrained and cannot expand in value, or the private sector creates additional elasticity by supplying its own 'safe' assets.

The IMF (2012) formally defines a 'safe' asset as a financial instrument that provides (1) low market and credit risks, (2) high market liquidity, (3) limited inflation risks, (4) low exchange rate risks and (5) limited idiosyncratic risks.

In practice, the definition of a safe asset often becomes fuzzy because it also involves geopolitical and psychological factors, such as trust, and belief. A safe asset is 'safe' only if others agree. Alongside, the history of safe assets shows that they share several properties:

1. Safe assets tend to rise in value during bad economic times, whereas riskier assets, such as equities and corporate and EM credits perform less well. In finance jargon, safe assets have a *negative beta* to the market.

2. Deep and liquid markets characterised by an ability to freely trade in large size around prevailing prices. It follows that capital controls can deny safe asset status.
3. Consistently lower yields than other assets. Krishnamurthy and Vissing-Jorgensen (2012) estimate that US Treasury yields are around 70 bps lower on average because of their better safety and liquidity features.
4. Greater fiscal capacity, as measured, say, by the low sensitivity of yields to an increase in the debt-to-GDP ratio, and the backing of a powerful, possibly military, State, e.g. USA.

The canonical safe asset is the 10-year US Treasury note, but, in practice, the list of safe assets includes any instruments that are used in an information-insensitive fashion, See G. Gorton, S. Lewellen, and A. Metrick, The Safe Asset Share, *American Economic Review* 102 (3), 2012; Safe Assets: Financial System Cornerstone? *IMF Global Financial Stability Report*, April 2012, and A. Krishnamurthy and A. Vissing-Jorgensen, Aggregate Demand for Treasury Debt. *Journal of Political Economy*, 120: 233–267, 2012.

Part of the reason for this extension in the risk-to-safe asset ratios is that the supplies of liquidity and government debt have lately been severely limited by austerity policies that restrict the issuance of government securities, and by the increasingly tighter regulations placed on traditional deposit-takers, such as high street banks, that ultimately limit the growth of their liabilities. These new liquidity rules and collateral requirements have increased the need for banks to hold high quality liquid assets, which, reduces their availability to support other transactions, including repos. Thus, the lack of available high-quality collateral can have a significant impact on liquidity in secured markets, especially during periods of financial stress. Even aside from official regulations, prudential rules have also materially increased the opportunity cost of holding insufficient liquid assets, so further increasing the demand for them. Consequently, the lack of collateral has been amplified by the weakened supply of liquidity, which together create a still greater demand for safe assets, so exaggerating the shortfall.

According to the IMF (2012): "...*heightened uncertainty, regulatory reforms, and crisis-related responses by Central Banks are driving up [safe asset] demand. On the supply side, the number of sovereigns whose debt is considered safe has fallen, which could remove some US$9 trillion from the supply of safe assets ... or roughly 16 per cent... Private sector production of safe assets as also declined as poor securitization in the US has tainted these securities, while some new regulations may impair [supply]...*" This reduced supply of 'safe' assets—here defined as government bonds in developed economies and cash and short-term instruments in Developed and Emerging economies—is shown in Fig. 11.4 as a percent of World GDP, alongside the annual growth rate of Global Liquidity. The new supply of international safe assets appears to have increased at around a 10% clip prior to the 2007–2008 GFC, but has since skidded lower to a barely positive pace. Even a decade of such sub-par growth would create a sizeable shortfall gap of some 80% compared to the pre-crisis trend. What's more, as the supply of safe assets has dwindled, so the expansion of Global Liquidity has similarly faltered, thereby significantly reinforcing the degree of excess demand and helping to explain the further plunge in Treasury bond term premia.

This shortfall matters because, unlike the traditional bank-based credit supply, the prevailing wholesale money market-based system essentially depends upon a steady supply of fresh collateral. Although the CICPs provide sources of new funding, they demand liquid, collateralised savings instruments which the financial system provides through repos. The rapid growth of CICPs has consequently boosted repo demand and, hence, furthered collateral needs. Structural shortages of Treasury securities have forced a large part of this institutional cash into collateralised and often 'newly-minted' private sector instruments. American households, for example, were encouraged from the early 2000s, often openly by politicians, to extend their mortgage financing. These loans could then be bundled

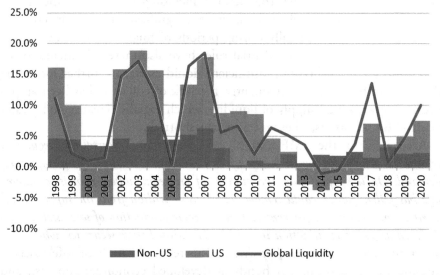

Fig. 11.4 Supply of global 'safe' assets (percent of world GDP) and growth of Global Liquidity (%yoy), 1998–2020 (Source *CrossBorder Capital*)

together into higher-graded mortgage-backed securities (MBS). This led to banks and shadow banks borrowing more institutional cash from the money markets and lending it on to households and other nontraditional borrowers, such as Emerging Market corporations. Events then worsened. Assured they could easily roll over these positions, in what had by the early 2000s become deep and liquid wholesale money markets, shadow bank lenders borrowed very short-term, often over horizons as slim as 7–14 days and often using MBS as collateral, but they simultaneously lent long-term, sometimes for 30 years thereby taking on huge *maturity risks*. The 2007–2008 GFC proved that the depth and liquidity of the money markets was not a reliable constant. The British bank *Northern Rock*, which held 10% of the UK mortgage market, became an early casualty of rapidly evaporating funding liquidity in August 2007. These tensions came on top of what anyway were likely to be higher *credit risks*, simply because the lenders faced new and largely unknown borrowers. Consider the heightened risks faced by borrowers when a 30-year security or loan, supported, say, by 14-day bills, is required to be refinanced a whopping 778 times up to its maturity. This huge refinancing burden provides plenty of opportunities for something to go wrong.

In the decade since the GFC, the structural shortage of safe assets has been met by the money markets repo'ing high quality collateral, such as Treasury notes and high-grade corporate bonds. However, the still limited supplies of government securities have added pressure on corporations to issue more debt. American capital markets have benefitted, not least because US dollar assets are in particular demand, but also because the US has the largest and most liquid corporate bond market Worldwide. Consequently, US credit spreads have also narrowed and issuance by US corporations has risen strongly. Low prevailing capital expenditure needs have meant that much of this extra cash has been channelled back into Wall Street equities through share buy-back programmes, thereby lifting stock prices. The close correlation between debt issuance and equity buy-backs is shown in Fig. 11.5. Meanwhile, Fig. 11.6 highlights that equity retirements have regularly averaged a net 1–2% of total US market capitalisation over the past decade, so diminishing the available pool of equity.

Yet, all this comes at a cost. A critical fact is that this collateral-based mechanism for liquidity creation is highly procyclical because the *quantity* of new liquidity created rests heavily on the *quality* of available corporate debt, which, in turn, depends on the state of the business cycle. This linkage warns that widening credit spreads can have outsized effects on the provision of liquidity. It is also potentially fragile, because the repo system could itself

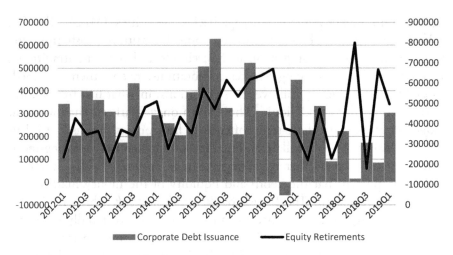

Fig. 11.5 US corporate debt issuance and net equity retirements, 2012–2019 (US dollars in millions) (Source *CrossBorder Capital*)

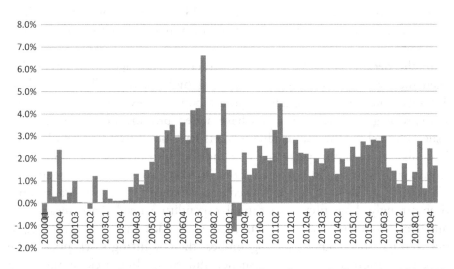

Fig. 11.6 US net equity retirements (percent of market capitalisation), 2000–2019 (Source *CrossBorder Capital*)

breakdown if corporate default risks increase, so driving investors into the safety of already scarce government bonds. Wall Street's sharp sell-off though December 2018 evidences accompanying jumps in both credit spreads and repo rates: between early November and late December 2018, US Single B High Yield (option-adjusted) spreads suddenly widened by over 200 bp to peak at 5.84%. This echoes the similarly fragile and procyclical system of liquidity provision that operated ahead of the 2007–2008 GFC, but which then centred on MBS (mortgage-backed securities) and other ABS (asset-backed securities). In 2007–2008, the deterioration in the US housing market proved to be an important trigger in destroying system-wide liquidity.

One solution to the 'safe' asset shortage is to force the Treasury to issue more long-term debt with, say, 30-year or even 100-year maturities. Quantitative easing policies that involve simply replacing government bonds with, say, Federal Reserve notes are far less effective because they soak up collateral, as Chapter 6 highlighted. Policy-makers must find the motivation to increase the overall government balance sheet, i.e. Treasury and Federal Reserve liabilities, and invent more innovative methods to free up collateral for the wholesale markets.

Notes

1. Helene Rey, IMF Mundell Fleming Lecture, 2015.
2. Frederick von Hayek, *Monetary Theory and the Trade Cycle*, 1933.
3. Henry Kaufman, *Tectonic Shifts in Financial Markets*, Palgrave, 2017.
4. Johnson & Johnson and Microsoft are the only two US companies rated-AAA the highest credit rating from S&P, down from 98 in 1992.
5. See https://www.ecb.europa.eu/press/key/date/2012/html/sp120726.en.html.
6. See   http://www.triffininternational.eu/images/global_liquidity/RTI-CSF_Report-Global-Liquidity_Dec2019.pdf.
7. Walter Bagehot, *Lombard Street*, 1873.
8. G. Gorton, S. Lewellen, and A. Metrick, The Safe Asset Share, *American Economic Review* 102 (3), and Global Financial Stability Report, International Monetary Fund, April 2012.

References

International Monetary Fund. 2012. Global Financial Stability Report, April.
Jordà, Òscar, Moritz Schularick, Alan M. Taylor, and Felix Ward. 2018. Global Financial Cycles and Risk Premiums. NBER Working Paper No. 24677, June.
Kaufman, Henry. 2017. *Tectonic Shifts in Financial Markets*. Cham: Palgrave.
Reinhart Carmen, M., and Kenneth S. Rogoff. 2009. *This Time Is Different: Eight Centuries of Financial Folly*. Princeton: Princeton University Press.
Rey, Hélène. 2015. IMF Mundell Fleming Lecture.
Schularick, Moritz, and Alan M. Taylor. 2012. Credit Booms Gone Bust: Monetary Policy, Leverage Cycles, and Financial Crises. *1870–2008, American Economic Review* 102 (2): 1029–1061.

12

The Financial Silk Road: Globalisation and the Eastwards Shift of Capital

The Financial Silk Road

The World's economic centre of gravity is being progressively pulled Eastwards, attracted by the huge economic opportunities in China, India and Central Asia. In 1950 it stood close to America's Eastern Seaboard. By 1980 it had notionally shifted into the mid-Atlantic and ironically around 1989 it passed from West to East Berlin, roughly coincident with the Fall of the Berlin Wall. It continued to move Eastwards passing through Helsinki in 2005, Moscow around 2010 and looks set to settle somewhere between India and China by the year 2050. Capital follows growth and it is marching remorselessly towards China and Central Asia along the old Silk Road, moving at a steady annual pace of 133 kilometres a year, equivalent to 3½ times the daily rate of an ancient camel train.[1] We have previously dubbed this capital shift the *Financial Silk Road*.[2] It reflects the shortage of capital in China and Asia relative to their sizeable investment opportunities. Trade along the old Silk Road was similarly driven by China's lust for silver as well as by the West's demand for silk, spices and tea. China's monetary system was tied to the silver peso, with more coins often circulating in China than in Mexico itself. It took over half a century for these sizeable trade and money flows to eliminate the profitable silver arbitrage between Europe and China.[3] This arbitrage reappeared in the early 1700s, when a Chinese population boom led to further large demands for silver coin. Thus, in both the sixteenth and eighteenth centuries the World economy was substantially reshaped as capital flowed from West to East.

© The Author(s) 2020
M. J. Howell, *Capital Wars*,
https://doi.org/10.1007/978-3-030-39288-8_12

In international markets, there are a few unrelated events. The first signs of this shift were clear even before the dust clouds from the crumbling Berlin Wall had settled. Almost overnight, State-owned companies were on the block around the World, offering foreign investors attractive new possibilities. Two months later in January 1990, Mexican President Salinas' keynote speech to the Davos World Economic Forum was so overshadowed by the delegates' obsession with Eastern Europe, that on his return he hastened NAFTA[4] negotiations and privatised Mexico's banks. The competition for foreign capital suddenly heated up. According to Mexican officials:

> ... he [Salinas] gives the keynote address and is extremely good and is well-received, and the next day, meetings on Hungary and Poland and East Germany started, and zoom, everybody was off listening to those meetings and what those other people had to say. (from New York Times, June 3rd, 1990)

In many ways, the top 500 US corporations have been foremost in leading this global capital shift, i.e. *globalisation*. Although they are still headquartered in America and they list their securities on the prominent New York exchanges, they otherwise outsource anywhere in the World to where components are cheapest and labour skills greatest, and they shift their profits to anywhere in the World where national taxes are lowest. The contrast with the Chinese economy could not be bigger. China's SOEs make-up her industrial core. They borrow from state banks (SOBs)[5] at artificially low rates, have preferential access to government contracts, and the SOEs and SOBs are used as convenient policy levers to balance the economy, lending and spending more when private companies are less willing to do so. They are also key engines of economic growth undertaking the necessary capital-intensive investments, including those in the leading-edge technologies, that underpin China's economy. China's goal is unambiguously to achieve national economic prosperity for the Chinese people, and her planners, SOBs and SOEs together undertake whatever is necessary to become the World's largest and most powerful economy. Since 1978, the Chinese economy has grown by an average of more than 9% per year. Although GDP growth has slowed recently and is likely to slow by more, it should still grow faster than almost any other major economy in the World, including the US, where real wages have stagnated for four decades, and huge wealth disparities and growing inequalities have materialised. China teaches that successful capitalism does not necessarily require political democracy. However, it does require vast inflows of industrial and financial capital, and many top US corporations have consequently been among the quickest to expand their Chinese operations.

A major conduit for these inward capital flows into China and elsewhere is foreign direct investment (FDI). FDI essentially consists of tangible investments in plant, equipment, buildings and businesses[6] located outside of the domestic economy. Japan has also been a consistently large net supplier of FDI, while the Emerging Markets and Frontier Markets are, in turn, consistently large net recipients of outflows from the developed economies as Fig. 12.1 confirms. FDI tends to embody the latest technologies and management skills. Consequently, it proves to be a major driver of growth particularly across China and other Emerging Markets. China has mostly received large-scale inward FDI, although lately its pace is slowing according to Fig. 12.2, following the combination of growing concerns over transferring proprietary technologies to China and the step-up of Chinese outward investment in her flagship *Belt and Road Initiative* projects. Aside from the period around unification, Germany has been a net supplier of FDI to the Rest of the World. Studies show that around half of this outward capital is reinvested in the neighbouring regions, so that the focus of Chinese FDI is predominantly in Asia and the focus of German FDI is mainly Europe. However, despite the apparent slowdown in Chinese net inward investment,

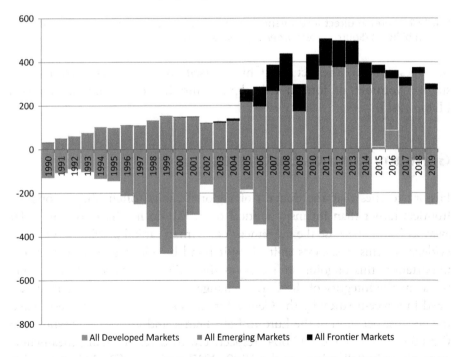

Fig. 12.1 Foreign direct investment flows (net) to major regions, 1990–2019 (US$ in billions) (Source *CrossBorder Capital*, UNCTAD)

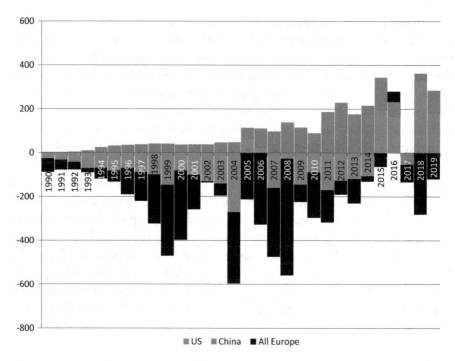

Fig. 12.2 Foreign direct investment flows (net) to US, China and Europe, 1990–2019 (US$ in billions) (Source *CrossBorder Capital*, UNCTAD)

this does not alter the fact that China herself also still needs to attract substantial volumes of foreign risk capital into her own domestic markets (Table 12.1).

Germany Lurches Eastwards

History teaches that the domain of regional capital often obeys economic frontiers rather than intrinsic political ones. We do not have to look as far away as China, because the movement of German capital provides up-to-date evidence of this Eastwards shift of capital and broader regional focus. More importantly, this ongoing shift exposes the frailties of the EU and possibly threatens the integrity of the Euro exchange rate system itself. This is underlined in a recent study by the Centre for European Policy,[7] which estimated the net cost per head of the Euro to Italy, France and Portugal at a whopping €73,605, €55,996 and €40,604, respectively, to date. Germans, meanwhile, enjoyed a windfall gain over the 1999–2017 period of €23,116 per capita. Ironically, in the context of the 2016 vote to exit the EU (i.e. Brexit), Britain

Table 12.1 Foreign direct investment flows (net) to major regions, 2000–2019 (US$ in billions)

	Developed economies	Emerging markets	Frontier markers	USA	China	Japan	UK	Germany	France
2000	−393.5	148.8	1.2	−80.8	37.5	−30.2	−201.3	140.7	−131.1
2001	−299.9	150.1	1.3	−100.9	37.7	−35.9	−49.1	−12.6	−41.0
2002	−160.7	120.9	1.2	−130.3	46.6	−29.5	−47.3	31.6	−0.1
2003	−244.2	127.8	5.2	−139.6	47.3	−27.3	−56.0	26.6	−10.0
2004	−637.7	140.7	9.3	−270.2	53.3	−29.2	−79.9	−32.7	−23.5
2005	−184.5	274.0	56.2	61.0	89.7	−45.3	97.8	−30.3	−30.6
2006	−344.9	285.0	89.3	21.2	98.0	−61.2	60.5	−57.4	−53.9
2007	−444.9	385.7	118.8	−159.6	139.0	−52.1	−156.0	−90.0	−48.3
2008	−642.9	437.9	146.1	−26.5	115.4	−84.7	−110.9	−68.2	−70.2
2009	−282.4	296.9	123.7	−144.3	89.6	−65.2	59.0	−46.1	−68.6
2010	−357.2	434.1	116.0	−88.5	186.4	−71.3	6.9	−58.6	−33.5
2011	−387.3	506.1	123.0	−169.4	228.4	−117.6	−47.7	−10.6	−19.5
2012	−264.1	497.1	121.6	−125.9	175.9	−117.9	31.1	−33.8	−18.3
2013	−307.0	494.7	105.8	−117.9	215.5	−145.0	42.9	−26.5	9.9
2014	−206.2	396.0	99.8	−105.3	149.0	−118.4	144.4	−83.3	−47.5
2015	10.4	374.7	36.8	193.5	66.2	−133.8	107.6	−66.2	−5.9
2016	86.4	274.9	37.3	167.0	−42.4	−139.8	197.3	−46.6	−37.4
2017	−250.6	329.7	39.5	−10.6	33.6	−151.8	−5.8	−57.2	−20.3
2018	−50.2	375.1	27.1	327.9	104.5	−138.5	11.5	−59.8	−63.7
2019	−252.6	298.7	24.6	179.8	80.6	−335.4	−39.8	−40.0	−10.4

Source CrossBorder Capital, UNCTAD

has recently benefitted from large-scale German FDI and access to low-cost skilled and semi-skilled EU workers. The benefit to UK economic growth has unquestionably been significant, evidenced by Britain's comparatively low unemployment rate. However, the contrast with economic conditions, and particularly youth unemployment rates, in the domicile EU economies of this immigrant labour is huge. Even more worryingly for these economies, the UK and others have been able to lure away their young entrepreneurs, a critical source of future economic growth. A key explanation for this 'brain drain' is the economic hollowing-out of several Southern European econo-mies caused by being straight-jacketed into the Euro. Currency unions have advantages, but they can also come with high costs. In Chapter 5 we explain this through real exchange rate adjustment and the role played by more flexi-ble asset prices and wages, when the nominal exchange rate is fixed. The big-gest cost, long evident in economies such as the US and UK is that the rich regions get richer and the poor regions get poorer. Not surprisingly, within the Eurozone economy Germany has consequently got significantly richer, whereas Italy and, particularly, Greece have become much poorer in both income and wealth terms. The collapse in asset values, notably real estate prices, across the smaller Eurozone economies has weakened their banking systems by eroding precious collateral, and thereby has held back economic recovery. America tries to eliminate her similar regional imbalances through taxation and social security payments, as well as through the location of her domestic military bases and government procurement programmes. The UK uses regional aid and has separate government departments to channel financial support towards underdeveloped regions, such as Wales, Scotland and Northern Ireland. In other words, a necessary component of any practi-cal currency union is a mechanism for fiscal transfers. The EU currently has a minimal regional support system and fragmented fiscal arrangements, but the scale of the economic imbalances between the member states that has unfolded in just the past twenty years demands far greater collective action. This is a controversial debate, and not least because when Brexit occurs, Germany will be the only large net contributor to the EU budget.

From a pure economic point of view, it seems probable that German capital, the powerhouse of the European industry, will continue to look Eastwards. Germany accounts for close to 40% of value-added in EU man-ufacturing, compared to between 10 and 15% for France. Already the out-ward FDI data show there is a stark divide opening up between German investments in Southern and Eastern Europe. Figure 12.3 compares the geographical shares of the German FDI stock in the years 2000 and 2018. Capital devoted to the US fell sharply from 29% of the total to under 17%

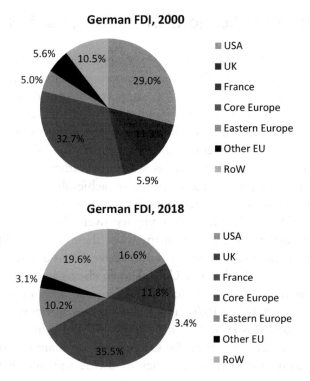

Fig. 12.3 German FDI holdings by geographical location, 2000 and 2018 (percentage of total) (*Source* Bundesbank, OECD, *CrossBorder Capital*)

over the period, but the share allocated to the UK managed to rise a tad to nearly 12%. The biggest swings occurred in the amounts allocated to France and 'Other EU' economies, which fell from a combined 11.5% to only 6.5% and the meaningful jump in the share devoted to Eastern Europe from 5 to 10.2%. The 'RoW' (Rest of the World) category embraces China and other Asian economies, including Central Asia, India and Russia. This too has doubled. These data evidence the ongoing shift in the World's economic centre of gravity from West to East. If we re-express this German data in simpler East versus West terms (and exclude the 'core' European economies i.e. Benelux, Denmark, Austria and Switzerland), the shift has been even more dramatic with the stock of investments in the 'West' falling from 51.8% of total German FDI in year 2000 to 34.9% by 2018. The equivalent share devoted to the 'East' roughly doubles from 15.5 to 29.8% and has been put in place in less than twenty years. Capital is essentially being sucked from the likes of Italy and Greece through German surpluses and is being redeployed into Eastern Europe.

Geopolitical Implications of Shifting Capital

Many in the West still see future dangers in terms of minor border disputes or rogue states. They also believe that democracy is integral to the success of Capitalism, which explains their support for pro-democracy uprisings, such as the 2011 Arab Spring and the Hong Kong demonstrators in 2019. What's more, according to this view, all free nations should inevitably develop like the West and remain at peace so that the West can eliminate unnecessary military spending. Yet, as we noted earlier China has already demonstrated that capitalist-like successes are achievable without extending Western-like democracy and freedoms. Many commentators consequently misread the 1989–1992 ideological victory over old-style Stalinist State Socialism as a final act, whereas, in many ways, the more embedded Russian and Chinese Leninist-style political models have essentially stayed put. We are, therefore, moving back into a Cold War era chess game of plodding diplomatic initiatives thwarted by frequent stalemates, with neither side ever really winning. Back in the 1970s and 1980s, three major powers dominated geopolitics—USA, Russia and China—following the split in the communist bloc engineered, at the time, by US Secretary of State Henry Kissinger. America subsequently followed a policy of divide-and-rule that paralleled the nineteenth-century British political diplomacy towards post-Napoleonic Europe, by keeping the opposition fragmented and otherwise preoccupied by smaller, local events. Today, policy experts are similarly advising US leaders to keep Russia and China apart, but for different reasons. Put another way, the US needs to get a 'fair' trade deal with China and carefully manage China's appetite for American technology and risk capital, while keeping Europe preoccupied and in awe of the constant Russian threat. In an ironic twist, Europe served as a convenient thorn in Russia's side in the 1970s and 1980s, but the tables have now turned, with Russia a nagging thorn for Europeans. The West was generally weakened economically by the 2007–2008 GFC, but the European Union (EU) suffered most. Now, for the first time since America's encouragement of the European project following the Treaty of Rome in 1957, the US no longer sees the EU as a diplomatic and geopolitical asset. What's more, capital is quitting Europe and it is now highly unlikely that Washington will allow the Eurozone to use the International Monetary Fund (IMF) again as a personal fiefdom to bailout its weakened regional banks. Indeed, many in the White House see Europe as a competitor and would happily see the EU broken up.

It seems that the European Union is already split economically and socially from the inside. It is saddled with the Euro, a corrosive currency mechanism that is still not working as promised, and the EU economies are likely to stagger from crisis to crisis until voters' patience is worn out. If it is to survive, Europe's monetary union must evolve into a full-scale federal state, with a single EU Treasury and uniform fiscal structure. This seems unlikely. The Eurozone is structurally divided into stubborn creditor and debtor blocs and each with a clashing macroeconomic agenda. Massive doses of QE (quantitative easing) by the European Central Bank (ECB) and a cyclical economic upturn have papered over these cracks in recent years, but Europe's underlying North–South divide remains chronic and unrelenting. We have already noted that German capital has very different interests from much of the rest of the EU. The old Franco–German axis that once formed the core of the EU has been effectively made obsolete by the Fall of the Berlin Wall in 1989. Any new attempt to reconstitute it would only highlight France's now much weaker position. This turnaround has been clearly evidenced by the Brexit process: whereas Britain largely negotiated with France to join the, then named, Common Market in 1972, she now has to persuade Germany in order to leave on decent terms.

On top, there is a risk that Eastern Europe will turn back towards Russia, possibly seduced by a Christian nationalism. Ultimately, the EU's core underlying problem remains: the conflicting needs of Germany and those of the South can be neither reconciled, nor healed by Economic and Monetary Union (EMU). The yawning gap in economic competitiveness and in debt burdens across Europe is far too great. Yet, the instinct of many of the EU's evangelical practitioners is march on regardless. Many of Europe's economies should not be sharing a common currency at all. Germany has championed a free-trade doctrine within Europe, economically bankrupting her neighbours in the process through the implicitly large undervaluation of the Deutschmark that was originally baked into the Euro at its creation. At the same time, the EU is relieved of vital large-scale military spending by leaning too heavily on US defence, so leaving herself exposed and unable to police her own borders were America to pull back. The EU is fast losing American geopolitical support, while at the same time she is ironically but less obviously also losing economic support as German capital marches Eastwards. In two decades, the Euro has facilitated the rapid deindustrialisation of Europe's Southern fringe and the shrinking of its wealth, while boosting the coffers of German business and arguably helping to finance its inevitable future expansion into Eastern Europe, Ukraine and ultimately Russia. In these economies, the consumers are younger, less indebted, more aspiring and so far they are untapped. At the same time, Europe's economic independence is compromised because it sits at the end of a Russian controlled gas pipeline (e.g. Nord Stream I and II), while further along her Eastern frontiers, she faces a plurality of unpredictable autocrats.

China, Russia, Iran and increasingly Turkey all dispute and often resist the post-Cold War settlement, namely the: (1) unification of Germany; (2) territorial dismemberment of the former Soviet Union and the absorption of previous Warsaw Pact nations into NATO; (3) a Middle-East dominated by the Sunni Saudis and supported by the US, who seeks to suppress Iraq and Iran and (4) America's uncontested dominance of Asia via friendly alliances and military bases across the region. All four malcontents have different aims and use different tactics, e.g. China is a major importer of resources and oil, but all are strategically focussed on Central Asia. Their common focus on Central Asia makes America's strategic position harder, leading America to question NATO and to disengage from the Middle East. On top, China is challenging US dominance in Asia. Russia is challenging the EU in Ukraine and through her attempts to re-establish influence over the Commonwealth of Independent States (CIS). And, Iran, via incursions into Syria and with tacit Russian help, is challenging Saudi power in the Middle-East and seeking to move the regional centre of power back to Tehran. All-in-all, capital is being sucked out of America and particularly Europe and shifting Eastwards along this *Financial Silk Road*, but more importantly it looks to be focussing on Central Asia. Geopolitical tensions will surely multiply?

Notes

1. Danny Quah, *The Global Economy's Shifting Centre of Gravity*, Global Policy, Volume 2, January 2011.
2. See *The Financial Silk Road*, Baring Securities, 1996.
3. In the late-1590s, the gold/silver ratio in China stood around 6:1, or more than twice the 13:1 ratio that then prevailed in Spain.
4. North American Free Trade Agreement.
5. State-owned enterprises (SOEs) and state-owned banks (SOBs) are widely used terms.
6. This includes service businesses and ownership is often technically defined by a shareholding of, say, 30% or more.
7. See Alessandro Gasparotti and Matthias Kullas, *20 Years of the Euro: Winners and Losers*, cepStudy, February 2019.

13

Measuring Liquidity:
The Global Liquidity Indexes (GLI)

The *CrossBorder Capital* Global Liquidity Indexes (GLI™)

CrossBorder Capital (CBC) track capital flows, assessing their impact on markets and economies. Their methodology derives from a comprehensive study of flow of funds data and the belief that changes in the sources of funds (i.e. financial flows) are more important than the uses of funds (i.e. economic spending categories). This is true by definition at major inflections in the funding cycle, which are measured through their regularly published *Global Liquidity Indexes* (GLI™). See www.liquidity.com. The GLI™ provide a practical example of how investors can measure and monitor liquidity.[1] They are a family of composite indexes that are designed to unambiguously assess *funding liquidity* conditions in a robust way across the same set of economies Worldwide. Coverage extends to developed, Emerging Market economies and Frontier Market[2] economies. Several key data series are gathered for each economy, comprising measures of Central Bank, private sector and net CBC flows. The multidimensional measurement of liquidity and the broad coverage adds to accuracy and conviction, and helps to eliminate 'false' signals. See Fig. 13.1.

The GLI™ have been regularly published since the early 1990s. They use the latest statistical techniques to extract common signals about the monetary climate from big data, exploiting the fact that these data sets have substantial co-movements. Data are collected from three main sources:

© The Author(s) 2020
M. J. Howell, *Capital Wars*,
https://doi.org/10.1007/978-3-030-39288-8_13

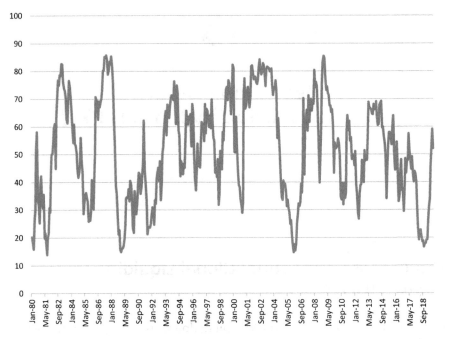

Fig. 13.1 CBC Global Liquidity Index, 1980–2019 (index 0–100) (Source *CrossBorder Capital*)

- Supranational Organisations, such as the International Monetary Fund (IMF), the United Nations (UN) and the Bank for International Settlements (BIS)
- National Treasuries and Central Banks, e.g. US Federal Reserve, People's Bank of China, ECB
- Trade Organisations, major lending corporations, money markets and shadow banks.

The GLI indexes can be shown to be Granger causal for many key economic and financial data series and they typically precede important asset price moves. The indexes tend to lead bond markets and forex markets by around 3–6 months; equity markets by 6–12 months and real economies by 15–20 months. They cover some eighty economies Worldwide and consist of baskets of z-scores ('normalised' statistical series), sampling around thirty data series per economy and covering traditional banks, Central Banks, shadow banks, corporations, households and foreign investors. This data is cleaned, cross-checked and assembled into a standard template to facilitate geographic and historic comparisons.

There are six types of variables potentially available for inclusion: (1) asset prices and credit costs; (2) credit spreads/risk premia; (3) leverage and credit growth; (4) off-balance sheet lending (e.g. shadow banks, securitisation); (5) lending surveys and (6) security new issuance data and ETF and mutual fund flows. CBC focus on #3 and #4 and part of #2, i.e. specifically:

- Growth rates in the volume of Broad Credit/Financial Savings
- Growth rates in the size of Central Bank balance sheets
- Net inflows of cross-border financial capital relative to the size of the domestic liquidity pool
- Leverage ratios of private credit providers
- Short-term credit spreads in money markets.

Lending surveys provide useful information, but experience shows that they are not predictive and tend to follow other credit measures with a long lag. Issuance data and ETF and mutual fund flows are also useful, but they are a 'use' not a 'source' of funds and again they are frequently non-predictive. Credit costs and asset prices are excluded for similar reasons, apart from very short-term credit spreads, such as LIBOR-OIS and TED,[3] which are used largely to 'cross-check' the flow data. The basic difference between the nominal liquidity flow data and the indexes is that the indexes are trend-adjusted; they are measured relative to current economic activity, and they are more comprehensive because they include certain key balance sheet ratios that plainly cannot be expressed as quantities. These indexes also implicitly incorporate monetary velocity.

The indexes are constructed through a three-stage process that systematically blends together both quantitative and qualitative data:

- Level 1: Raw data
- Level 2: Transformation and Normalisation
- Level 3: Index Construction.

In practice, index construction involves several choices: (1) data frequency; (2) number of variables included; (3) time span covered in each reference period and (4) weighting system. Since an index is a benchmark it needs to be scaled either relative to its own fluctuations or compared to some specific historic reference point: both involve the choice of appropriate timescale. A longer span might seem better, but this is more likely to include periods of structural change that may compromise the index. In contrast, a shorter period may be more stable, but too little history will give insufficient perspective. Similarly, high frequency data, say daily, might be preferable to monthly or quarterly because it facilitates more frequent decision-making. However, the cost to the index is that daily data probably contain more 'noise' and so are less reliable. CBC compromises by using monthly data. The number of signalling variables to include in the index is subject to a similar paradox because again more might seem better than less. However, the problem with gathering lots of variables is that the sample could become lop-sided, including too many of a readily available type that correspondingly bias as the index in a certain direction and so 'over signal'. This problem is mitigated by grouping variables according to type into separate sub-indexes, e.g. Central Bank liquidity, CBC flows, and by considering the statistically significant number of around thirty different variables by economy rather than, say, 100. The data components that make up each sub-index are detrended and volatility-adjusted to ensure they are stationary.

The resulting GLI™ essentially consist of 'normalised' growth rates and balance sheet ratios. The idea is that financial markets respond to shocks, which are scaled according to their standard deviations. Investors will grow accustomed to a steady flow of liquidity, but react when the growth rates suddenly change. The GLI™ are similar to standard diffusion indexes. They are made up from multiple sub-components that are algorithmically weighted together and then expressed as normalised z-scores. Given that it is difficult to compare what is 'loose' or 'tight' across indicators, z-scores calculate how spread-out the standardised data are. A diffusion index measures the extent that this data, etc. are dispersed or 'diffused' within each specific group. The more dispersed the collective readings, the greater the confidence we should have in concluding whether liquidity is 'loose' or 'tight'.

These individual component z-scores are combined using a likelihood-based methodology that produces its strongest signals when all measures are aligned and is not biased by large extreme readings from one or two sub-components. The resulting aggregate z-score is not a simple sum of components, but it incorporates a 'confidence' effect. This makes it nonlinear. Thus, if all sub-components have 'high' z-scores, the aggregate z-score for a composite index or sub-index will be much higher because it works from joint probabilities. Each index level z-score, e.g. Central Bank Liquidity, is expressed as a 'normalised' range 0–100, with its mean set at 50; one standard deviation (1sd) drawn at 60; 2sd at 80;—1sd at 40 and—2sd at 20. A GLI™ index or sub-index reading over 50 represents an increase in liquidity within the financial sector of that economy compared to its 41-month trend. A reading under 50 represents a decrease in liquidity below trend. An increase (decrease) compared to the previous month indicates an acceleration (deceleration). The larger the index value, the faster the implied rate of change.

An example is shown in Fig. 13.2 for the US Federal Reserve Liquidity sub-index and its five key sub-components, such as overall balance sheet growth, banks' excess reserves and holdings of government debt. These, sometimes over-lapping, sub-components are chosen in order to provide an unambiguous measure of quantitative policy easing and tightening actions. They are combined into the US Federal Reserve Liquidity Index (range 0–100), which should be read as a cumulative probability score. When the sub-components reinforce each other with a similar message, the index takes on a more extreme value. Disparate sub-component values are more likely to give a neutral index reading. Similarly, Fig. 13.3 shows the co-movement between the three sub-indexes that make up overall Emerging Market Liquidity—Central Bank liquidity, private sector liquidity and CBC cross-border capital flows—alongside the aggregate Emerging Market Index itself.

There are essentially two choices with regard to how these sub-indexes are weighted together into the national and aggregate GLI™ indexes: (1) size-based weights and (2) weights dependent on data performance. Size-based are determined by the outstanding stock of liquidity in each category. Performance weights typically mean either regression-based loadings determined by the correlation of the components to a target data series, or principal components where the weights are determined by their contribution to the first principal component of common variation in the data. Because both approaches have their advantages and disadvantages, CBC adopt a hybrid approach by using an optimised combination of principal component weights and weights determined by the outstanding stock of liquidity. In practice, this gives Central Bank liquidity a higher loading in the index

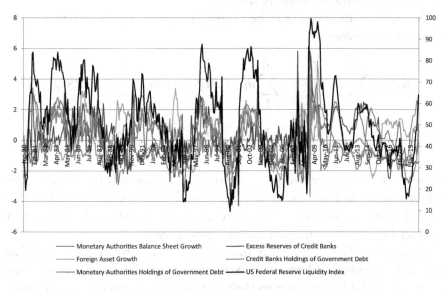

Fig. 13.2 CBC US Central Bank liquidity index and major sub-components, 1980–2019 (index 0–100 and z-scores) (Source *CrossBorder Capital*)

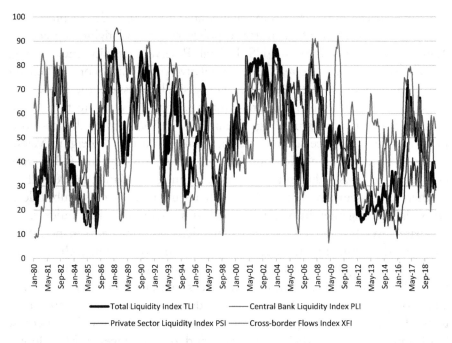

Total Liquidity Index TLI ——— Central Bank Liquidity Index PLI
——— Private Sector Liquidity Index PSI ——— Cross-border Flows Index XFI

Fig. 13.3 CBC Emerging Market liquidity index and sub-indexes, 1980–2019 (index 0–100) (Source *CrossBorder Capital*)

than its size-weighting alone would merit. On average, CBC ascribe 32% to each of Central Bank and private sector liquidity; 20% to cross-border flows and 16% to short-term liquidity spreads.

The index methodology can be expressed mathematically in terms of the following expression:

$$\text{GLI}_t = \sum_1^{80} w_i \cdot \left[pc_1 \cdot \sum_1^{10} u_k \cdot \text{CBL}f_{i,k,t} + pc_2 \cdot \sum_1^{15} v_l \cdot \text{PSL}f_{i,l,t} \right.$$
$$\left. + pc_3 \cdot \sum_1^{5} x_m \cdot \text{CS}f_{i,m,t} + pc_4 \cdot \text{CBF}f_{i,t} \right]$$

where w_i is a country weight; pc_i principal component-based sub-index weights; u_k, v_l and x_m factor weights; $\text{CBL}f_i$, $\text{PSL}f_i$, $\text{CS}f_i$ and $\text{CBF}f_i$ the Central Bank, private sector, short-term credit spreads and cross-border liquidity factors. t denotes each monthly time period.

The resulting Global Liquidity Index (GLI™) is reported in Fig. 13.4. The indexes for regional and national economies are weighted together to create the aggregate GLI, according to their relative sizes, based on the outstanding stock of liquidity measured in US dollar terms, in the base year, which

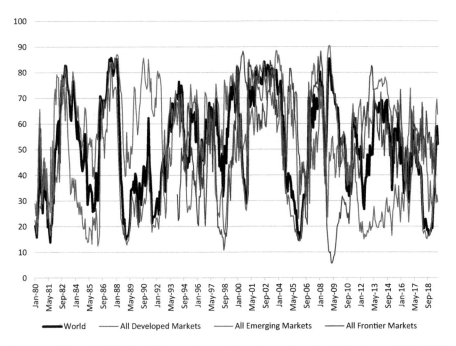

Fig. 13.4 CBC Global Liquidity Index and main regional sub-indexes, 1980–2019 (index 0–100) (Source *CrossBorder Capital*)

is currently year 2010. Alongside, CBC report the major regional components—Developed Markets, Emerging Market economies and Frontier Market economies. There are some clear anomalies, such as the strength of Emerging Market liquidity in the early 1990s as cross-border flows raced to take advantage of the geopolitical shifts; the large slump in Emerging Market liquidity from around 2012–2016 and again through 2018–2019 following China's two monetary squeezes, and the precipitous drop in Frontier Market liquidity ahead of the 2007–2008 GFC.

Notes

1. For alternative approaches, see Office of Financial Research, OFR Financial Stress Index, www.financialresearch.gov/financial-stress-index/ and Somnath Chatterjee, Ching-Wai (Jeremy) Chiu, Thibaut Duprey, and Sinem Hacioglu Hoke, *A Financial Stress Index for the United Kingdom*, BoE WP#697, December 2017.
2. See, for example, the MSCI definitions of these groups.
3. TED is the Treasury bill/Eurodollar spread; OIS is the overnight indexed swap rate.

14

Conclusion: A High-Water Mark?

Peak Liquidity: Will Globalisation Be the First Victim of the Capital Wars?

The stone wall protecting the Union positions along Cemetery Ridge on the Civil War battlefield at Gettysburg has long symbolised the *High-Water Mark of the Confederacy* touched by rebel Americans in 1863. There is no such pointer on the trading screens of international finance, but one senses that the tide of Global Liquidity may also be going out? Instrumental in this shift is the unfolding US policy of no longer fully embracing China, but instead explicitly containing China's economic and geopolitical challenge by, among other things, controlling trade, technology transfer and capital flows. Equally, China claims she has already adopted a similar policy to thwart US dollar hegemony. Although, to date, the retreat from globalisation towards a regionalism, based as much on ideology as geography, has centred on trade rather than capital flows, could we be reaching the equivalent High-Water Mark of Global Liquidity, i.e. 'Peak Liquidity'? We foresee a deglobalisation and new regionalism, with geopolitics dictating the realm of capital, and China, at least in the eyes of many in the US, taking on the rebel role.

Trade wars by themselves are not always easy to win. Yet, win or lose, there is far more to economic dominance than trade in goods, and there are many more ways to hurt an industrial competitor than with tariffs. Flows of capital and technology matter at least as much and arguably more than flows of goods. Today, the central axis of China/US competition runs through leading-edge technologies, such as artificial intelligence (AI), 5G networks,

© The Author(s) 2020
M. J. Howell, *Capital Wars*,
https://doi.org/10.1007/978-3-030-39288-8_14

digital money and quantum computing, each of which has the potential to reshape the geopolitical balance of power in economic, cybersecurity and military spheres. Consequently, capital protectionism and limits on technology transfer likely pose a much greater economic threat to China and others than basic trade protection. China needs to import 'intelligent' and risk-seeking capital to maintain her growth and stability, evidenced by her recent removal of a longstanding hurdle to foreign investment and the unsolicited bid made in September 2019 by the Hong Kong Stock Exchange to buy the London Stock Exchange. This would open an important conduit for capital to flow Eastwards and it almost certainly appears to be Beijing-inspired. Only days earlier, the State Administration of Foreign Exchange (SAFE) announced that international investors would no longer be limited by quotas[1] when buying Chinese stocks and bonds, so removing a barrier to inward foreign investment that had been in place for almost two decades. Capital wars matter.

We began by posing the question that if finance drives the World economy, then who or what drives finance? We have also seen that Central Banks have power, but not always control. Liquidity provision is increasingly a global phenomenon, resting on a potentially wobbly collateral base, but largely under America's and China's direction. Alongside, and at least for now, the US Dollar continues to play a pivotal role, particularly in the cross-border markets. In fact, we noted the paradox that in the decades since the demise of the Bretton Woods fixed exchange rate system, the World has become even more-dollar centric. Put another way, despite the slide in the relative size of the American economy, global investors are still dependent on decisions made by the US Federal Reserve and US Government. Ironically, the politically sensitive US trade deficit is largely explained by the competitiveness of America's financial markets, rather than by the assumed uncompetitiveness of her industry.

We reject the conclusion sometimes made that the World is inevitably moving towards a multipolar exchange rate system: a bilateral (or possibly if we include the Euro a trilateral) outcome seems the more plausible. An analogy is often made with the late-nineteenth century, when although Britain *prima facie* oversaw the gold standard, vital support for the system was periodically provided by both France and Germany. In practice, these arrangements seem little different from the current state, where the US dollar sits happily alongside other units, such as the Yen, Euro and Sterling. But it does not alter the reality that some two-thirds to three-quarters of real and financial market activity is transacted and settled in the dominant US unit.

All these facts ensure that the financial cycle will continue to be highly procyclical, sometimes fragile and always unpredictable. They may, in turn, explain our central proposition: why, as the investment World gets bigger, it also becomes more volatile? Global Liquidity provision has unquestionably become more erratic in the last three decades. The main supplier of the global currency to World markets is a large, low productivity growth economy, with highly developed financial markets and a capital surplus. The major user, increasingly through its GVCs (global value chains), is a large, high productivity growth economy, with underdeveloped financial markets and a greater need to import risk capital. This stark division characterises the growing economic rivalry between America and China: China may now enjoy the industrial power, but America remains the financial powerhouse with China forced to lean too heavily on the US dollar, which itself represents a further risk for global markets.

The Financial Silk Road

We have argued that the Fall of the Berlin Wall in 1989 symbolised the key economic and geopolitical changes: as the shaky two-stroke Trabants[2] trundled Westwards, they were overtaken by a surge of Western capital rushing Eastwards, eventually leading to the economic enfranchisement of 2–3 billion 'new producers'. These forces also hastened China's own economic reforms that were started by Deng Xiaoping[3] just a few years earlier and they encouraged similar reform movements across Latin America, led by Mexico's privatisation programme and her negotiations towards NAFTA under President Carlos Salinas. The borders between spheres of economic influence are being redrawn as a result: China appears to be consolidating her influence in Asia, while at the same time expanding Westwards via the *Belt and Road Initiative* into Central Asia and ultimately into European and African markets. Europe's own intensions are voiced through German capital, and the evidence already shows that Germany is redeploying her capital in the East, with Ukraine and Russia as likely future targets, and possibly then moving into parts of the Middle-East, including Turkey and Iran. US capital is left to expand Southwards into Latin America and to pick-up what scraps of influence it can retain in Europe and Asia, such as in Japan, Taiwan, Korea, South-East Asia and, possibly, India. It seems that the boundaries and many of the institutions of the post-WW2 settlement are finally being redrawn.

Risk capital is forever being pushed out from the large money centres in cyclical waves, but it is simultaneously being pulled towards faster growth economies. Risk capital facilitates economic 'catch-up', which many acknowledge as the only guaranteed source of growth in the modern industrial era. China's and other Emerging Markets' resulting rapid productivity growth effectively forced the US, through a convoluted real-exchange adjustment, to run a near-permanently loose monetary policy and for World markets to suffer the bubble consequences. The still nascent financial systems in China and other Emerging Markets have let this loose US money spillover via capital inflows and so fuel multiple local credit booms. Alongside, the new industrial competition spurred cost-cutting and ate into profit margins and economic growth in the West, forcing many firms to trim or even abandon new capital spending plans, since marginal returns on capital fell too low. Many businesses focussed instead on raising the average return on capital by slashing operating costs on their existing capital. By sweating on-site assets harder, they boosted industrial cash flows, which were channelled through wholesale money markets, rather than into high-street banks, or into large merger deals, which concentrate global industries, and share-buybacks that raise financial leverage. Financial markets were forced to focus more on capital distribution and refinancing, rather than serving as traditional capital-raising mechanisms. This changing role makes balance sheet capacity, i.e. the volume of liquidity, far more important in order to meet the exhausting and persistent demands for debt rollovers, than the cost of capital, i.e. interest rates, to finance the now seemingly less frequent, new capital projects. Also, by encouraging the build-up of corporate and institutional cash pools (CICPs) these new forces effectively reversed the polarity of the international financial system. The resulting excess demand for 'safe' assets has reinforced the procyclicality of Global Liquidity and added a worrying element of fragility.

This trend carries with it social and political costs. In the West, as cost-cutting ripped through middle-class work forces, it enfranchised top management's valuable share options. By shaking-up employment patterns, many routine cognitive and semiskilled manual jobs have since been lost. Hours worked have dived and new jobs have largely come in the 'low-hour' industries and in the gig economy. Hurt by low wage growth, Western households were encouraged to borrow and mortgage more in order to keep up their rates of consumer spending. As industries turned towards 'asset-lite' business models, capital spending fell, notably in oil and retailing, and what has been left is concentrated in the hi-tech sectors. Debt has multiplied in industries like healthcare and technology, largely off-setting the slump in new debt flows going into more traditional industrial businesses, such as energy, autos and chemicals. These changes, reinforced by the prevailing negative demographic forces, have weakened underlying economic growth. Despite reportedly high aggregate rates of employment, social alienation, arising from a lack of job opportunities, has discouraged workers. The resulting gaping wealth disparities are destroying the middle ground in politics, leading to the so-called populist policies that are now polarising into left and right-wing extremes. Capital matters.

The Rise of the Repo

History shows that as the economic system evolves, integrates and concentrates, large entities and vested interests have a tendency to control and limit price movements. These sticky prices and wages have forced more adjustment on to quantities and asset prices, and hence on to balance sheets and incomes. China's entry into the WTO in 2001 both furthered the extensive growth of regional supply chains and accelerated the intensive use of the US dollar within these platforms. This has both underscored and broadened the need for national currency stability against the US unit, in turn, leading to large increases in the size of forex reserve cushions across many Emerging Market economies and the parallel establishment of Sovereign Wealth Funds to help manage these cash pools: a period frequently dubbed 'Bretton Woods II' by commentators. Added to the equally massive pools of US dollar cash newly built-up by mature Western industrial corporations, these flows from the East account for a large part of the concentrated CICPs that have since outgrown the ability of traditional high street banks to provide safe, liquid assets. The rise of the repo and the resulting demands for evermore dollars, both to hold as safe assets and to use as means of circulation in supply chains, set against the slow official supply, has forced their increasing substitution via private sector provision. This drive for greater financial elasticity, in turn, has fuelled a jump in cross-border flows outside of the realm of US Federal Reserve interest rate and regulatory control, so providing an additional source of leverage both directly and indirectly through the Eurodollar markets. These offshore pools of footloose capital are ready sources of unregulated wholesale funding. They carry no national flags, know few boundaries, and can shift rapidly at speeds only limited by the latest communication technologies, so amplifying the cycle of Global Liquidity.

It seems, in conclusion, that the financial market volatility that once characterised the nineteenth and early twentieth centuries is back. This long arc of history warns that while capitalism undeniably excels at aggregate wealth creation, it does so by collapsing the industrial cost structure and erecting a towering financial superstructure. Left unchecked, free markets create high street price deflation, but alongside they lead to asset price inflation and more market volatility when these asset bubbles burst. Western private sectors need more and more debt to grow, but the greater the flow of debt the poorer its quality and the more future balance sheet capacity is, ultimately, required to refinance it. Balance sheet capacity is another way of expressing financial liquidity. However, this liquidity is built from the same safe asset pool that is being adulterated by flaky private sector debts. In this vicious spiral, more poor-quality debts are being funded by still more poor-quality private sector debts.

The history of money teaches that payment systems require a level of liquidity backstopping that no private entity, and often only large States, can provide. In other words, these market-based solutions to the safe asset shortage can only work up to a point. Yet, the efficacy of the State in controlling the monetary system waxes and wanes. Their relationship is frequently fraught, and it inevitably becomes a struggle between the private sector's quest for greater elasticity and the regulations imposed on them through new instruments and stronger authorities in order to restrain the growth of debt. Capitalism needs a stable credit instrument that can support capital accumulation and expansion. Gold is not sufficiently elastic and the supply of State money is often at odds with low inflation policies and the 'sound money' ideology. The US dollar has worked, but it remains to be seen whether the US dollar system can withstand another World crisis? The private sector always innovates to create new substitutes, but these tend to be outside State control and support, and highly procyclical. The extreme swings in the Global Liquidity cycle owe much to the mechanism of private sector provision and particularly to changes in unofficial sources of high-powered money, or what we have called the *shadow monetary base*. It follows that in downturns when liquidity is most needed, it simply is not there. A more fragile and more procyclical financial system results.

Admittedly, there are positives. The mass *financialisation* of the US and World economies over the past two decades has left many investors far richer on paper than they were even at the top of the dot-com bubble in the year 2000. Behind this paper wealth lies an over-abundant supply of cheap footloose, Global Liquidity, much of it the result of unconventional monetary policies. With Central Banks creating new money and policy-makers and corporations retiring financial instruments from the general marketplace, the pool of available assets (particularly higher quality assets) for the private sector to buy has shrunk significantly, whereas the amount of money chasing those assets has grown. Excess demand or *money power* therefore underpins these higher asset valuations. Since the late-1990s, when many allege that the Greenspan-led, Federal Reserve started to veer fatally towards persistently loose money, nominal US GDP has grown at an average annual 4–5% clip. But the returns earned by equities, residential and commercial real estate, agricultural land, Treasury securities, investment-grade and high-yield corporate bonds, junk bonds and leveraged loans have all outpaced the underlying economy from which they notionally derive their strength. Thus, it is easy to see why the possibility of future tighter monetary policies rings alarm bells for many investors.

Set against this threat, policy-makers are limited in what they can do even when using latest tools to ensure stability. "*By sticking to the new orthodoxy of monetary policy and pretending that we have made the banking system safe, we are sleepwalking towards that crisis*", warned former Bank of England head Mervyn King at the IMF annual meetings in 2019. Latest estimates put the natural rate of interest in the US around 2–2½%, or roughly where the Federal Reserve's policy rate has recently hovered. This low ceiling means that when the next crisis hits, US policy-makers will have limited scope for further reducing nominal interest rates. Rate-cutting remains their instinct, and what is true for the Federal Reserve is truer still for other major Central Banks, namely the European Central Bank and the Bank of Japan. Admittedly, some policy-makers have at times experimented with negative interest rates, but this comes at the cost of potentially undermining the vital repo mechanism and damaging commercial banks' profitability. In other words, negative or near-negative interest rates may perversely destroy liquidity supply.[4] Prudent Central Bankers are surely unwise to extend these experiments? A major tenet of liquidity theory is that interest rates are not the price of money. Rather this is the exchange rate. Low interest rates reflect either a poor return on industrial capital and/or a large excess demand for 'safe' assets. By maintaining austerity policies, cutting interest rates and not expanding the volume of liquidity in their financial systems, policy-makers risk destroying the credit mechanism, much as they did in the early-1930s.

A thoughtful recent study of inflationary and deflationary forces by Rick Rieder[5] Blackrock's fixed income head enumerates the immense secular deflationary forces that have reappeared since the 1970s. An active capitalism always creates cost deflation. To his list of declining baby boomers, greater female labour participation, China, new technologies and the quiescence of OPEC, we might also choose to add the effects of increasing returns from large-scale production, but the key point here is that 'money' is nowhere mentioned as a factor. In fact, set against the scale of these tectonic supply-side shifts, Central Banks could even stand accused of tiptoeing around. For at least two decades, the US Fed has followed a national 2% price inflation target. If high street inflation is no longer—to use the long-cherished statement by monetarism's celebrated high priest Milton Friedman—*always and everywhere a monetary phenomenon* and if the much-loved Phillips Curve is dead, they have been wasting their time. But even more than this, they have been ignoring the one area where monetary policy does matter namely financial stability. Targeting low inflation during the deflationary supply shocks, caused by globalisation and China's entry into the WTO, has resulted in asset bubbles. Central Banks have seemingly refused to recognise the implications of this for financial stability. Not surprisingly, the two big debates in monetary theory now concern the future roles of digital money and MMT (Modern Monetary Theory). Both reflect underlying doubts over the ability of the Central Banks to master our Byzantine-like global financial system.

Refinancing Versus New Financing Systems

What comes next? The Central Banks and the Regulators need to re-focus on financial stability and specifically the provision of sufficient volumes of 'safe' assets and liquidity, rather than trying to fine-tune high street inflation. Inflation is largely a real economy and not purely a monetary phenomenon: in short, China's low costs have proved Milton Friedman wrong! Policy-makers will be forced to again resort to quantitative easing policies (QE) and so expand Central Bank balance sheets, probably significantly, to replace the funding capacity permanently lost in the 2007–2008 GFC. Funding measures gross, rather than net, credit flows and is essential in facilitating much-needed debt rollovers. Think of this as a future QE4, QE5, QE6, et al. Policy-makers must ensure that there is adequate liquidity in the system, not least because we live in a World where debt refinancing is far more important than the funding of new capital. In short, the *capacity of capital*, i.e. the financial sector balance sheet size outweighs the *cost of capital*, i.e. the level of interest rates. This suggests that the entire debate surrounding Peoples' QE and MMT is misdirected because our economic problems and low rate of new investment have little to do with the lack of money, per se. Central Banks are able to purchase State debt in the secondary markets, but they are not supposed (nor, in most cases, legally permitted) to buy primary issues. Yet, there is an unambiguous and large appetite for government debt as shown, not only by the low prevailing yields, but, more importantly, by the hugely negative term premia readings. These are predominantly caused by an excess demand for 'safe' asset Treasuries, which may total the whopping equivalent of a cumulative 80% of World GDP since the GFC.

Understanding this changing financial structure is always a critical factor in getting policy right. Some argue persuasively that this dimension is often missing (Kaufman 2017). The real issue is not 'too big to fail', but 'too interconnected to fail'. Essentially, the modern financial system has become a vast refinancing system more than a new financing system. Central Banks, the overseers, are monopoly suppliers of currency but only one among many providers of credit. They may influence the level of interest rates, but as the 2007–2008 financial crisis underscored, they do not set them. On the other hand, the credit cycle cannot be either understood or controlled if it is not properly monitored. Policy-makers need to re-establish expertise for tracking the volume of credit and liquidity. What's more, there should be a general move towards an asset-based framework for control, focussed on credit quality, rather than today's much compromised liability-based systems that limit funding. A steady supply of safe assets is critical. The bottom line is that targeting interest rates with the (sole) objective of controlling fast disappearing consumer price inflation is no longer adequate. A better intermediate objective is the encouragement of currency blocs, with greater exchange rate adjustment allowed between these blocs than within them, alongside the establishment of more efficient tools to quell excessive credit growth within each bloc in order to maintain financial stability, including the issuance of longer duration instruments, e.g. 30, 50 and 100-year government bonds, and by adopting ways to limit the negative effects of excessive capital flows. But above all, avoiding systemic risks means ensuring adequate levels of Global Liquidity.

Coming Decades: The Internationalisation of the Yuan

Today, the three most important sources of Global Liquidity come from the US Federal Reserve, the People's Bank of China (PBoC) and cross-border flows of capital. The latter, in turn, depend greatly on movements in the US dollar exchange rate, which are to some degree under the control of the US Fed and, ironically, also in the hands of the PBoC. Each of these three primary sources of liquidity needs to expand. The greatest change in the economic and financial landscape in the last two decades has unquestionably been the rise of China. China accounted for 5.9% of Global Liquidity in the year 2000, but today she commands a whopping

27.5% share, besting even America. Being a major dollar user, China has historically helped to stabilise the US dollar region by delivering timely fiscal boosts whenever her offshore export economy requires. Although Chinese industry continues to expand, her financial system remains, in many ways, remarkably immature. This explains both why she has had to become a heavy dollar-user and why the Chinese Authorities, rather than private firms, are forced to re-cycle these dollars. China's submissive role in her choice of currency cannot continue. We ought to recall the earlier quote from Chapter 1 that signals China's aspirations:

> ...we should promote the Renminbi to be the primary currency of Asia, just as the US dollar first became the currency of North America and then the currency of the World ... Every globalisation was initiated by a rising empire ... As a rising super power, the 'One Belt, One Road' strategy is the beginning of China's own globalisation ... it is a counter-measure to the US strategy of shifting focus to the East. (excepts from a speech by Major-General Qiao Liang, Chinese PLA, April 2015)

Although history teaches us that nations often eclipse their industrial rivals economically several decades before their currencies come to dominate, this still suggests that the next development phase across World financial markets will almost certainly feature the rise of the Yuan. The oft-used counterargument summoned against the Yuan is that trust, being a vital dimension of currency adoption, demands a truly democratic State. This claim would not have impressed the Romans and plainly did not derail the widespread circulation of the denarii.[6] Nor will it hold sway with those regional neighbours eager for Chinese investment. With Chinese money already a force, 'PBoC-watching' will become at least as important for investors over coming years as the science of 'Fed-watching' is today.

How can China rival and ultimately destroy the dominant US dollar system? Her obvious strategy will be to broaden the Chinese gross international balance sheet, as adumbrated earlier in Chapter 9, by invoicing more trade in Yuan; developing a Yuan trade credit markets, which would allow Chinese banks to lend more to foreigners, and further opening up the large domestic Chinese Yuan-denominated bond market to international capital. A major part of this strategy likely involves the establishment and use of a digital Chinese Yuan. Allegedly, China is already well-advanced. We think of encrypted digital monies as cash substitutes that, unlike existing electronic monies, eliminate intermediaries and so allow person-to-person transfers. Digital monies, i.e. cryptocurrencies, disintermediate banks because they internalise clearing and settlement. They also potentially disintermediate the US dollar and weaken US financial power. Already dominant Chinese payment platforms, such as Alipay and WeChat, could soon have the facility to accommodate a State-issued digital currency via an e-wallet. There is a neat historical symmetry here, because China, the originator of paper money more than a millennium ago, may be the first major nation where it is superseded by more flexible electronic and digital monies. Developing a captive market for Yuan in neighbouring economies, such as Central Asia, and providing development aid and government loans denominated in Yuan, would also help further China's goal. In addition, China will likely attempt to reposition more of her supply chains onshore. This would reduce imports of manufactured goods, and it would align with her controversial *Made in China 2025* policy.[7] As we emphasised earlier, under existing arrangements China is, paradoxically, forced to re-export US dollars, when she ideally needs to export both electronic and digital Yuan. Not only should we expect to see an acceleration of these initiatives in coming years, but we must also question whether this rivalry will compromise the ability of global liquidity and private sector financial balance sheets to expand, and/or affect the future availability of the Federal Reserve's often vital US dollar swap lines?

Yet, the Yuan is unlikely to see a straight-line path to dominance because the existentialist threat posed to the US dollar hegemony and the entire Western financial system will stir-up countervailing geopolitical forces and likely spur attempts to halt the free flows of capital. The vast US dollar international payments system, outlined in Chapter 8, stands as a key part of American foreign policy, and, given the resulting benefit from lower US Treasury funding costs, a vital component of US budgetary policy. Similar existential attacks were sometimes successfully fought-off by previous World monetary regimes. Arguably, the US dollar has recently held back the challenge of the Euro, which largely succumbed following the 2010–2012 European banking crisis. The British pound-gold standard was also once challenged by the French-led and silver-backed *Latin Monetary Union* (1865–1873). Although ended de facto by the new Kingdom of Italy and France's defeat in the Franco-Prussian War (1870–1871), the challenge essentially failed because the Vatican State persistently cheated (OMG) by issuing silver coins of lower fineness. But, put into context, these represent the financial equivalents of military skirmishes. The ultimate battle in this Capital War must surely involve a fight for supremacy between, the US dollar, the Chinese Yuan and digital/cryptocurrencies, and arguably, as we have suggested, against the latter two forces united into one single foe. The ironclad question that policy-makers, business leaders and investors need to ask is: could the digital Yuan ever become the twenty-first century's 'safe' asset? We must be prepared for this next potential stage of Chinese development and power.

History not economics deserves the final word. The Franco-Prussian War was ultimately settled by massive indemnity payments hoisted on France by the victorious Germans. Germany threatened to occupy large parts of Northern France until these bills, totalling a whopping one quarter of French GDP, were settled. In the event, France paid her debts two years early. She handed over her gold reserves to Germany and raised billions through the new Thiers issue of government bonds. These bonds were heavily over-subscribed in France and across Europe. At a stroke, the pool of international 'safe' assets was sizably enlarged. Previously inert savings were mobilised, and credit boomed and spread outwards cross-border. Admittedly, with hindsight, the scale of the subsequent boom proved too great and another financial crisis ultimately followed. The so-called Panic of 1873 was arguably the first truly World crisis, embracing Britain and mainland Europe, and touching the shores of America, where it became better known through the speculative railroad bubble, the failure of bankers Jay Cooke & Co., the US Coinage Act, which demonetised silver and the resulting sound money policies of Civil War hero General Ulysses S. Grant's Second Presidential Administration. All-in-all, it emphasises the importance of 'safe' asset creation and the then adolescent power of Global Liquidity. And, it is Global Liquidity, namely flows of savings and credit, that drives stocks, bonds and asset markets… NOT the economy.

We offer four conclusions:

- As the investment World gets bigger and more interconnected by rapid flows of international capital, it becomes more volatile.
- This derives from an increasingly procyclical monetary system, dominated by private sector credit and debt, featuring global supply chains, based around the USD, and driven by fast-moving flows of *Global Liquidity.*
- Policy-makers fail to understand the changing financial structure; the reversal of financial polarity; the rise of CICPs and the focus of institutions on refinancing, rather than new money-raising. This results in inappropriate and ultimately destabilising monetary policies.
- Regionalism, possibly based on digital monies, will consequently replace globalisation as capital rivalry limits cross-border trade, technology transfer and the free-flow of risk capital.

Notes

1. Ironically, only one-third of the US$300 billion QFII (qualified foreign institutional investor programme) has been taken up.
2. Trabants: vehicles manufactured in East Germany by VEB Sachsenring and powered by a 2-stroke 500 cc engine, were themselves a sorry symbol of Communist technical achievement. Nicknamed the 'sparkplug with a roof', the Trabant had no fuel gauge, a one-piece steel chassis and featured *duroplast* plastic bodywork made from recycled cotton waste from the Soviet Union.
3. Coincidently, Deng announced he was standing down on November 9, 1989, the day the Berlin Wall fell.
4. See Markus K. Brunnermeier and Yann Koby, *The Reversal Interest Rate*, Princeton, January 2019.
5. Blackrock, *The Monetary Policy Endgame*, September 2019.
6. The standard Roman silver coin, originally worth 10 asses.
7. *Made in China 2025* is China's official plan to rival US manufacturing by focussing on high-technology industries, such as pharmaceuticals, automotive, aerospace, semiconductors, IT and robotics. It targets an increase in the Chinese-domestic content of core materials to 40% by 2020 and 70% by 2025.

Reference

Kaufman, Henry. 2017. *Tectonic Shifts in Financial Markets*. New York: Palgrave.

Appendix:
Inflation, Deflation and Valuations

We originally noted in Chapter 2 that inflations and deflations affect asset allocation and, by implication, via its effect on the P/M (price-to-money) ratio introduced in Chapter 10 it will influence the valuation of assets, such as the traditional P/E multiple. These assertions are explained in this section.

The diagram in Fig. A.1 depicts the theoretical P/E multiple and the (inverted) government bond yield, both drawn against the annual rate of inflation on the bottom axis. The behaviour of real assets is also indicated. Equity valuations include an additional risk premium based on the odds of default and of inventory valuation losses during deflationary periods. Similarly, although these factors likely reverse during periods of inflation, the drag of higher bond yields on equity valuation levels causes the relationship between equity P/E multiples and inflation to take-on this humped pattern. In contrast, bond valuation (and by implication, contra-wise, the valuation of real assets) display a smooth downward sloping valuation curve. The humped relationship implies two features: (1) equities enjoy their peak valuation levels when price inflation is low, say, 1–2% at an annual rate, and (2) the correlation between movements in equities and bonds crucially depends upon the underlying inflation regime. The diagram implies that in deflations and in low inflationary periods up to the inflation threshold that defines the equity valuation peak, bonds and equities are negatively correlated. Thereafter, at higher inflation rates, the valuations of bonds and stocks are positively correlated. In this latter case, it is possible that this valuation-based correlation could break-down at the level of asset prices, when equity earnings are sufficiently strongly positively affected by

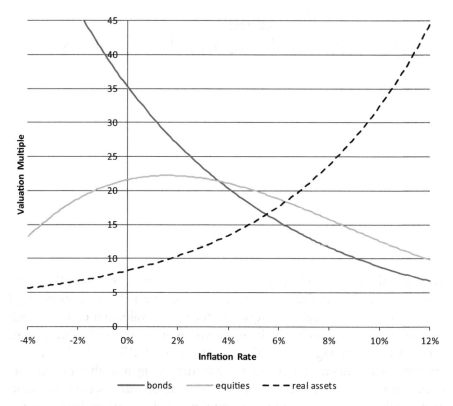

Fig. A.1 Theoretical P/E multiple, real assets and bond yields (inverted) versus inflation (Source *CrossBorder Capital*)

rising inflation. Nonetheless, the underlying argument helps to explain the puzzling change in the correlation pattern between bonds and stocks witnessed in recent years.

The Japanese markets provide a clear example of this changing correlation structure. During the late-1980s, the correlation coefficient between stocks and bonds averaged around 0.6, at a time when Japanese consumer price inflation stood close to an annual rate of 2½%. By the late-1990s, Japanese annual inflation had turned negative at around minus ½%, causing the correlation between stocks and bonds to collapse to minus 0.4. More recently, with inflation on the wake of the 2007–2008 GFC tumbling lower to average around minus 1% annually, the Japanese stock/ bond correlation has tumbled to minus 0.6. In other words, bonds provide a good hedge to equities during periods of low inflation and price deflation.

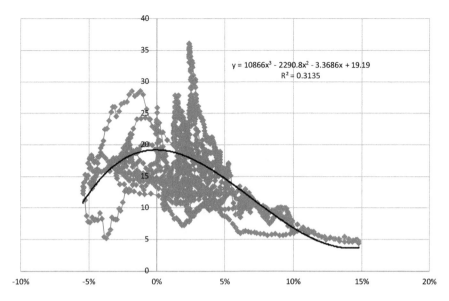

Fig. A.2 US CAPE and inflation (rolling 5-year averages), 1881–2019 (Source *CrossBorder Capital*, US Federal Reserve, Shiller)

This analysis emphasizes that asset valuation is conditional on inflation: it is not an absolute criterion. High street inflation is a common factor that links the valuation of asset markets, and this fact may explain why investors often compare the relative valuations of equities and bonds. Asset allocation is seriously affected by inflations and deflations, because both can disturb future liabilities. In other words, this common factor facilitates an arbitrage between the equity and bond markets. It could also explain why relative valuation, using, say, an earnings or dividend discount model, has often proved a better investment tool than separately comparing bonds, by their yields, and equities, by their P/E multiples.

The empirical data reported in Fig. A.2 seem to confirm the other feature of Fig. A.1, namely the valuation peak coinciding with low inflation. Although the Japanese data also evidence this feature, we spotlight the US case, using data extracted from the Shiller database,[1] from 1880 onwards. The diagram plots the five-years average of the US CAPE (cyclically-adjustedP/E) against the five-year average rate of consumer price inflation. We have fitted a cubic relationship, which shows a peak CAPE at close to zero inflation, although the data also support our proposition that equity valuations are highest at low positive inflation rates. The message is that inflation matters hugely to asset allocation decisions.

A Note on Data Sources

Unless otherwise stated all the data sources for the charts and tables come from the *CrossBorder Capital* databases and have been downloaded from www.liquidity.com between March and October, 2019.

This website provides liquidity and capital flow data denominated in both nominal US dollar and local currency terms, as well as the proprietary GLI indexes. The databases cover some 80 economies Worldwide and provide monthly and, sometimes, weekly data spanning the years from 1980. onwards. They are published in both real time and point-in-time formats.

Note

1. See http://www.econ.yale.edu/~shiller/data.htm.

Further Reading

1. *Inside the Yield Book* (1972)—**Marty Leibowitz and Sidney Homer**
   This book proved ground-breaking. It established bond math and made fixed-income investing into a science. Behind the scenes, Marty re-introduced two seminal ideas—the notional of a continuous yield curve that could be arbitraged, and Macaulay duration.

2. *A History of Interest Rates* (1977)—**Sidney Homer**
   Few may have read it from cover-to-cover, but this widely-referenced work thoroughly catalogues interest rates from ancient times through Medieval Europe to the post-1990 World, including America, Asia, and Africa. In the words of Henry Kaufman: 'No book has its peer'.

3. *Interest Rates, the Markets, and the New Financial World* (1986)—**Henry Kaufman**
   This is probably the book that most influenced me when I joined Salomon. Its prescience is still remarkable. Henry managed to foresee the future instability in credit markets and warned accordingly. Its analysis of flow of funds and liquidity was eye-opening, and I often refer back to its analysis of the yield curve.

4. *Money in a Theory of Finance* (1960)—**John Gurley and Edward Shaw**
   Gurley and Shaw pioneered the concept of 'liquidity' and credit creation by non-bank financial institutions, or what we now dub 'shadow banks'. It's a heavy-going read, but the idea that traditional banks and money were both losing their financial dominance was new.

© The Editor(s) (if applicable) and The Author(s),
under exclusive license to Springer Nature Switzerland AG 2020
M. J. Howell, *Capital Wars*,
https://doi.org/10.1007/978-3-030-39288-8

5. *The General Theory of Employment, Interest and Money* (1936)—John Maynard Keynes

This widely-known book is either loved or reviled. Keynes was originally a Cambridge monetary theorist. Two of his main insights were, first, the existence of separate industrial and financial circuits for money and, second, the fact that financial sector problems, e.g. a 'liquidity trap', could disrupt real economic activity and employment.

6. *Das Kapital* (Volume 3, 1894)—Karl Marx

A controversial choice, but as an economic historian Marx was the best chronicler of nineteenth-century capitalism, and here in this posthumously published volume is some of the best granular descriptions of money markets and financial crises anywhere, all peppered with cynical socialist invective. The alternative choice is Walter Bagehot's Lombard Street, but Marx gets the edge for writing about World financial markets and not just London.

References

Adrian, Tobias, and Hyun Song Shin. 2007. Liquidity and Leverage. BIS Annual Conference, September.

Adrian, Tobias, and Hyun Song Shin. 2008. Money, Liquidity and Financial Cycles. FRBNY Current Issues, January/February.

Adrian, Tobias, and Hyun Song Shin. 2009. Money, Liquidity and Monetary Policy. New York Fed Staff Papers, January.

Adrian, Tobias, Erkko Etula, and Tyler Muir. 2014. Financial Intermediaries and the Cross-Section of Asset Returns. *Journal of Finance* 69 (6) (December): 2557–2596.

Adrian, Tobias, and Bradley Jones. 2018a. Shadow Banking and Market-Based Finance. IMF Working Paper No. 14/18.

Adrian, Tobias, and Nina Boyarchenko. 2018b. Liquidity Policies and Systemic Risk. *Journal of Financial Intermediation* 35 (Part B, July): 45–60.

Alessi, L., and C. Detken 2011. Quasi Real-Time Early Warning Indicators for Costly Asset Price Boom/Bust Cycles: A Role for Global Liquidity. *European Journal of Political Economy* 27 (3): 520–533.

Allen, Franklin, and Douglas Gale. 2007. *Understanding Financial Crises*. Oxford: Oxford University Press.

Bagehot, Walter. 1873. *Lombard Street*. London: Henry S. King & Co.

Baks, K., and C. Kramer. 1999. Global Liquidity and Asset Prices: Measurement, Implications and Spillovers. IMF Working Paper No. 99/168.

Bank for International Settlements. 2019. Triennial Central Bank Survey of Foreign Exchange and Over-The-Counter (OTC) Derivatives Markets in 2019. https://www.bis.org/statistics/rpfx19.htm.

Bank for International Settlements—Committee on the Global Financial System. 2011. Global Liquidity—Concept, Measurement and Policy Implications. CGFS Paper No. 45, November.

Bank of England. 2007. Financial Market Liquidity. *FSR*, April.

Bank of England. 2010. Quantitative Easing Explained. *BoE Website*.

Banque de France. 2018. Financial Stability Review No. 2, April.

Baring Securities. 1996. *The Financial Silk Road*. London.

Berger, Allen N., and Christa H.S. Bouwman. 2008. Financial Crises and Bank Liquidity Creation. Working Paper, August.

Bernanke, Ben S. 2005. The Global Saving Glut and the U.S. Current Account Deficit. Federal Reserve Board, Remarks made at the Sandridge Lecture, Virginia Association of Economists, Richmond, Virginia, March.

Bernanke, Ben S. 2008. Liquidity Provision by the Federal Reserve. Speech, Board of Governors of the Federal Reserve System, May 13.

Bernanke, Ben S., and Mark Gertler. 1995. Inside the Black Box: The Credit Channel of Monetary Policy Transmission. *The Journal of Economic Perspectives* 9 (4) (Autumn): 27–48.

Bernstein, Peter. 1992. *Capital Ideas*. New York: The Free Press.

Bierut, Beata. 2013. Global Liquidity as an Early Warning Indicator of Asset Price Booms: G5 Versus Broader Measures. DNB Working Paper No. 377, May.

Bookstaber, Richard. 2000. Understanding and Monitoring the Liquidity Crisis Cycle. *Financial Analysts Journal* 56 (5) (September/October): 17–22.

Borio, Claudio. 2012. The Financial Cycle and Macroeconomics: What Have We Learnt? BIS Working Papers No. 395, December.

Borio, Claudio, and Philip Lowe. 2002. Asset Prices, Financial and Monetary Stability: Exploring the Nexus. BIS Working Papers No. 114, July.

Borio, Claudio, and Haibin Zhou. 2008. Capital Regulation, Risk-Taking and Monetary Policy: A Missing Link in the Transmission Mechanism? BIS Working Papers No. 268, December 17.

Borio, C., and M. Drehmann. 2009. Assessing the Risk of Banking Crises-Revisited. *BIS Quarterly Review*, March, 29–46.

Borio, Claudio, and Anna Zabai. 2016. Unconventional Monetary Policies: A Re-appraisal. BIS Working Papers No. 570, July.

Borio, Claudio, Mathias Drehmann, and Dora Xia. 2019. Predicting Recessions: Financial Cycle Versus Term Spread. BIS Working Papers No. 818, October.

Bruno, Valentina, and Hyun Song Shin. 2015. Capital Flows and the Risk-Taking Channel of Monetary Policy. *Journal of Monetary Economics* 71 (April): 119–132.

Brunnermeier, Markus K., and Lasse Heje Pedersen. 2009. Market Liquidity and Funding Liquidity. *The Review of Financial Studies* 22 (6) (June): 2201–2238.

Brunnermeier, Markus K., and Yuliy Sannikov. 2014. A Macroeconomic Model with a Financial Sector. *American Economic Review* 104 (2): 379–421.

Brunnermeier, Markus K., and Yann Koby. 2019. The Reversal Interest Rate. Princeton Working Paper, January.

Bullard, James. 2010. The Seven Faces of the Peril. Federal Reserve of St. Louis.

Carlstrom, Charles T., and Sarah Wakefield. 2007. The Funds Rate, Liquidity and the Term Auction Facility. Federal Reserve Bank of Cleveland, December.

Carney, Mark. 2019. Pull, Push, Pipes. Speech, Tokyo, Bank of England, June 6.

Champ, Bruce, and Sarah Wakefield. 2008. Monetary Policy: Providing Liquidity. Federal Reserve Bank of Cleveland, January.

Chatterjee, Somnath, Ching-Wai (Jeremy) Chiu, Thibaut Duprey, and Sinem Hacioglu Hoke. 2017. A Financial Stress Index for the United Kingdom. Bank of England Working Paper No. 697, December.

Clower, Robert W. 1967. A Reconsideration of the Microfoundations of Monetary Theory. *Western Economic Journal* 6: 1–8.

Clower, Robert W. 1965. The Keynesian Counter-Revolution: A Theoretical Appraisal. In *The Theory of Interest Rates*, ed. F.H. Hahn and F. Breechling. IEA.

Committee for Global Financial Stability. 2011. Annual Report, Basel.

Coimbra, Nuno, and Hélène Rey. 2019. Financial Cycles with Heterogeneous Intermediaries. NBER Working Paper No. 23245 (Revised).

Copeland, Morris. 1952. *A Study of Moneyflows in the United States.* NBER.

Cour-Thimann, Philippine, and Bernhard Winkler. 2013. The ECB's Non-standard Monetary Policy Measures the Role of Institutional Factors and Financial Structure. ECB Working Paper Series No. 1528, April.

D'Arista, Jane. 2002. Rebuilding the Transmission System for Monetary Policy. Financial Markets Center, November.

D'Arista, Jane. 2009. Rebuilding the Framework for Financial Regulation. Economic Policy Institute. Briefing Paper No. 231, May.

Darmouni, Olivier M., and Alexander Rodnyansky. 2017. The Effects of Quantitative Easing on Bank Lending Behavior. *The Review of Financial Studies* 30 (11) (November): 3858–3887.

Detken, C., O. Weeken, L. Alessi, D. Bonfim, M.M. Boucinha, C. Castro, S. Frontczak, G. Giordana, J. Giese, N. Jahn, J. Kakes, B. Klaus, J. H. Lang, N. Puzanova, and P. Welz. 2014. Operationalizing the Countercyclical Capital Buffer. ESRB Occasional Paper No. 5.

Di Maggio, Marco, Amir Kermani, and Christopher J. Palmer. 2018. How Quantitative Easing Works: Evidence on the Refinancing Channel. MIT Working Paper, June.

Drehmann, Mathias, and Kleopatra Nikolaou. 2009. Funding Liquidity Risk. ECB Working Paper No. 1024, March.

Drehmann, Mathias, Claudio Borio, and Kostas Tsatsaronis. 2011. Anchoring Countercyclical Capital Buffers: The Role of Credit Aggregates. BIS Working Paper, November.

ECB. 2002. The Liquidity Management of the ECB. *Monthly Bulletin*, May.

ECB. 2012. Global Liquidity: Concepts, Measurement and Implications from a Monetary Policy Perspective. *ECB Monthly Bulletin*, October.

Eggertsson, Gauti B., and Michael Woodford. 2003. The Zero Bound on Interest Rates and Optimal Monetary Policy. *Brookings Papers on Economic Activity* 2003 (1): 139–211.

Emmerson, Charles. 2013. *1913: In Search of the World Before the Great War*. New York: PublicAffairs.

Espinoza, Raphael A., and Dimitrious P. Tsomocos. 2008. Liquidity and Asset Prices. Working Paper, July.

European Central Bank. 2016. Dealing with Large and Volatile Capital Flows and the Role of the IMF. Occasional Paper No. 180, September.

Federal Reserve Board. 2012. Shadow Banking After the Financial Crisis, Remarks by Daniel K. Tarullo, June.

Financial Services Authority. 2008. Liquidity Risk Metrics, March 20.

Financial Stability Board. 2019. Global Monitoring Report on Non-bank Financial Intermediation, February.

Fisher, Irving. 1933. *Booms and Depressions*. New York: Adelphi Company.

Fornari, Fabio, and Aviram Levy. 2000. Global Liquidity in the 1990s. BIS Conference Papers No. 8, March.

Gagnon, J. 2016. Quantitative Easing: An Underappreciated Success. PIIE Policy Brief No. 16-4. Washington, DC.

Galí, Jordi. 2008. *Monetary Policy, Inflation, and the Business Cycle: An Introduction to the New Keynesian Framework and Its Applications*, 2nd ed. Princeton: Princeton University Press.

Geanakoplos, John. 2002. Liquidity, Default and Crashes: Endogenous Contracts in General Equilibrium. Cowles Discussion Paper No. 1316R, June.

Gerdesmeier, Dieter, Hans-Eggert Reimers, and Barbara Roffia. 2010. Asset Price Misalignments and the Role of Money and Credit. *International Finance* 13 (3) (December): 377–407.

Gertler, Mark. 1988. Financial Structure and Aggregate Economic Activity: An Overview. *Journal of Money, Credit and Banking* 20 (3) (August): 559–588.

Goldberg, Linda S., and Robert Lerman. 2019. The U.S. Dollar's Global Roles: Where Do Things Stand? Liberty Street Economics, February.

Goldsmith, Raymond W. 1985. *Comparative National Balance Sheets: A Study of Twenty Countries, 1688–1978*. Chicago: University of Chicago Press.

Gopinath, G. 2016. The International Price System. Jackson Hole Economic Symposium.

Gopinath, Gita, and Jeremy C. Stein. 2018. Banking, Trade, and the Making of a Dominant Currency. NBER Working Paper, March.

Gorton, G., S. Lewellen, and A. Metrick. 2012. The Safe Asset Share. *American Economic Review* 102 (3): 101–106.

Gourinchas, Pierre-Olivier, and Helene Rey. 2007. International Financial Adjustment. *Journal of Political Economy* 115 (4) (August): 665–703.

Gourinchas, Pierre-Olivier, Helene Rey, and Maxime Sauzet. 2019. The International Monetary and Financial System. LBS Working Paper, April (Forthcoming, *Annual Review of Economics*).

Graham, Benjamin, and David Dodd. 1934. *Security Analysis*. New York: McGraw-Hill.

Griese, Julia V., and Christin K. Tuxen. 2007. Global Liquidity and Asset Prices in a Cointegrated VAR, July.

Gurley, J., and E. Shaw. 1960. *Money in a Theory of Finance*. Washington, DC: Brookings.

Harman, Jeremiah. 1819. Report from the Secret Committee of the Bank Resuming Cash Payments. Bank of England.

Hawtrey, Ralph G. 1928. *Currency and Credit*, 3rd ed. London: Longmans.

Hayek, Frederick von. 1933a. *Prices and Production*. London: Mises Institute.

Hayek, Frederick von. 1933b. *Monetary Theory and the Trade Cycle*. London: Mises Institute.

He, Zhigu, and Arvind Krishnamurthy. 2012. A Model of Capital and Crises. *Review of Economic Studies* 79 (2): 735–777.

Hicks, John. 1939. *Value & Capital*. Oxford: Clarendon Press.

HMSO. 1959. Committee on the Working of the Monetary System: (Radcliffe) Report. Cmnd 827.

Holmstrom, Bengt, and Jean Tirole. 2001. LAPM: A Liquidity-Based Asset Pricing Model. *Journal of Finance* 56 (3) (October): 1837–1867.

Homer, Sidney. 1991. *A History of Interest Rates*. New Brunswick: Rutgers.

Horn, Sebastian, Carmen Reinhart, and Christoph Trebesch. 2019. China's Overseas Lending. Kiel Working Paper No. 2312, June.

Howell, Michael J. 2017. *Further Investigations into the Term Structure of Interest Rates*. London: University of London.

Howell, Michael J. 2018. What Does the Yield Curve Slope Really Tell Us? *The Journal of Fixed Income* 27 (4): 22–33.

Howell, Michael J. 2019. Measuring Bond Investors' Risk Appetite Using the Interest Rate Term Structure. *The Journal of Investing* 28 (6) (October): 115–127.

International Monetary Fund. 2010. Global Liquidity Expansion: Effects on 'Receiving' Economies and Policy Response Options. Global Financial Stability Report, April.

International Monetary Fund. 2012. Global Financial Stability Report, April.

Jevons, William Stanley. 1884. *Investigations in Currency and Finance*. London: Macmillan.

Jordà, Òscar, Moritz Schularick, Alan M. Taylor, and Felix Ward. 2018. Global Financial Cycles and Risk Premiums. NBER Working Paper No. 24677, June.

Kaldor, Nicholas. 1992. *The Scourge of Monetarism*. Oxford: Oxford University Press.

Kaufman, Henry. 1986a. Debt: The Threat to Economic and Financial Stability. *Economic Review*. Federal Reserve of Kansas.

Kaufman, Henry. 1986b. *Interest Rates, the Markets and New Financial World*. Time Books.

Kaufman, Henry. 2017. *Tectonic Shifts in Financial Markets*. Cham: Palgrave.

Keynes, John Maynard. 1936. *The General Theory of Employment, Interest and Money*. London: Macmillan.

Keynes, John Maynard. 1930. *A Treatise on Money*, 2 vols. London: Macmillan.

Kohn, Donald L. 2009. Monetary Policy Research and the Financial Crisis: Strengths and Shortcomings, Speech. Board of Governors of the Federal Reserve System, October 9.

Krishnamurthy, Arvind, and Annette Vissing-Jorgensen. 2011. The Effects of Quantitative Easing on Interest Rates: Channels and Implications for Policy. Brookings Papers.

Krishnamurthy, A., and A. Vissing-Jorgensen. 2012. Aggregate Demand for Treasury Debt. *Journal of Political Economy* 120: 233–267.

Krishnamurthy, Arvind, and Annette Vissing-Jorgensen. 2013. The Ins and Outs of LSAPs. Jackson Hole Economic Symposium.

Lane, Philip R., and Peter McQuade. 2013. Domestic Credit Growth and International Capital Flows. ECB Working Paper No. 1566, July.

Lane, Philip R., and Gian Maria Milesi-Ferretti. 2008. The Drivers of Financial Globalization. *American Economic Review* 98 (2): 327–332.

Leibowitz, Martin L. 1986. Total Portfolio Duration [from *Investing*, Probus, 1992].

Leibowitz, Martin L. 2004. *Franchise Value.* Hoboken: Wiley.

Leibowitz, Martin L., Eric H. Sorensen, Robert D. Arnott, and H. Nicholas Hanson. 1989. A Total Differential Approach to Equity Duration. *Financial Analysts Journal* 45 (5) (September/October): 30–37.

Lombardi, Marco, Madhusudan Mohanty, and Ilhyock Shim. 2017. The Real Effects of Household Debt in the Short and Long Run. BIS Working Paper No. 607.

Lucas, Robert E. 1984. Money in a Theory of Finance. Carnegie-Rochester Conference Papers No. 21.

Macaulay, Frederick R. 1938. *Some Theoretical Problems Suggested by the Movements of Interest Rates, Bond Yields and Stock Prices in the United States Since 1856,* NBER.

Mandelbrot, Benoit, and Richard L. Hudson. 2004. *The Misbehavior of Markets: A Fractal View of Financial Turbulence.* New York: Basic Books.

Mian, Atif, Amir Sufi, and Emil Verner. 2017. How Do Credit Supply Shocks Affect the Real Economy? Evidence from the United States in the 1980s. NBER Working Paper, August.

Minsky, Hyman P. 1957. Central Banking and Money Market Changes. *Quarterly Journal of Economics* 71 (2) (May): 171–187.

Minsky, Hyman P. 1992. The Financial Instability Hypothesis. Jerome Levy Institute Working Paper No. 74, May.

Mishkin, Frederick S. 2007. Financial Instability and the Federal Reserve as a Liquidity Provider. Speech, Board of Governors of the Federal Reserve System, October 26.

Miranda-Agrippino, S., and H. Rey. 2019. US Monetary Policy and the Global Financial Cycle, March 28.

Moreira, Alan, and Alexi Savov. 2017. The Macroeconomics of Shadow Banking. *Journal of Finance* 72 (6) (December): 2381–2432.

Nikolaou, Kleopatra. 2009. Liquidity (Risk) Concepts: Definitions and Interactions. ECB Working Paper No. 1008, February.

Pedersen, Lasse Heje. 2008. Liquidity Risk and the Current Crisis. *Vox*, November 15.

Qiao Liang, Major-General. 2015. Speech, Chinese PLA, April.

Quah, Danny. 2011. The Global Economy's Shifting Centre of Gravity. *Global Policy* 2 (1) (January): 3–9.

Reinhart Carmen, M., and Kenneth S. Rogoff. 2009. *This Time Is Different: Eight Centuries of Financial Folly*. Princeton: Princeton University Press.

Rey, Hélène. 2013. Dilemma Not Trilemma: The Global Financial Cycle and Monetary Policy Independence. Jackson Hole Conference, August 2013.

Rey, Hélène. 2015. IMF Mundell Fleming Lecture.

Ruffer, Rasmus, and Livio Stracca. 2006. What Is Global Excess Liquidity, and Does It Matter. ECB Working Paper No. 696, November.

Schularick, Moritz, and Alan M. Taylor. 2012. Credit Booms Gone Bust: Monetary Policy, Leverage Cycles, and Financial Crises. *1870–2008, American Economic Review* 102 (2): 1029–1061.

Shin, Hyun Song. 2012. Global Banking Glut and Loan Risk Premium. *IMF Economic Review* 60: 155–192.

Shostak, Frank. 2000. The Mystery of the Money Supply Definition. *Quarterly Journal of Austrian Economics* 3 (4) (Winter): 69–76.

Singh, Manmohan. 2013. Collateral and Monetary Policy. IMF Working Paper No. 13/186, August.

Singh, Manmohan, and Peter Stella. 2012. The (Other) Deleveraging: What Economists Need to Know About the Modern Money Creation Process. *CEPR VOX*, July 2.

Singh, Manmohan, and Rohit Goel. 2019. Pledged Collateral Market's Role in Transmission to Short-Term Market Rates. IMF Working Paper No. 19/106, May.

Sprinkel, Beryl W. 1964. *Money and Stock Prices*. Homewood: Irwin.

Stanton, Bernard F. 2007. *George F. Warren—Farm Economist*. New York: Cornell University Press.

Strahan, Philip. 2008. Liquidity Production in 21st Century Banking. NBER Working Paper No. 13798, February.

Stein, Jeremy C. 2012. Monetary Policy as Financial-Stability Regulation. *Quarterly Journal of Economics* 127 (1): 57–95.

Stigum, Marcia L. 1987. *Money Market*, Rev. ed. New York: McGraw-Hill.

Taleb, Nassim Nicholas. 2008. *Black Swan*. London: Penguin.

Taylor, Lance. 2008. Notes on Liquidity. *New School for Social Research*, April.

Thornton, Henry. 1802. *An Enquiry into the Nature and Effects of the Paper Credit of Great Britain*. London.

Tooze, Adam. 2018. *Crashed*. London: Penguin.

Tucker, Paul. 2004. Managing the Central Bank's Balance Sheet: Where Monetary Policy Meets Financial Stability. *BoE Quarterly Bulletin*, Autumn.

Tucker, Paul. 2018. *Unelected Power*. Princeton: Princeton University Press.

Vlieghe, Gertjan. 2016. Monetary Policy Expectations and Long-Term Interest Rates. Speech at London Business School, Bank of England, May.

Woodford, Michael. 2003. *Interest and Prices: Foundations of a Theory of Monetary Policy.* Princeton: Princeton University Press.

Zero Hedge. 2019. 12 Reasons Why Negative Rates Will Devastate the World, August 19.

Zucman, Gabriel. 2013. The Missing Wealth of Nations. *Quarterly Journal of Economics* 128 (3) (August): 1321–1364.

Index